pulling the pieces together

PMP® Exam Practice Questions and Solutions

Why the best answer is best and the wrong answers are wrong

Aileen Ellis, PMP®

Release 1.5d

Published by

AME Group Inc.
175 Palm Springs Drive
Colorado Springs, CO 80921
Phone: 719-659-3658
www.amegroupinc.com
aileen@amegroupinc.com

© November 2005 AME Group, Inc.

First Edition November 2005

ISBN 0-9774381-0-4

Preface

Aileen Ellis of AME Group Inc. has been helping professionals prepare for the PMP® Exam since 1998. With years of experience working with thousands of students, AME Group has learned how students best prepare for the PMP® Exam. Beginning in 2005 Ms. Ellis and AME Group Inc. expanded their focus to include the CAPM® Exam.

In the classroom, the comment heard over and over again is: "I get why the right answer is right, but please explain why my answer is not as good." In response to that comment, as well as the request for more sample questions, this book was developed.
AME Group started testing these questions in the classroom in 2001 and has continued to update and modify them for optimum learning. The detailed explanations of the wrong answers provide students with four times the learning in every sample question.

Many students preparing for the PMP® exam assume they will score very high on practice tests. Don't worry about your score initially. Think of these questions as part of your learning experience, which will inevitably help to boost your exam scores.

What makes *PMP® Exam Practice Questions and Solutions* different from other sample question books? The AME Group has designed the book with the goal of not only helping students pass the exam but also obtain high exam scores. To achieve this goal, this book:

- Is solely focused on the PMP® exam. Focus your time studying what is on the PMP® exam.

- Includes not only a good description of why the right answer is right, but why the three wrong answers are wrong. You will get four times the learning from each question. Other books tell you the right answer, but do they really explain why the wrong answer is wrong? How many times have you understood that the right answer is good, but still not fully understood why your answer was wrong? In this book, there is as much focus on the wrong answers as on the right answers to set the record straight.

- Provides references—many to the *PMBOK® Guide*—for each correct answer. How many times have you wanted to read more about the content of the question in order to prepare for more exam questions similar or related to the topic, but have had no reference?

- Focuses on the exam content, not on the topics of interest to the writers. Focus your time on studying what is on this exam…instead of what is on other exams.

- Grooms students to answer exam questions correctly by practicing test-taking strategies. See Part One for these strategies explained in detail along with sample questions using each of the techniques.

About the Author

Aileen Ellis, the president of AME Group Inc. has helped more than 3,000 students obtain those coveted letters: PMP®. Working with thousands of students from dozens of countries, Ms. Ellis has gained a thorough understanding of the ins and outs of the *PMBOK® Guide*, the exam content, and proven test-taking strategies.

Ms. Ellis began teaching Exam Preparation Courses in 1998. Over the years she has mastered how students learn best and has incorporated those lessons and methods into her books. Her approach is focused on understanding the Project Management Processes and their interactions, with limited memorization. Along with teaching Project Management courses around the world, Ms. Ellis also leads workshops to help students study for and pass the CAPM® and PMP® exams through review of content and hundreds of sample questions.

Ms. Ellis lives in Colorado Springs with her husband, Terry, and their two young children, Nick and Alex. When not teaching, coaching or writing, Ms. Ellis spends her days hiking the Colorado mountains.

Courses Available - AME Group Inc.

CAPM® Exam Preparation Course- AME Group Inc.
and
PMP® Exam Preparation Course- AME Group Inc.
and
PgMP Exam Preparation Course- AME Group Inc.

These three and four-day courses incorporate accelerated learning with content and hundreds of sample questions to:

- Improve your chances of passing the exam on your first attempt
- Focus your study efforts on exactly what you need to pass the exam
- Decrease your study time
- Make preparing for the exam a fun experience (Yes… we have students who have said, "Preparing for the exam is fun!".. and yes they passed)

Note: AME Group also is available to facilitate onsite exam preparation courses to specifically coach your team on how to pass these exams

Online Questions and Solutions!

(www.amegroupinc.com)

CAPM® Exam- Sample Questions and Solutions
and
PMP® Exam- Sample Questions and Solutions
(over 500 additional questions than found in this book-updated weekly)

and
PgMP Exam- Sample Questions and Solutions (Spring 2008)

- Complete set of sample questions with detailed solutions sorted by domain or knowledge area
- Determine where you need to focus your studies
- Study what you don't know, not what you know
- Hundreds more situation questions for the *PMP® and PgMP Exam* with new questions added every week

Practice Questions and Solutions Books!
(www.amegroupinc.com)

CAPM® Exam- Sample Questions and Solutions
and
PMP® Exam- Sample Questions and Solutions
and
PgMP Exam- Sample Questions and Solutions (Coming 2008)

- Complete set of sample questions with detailed solutions by knowledge area
- Determine where you need to focus your studies
- Study what you don't know, not what you know
- Hundreds of situation questions for the *PMP® and PgMP Exam*

Exam Preparation Study Guides!
(www.amegroupinc.com)

CAPM® Exam- Study Guide (coming soon)
and
PMP® Exam- Study Guide (coming soon)
and
PgMP Exam- Study Guide (coming soon)

- Complete explanation of the required PMI Standards - not a repeat
- Clear explanations of what you need to pass the tests and only what you need to pass the tests
- Sample documents such as Project Charter, Scope Statement, Scope Management Plan, etc.

For more information on courses, books and online programs visit:

www.amegroupinc.com

Introduction

The first step to prepare for the PMP® exam is to go to www.pmi.org and print the Project Management Professional (PMP®) Credential Handbook. Use this handbook and apply for the exam, now!

About the Book

The sole purpose of the book is to help you focus your study efforts so as to improve your chances of passing the exam on your first try.

If you need more than the sample questions provided in this book please go to www.amegroupinc.com to purchase 60 days of access to over 500 additional questions and solutions.

This book is divided into three parts:

Part One addresses question strategy
This section begins with AME Group's Exam Question Strategy. You will be amazed at how much strategy can help you on this exam when answering questions where your content knowledge may not be enough. Review this area before the rest of the book and then come back to it after you have covered the content in other sections.

Part Two addresses types of questions
Knowing the type of exam questions and how to approach each can take you a long way in your question approach. The PMP® exam includes:
- Input/output, tool and technique questions
- Questions that ask, *What would you do first?* (PMI® Methodology)
- Definitional type questions
- Professional Responsibility questions

Part Three focuses on sample questions and solutions

Each section in part three is set up in the same format:

- What you should *know* about the section
- At least 40 questions per section with detailed explanations of the right and wrong answers
- Author suggestions:
    o Take 10 questions, score yourself, and review your answers.
    o With each answer, those you get right, those you get wrong, read through the detailed solutions provided.
    o Go to the *PMBOK® Guide* and read all you can on the topic.
    o After you have conquered 10 questions, move onto the next 10.

Part One: Exam Question Strategy

1. Read the question and ask yourself first: *What knowledge area am I in?* Also ask yourself, *What process group am I in?* Once you can identify the knowledge area and the process group, you may then be able to identify the actual process step. Think of the objective of that process step as well as the inputs /tools and techniques/ outputs of this step to give you a clue.

2. Look for qualifier words in the question. Frequently used qualifier words include *every, always, never, all*, etc.

Note: PMI® has both "bad words" and "good words." For example:

Bad words	**Good words**
Frequently	Timely
Punish	Coach
Force	Encourage

3. Identify the type of question.

- Input/output, tool and technique questions
- Questions that ask, *What would you do first?* (PMP Methodology)
- Definitional type questions
- Professional responsibility questions

4. As you practice for the exam, read each question and write the question number on a piece of paper. Identify and eliminate any wrong answers. It is better to "guess" between two choices than four choices. In doubt, remember that words from the *PMBOK® Guide* are more likely to be correct than non-*PMBOK® Guide* words. Use definitions, common sense, etc. Let's take a look at an example:

1. What is the right answer?
    a. this answer I know is wrong, so I will put a line through "a"
    b. this answer I am not sure of, so I will put a "?" next to "b"
    c. this answer I know is wrong, so I will put a line through "c"
    d. this answer I believe is the correct answer, so I will circle "d"

Your handwritten page should look something like this:
1. ~~a~~
   ? b

Now go back and look at "b" and see if there is a way to eliminate this answer.

Part Two: Types of Questions

On the exam you are likely to encounter at least four different types of questions.

- Input/output, tool and technique questions
- Questions that ask, *What would you do first?* (PMI Methodology)
- Definitional type questions
- Professional responsibility questions

1. Input/Tool and Technique /Output Questions

PMI thinks of methodology in terms of inputs/tools and techniques/ outputs.

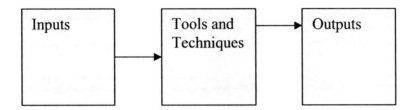

The outputs of one step are often the inputs of another step. Inputs and Outputs are usually (but not always) documents.

INPUTs and OUTPUTs are documents or documentable items. Learn to recognize this list of **typical inputs and outputs**:

- information
- policies
- plans
- detail
- outputs
- constraints
- assumptions
- change requests

- updates
- lesson learned
- reports
- descriptions
- criteria
- WBS
- changes
- baselines

- lists
- diagrams
- estimates
- dependencies
- capabilities action
- PM Identified
- formal acceptance
- registers

TOOLS and TECHNIQUES are mechanisms applied to the INPUTS to create OUTPUTS. Learn to recognize this list of **typical tools and techniques**:

- methodology
- methods
- skills and knowledge
- estimating, systems
- EVM, meetings
- procedures

- management
- measurement
- analysis
- identification
- judgment
- templates

- decomposition
- additional planning
- inspection
- simulation
- software

Many of these questions will ask: *Which of the following is not an input of ...?* Or, *Which of the following is not a tool and technique of...?* If you can identify if each answer is an input (document) or tool and technique (things we do to documents to create other documents), you may easily be able to eliminate one, two, or three of the wrong answers.

Let's take some sample questions. Yes, you are going to do some questions and get them right without seeing the *PMBOK® Guide* content.

Input /T&T/ Output Question #1
Which of the following is *not* an input of cost control?

    a.   cost baseline
    b.   performance reports
    c.   cost change control system
    d.   project management plan

Of course, we have not covered cost control yet, but use the ideas above to help you.
Step one: We are definitely in the cost control process group because the question states "cost control." Cost control deals with controlling changes to the project budget.
Step two: The qualifier word here is *not*. I realize I am looking for the answer that *does not belong*.
Step three: This is definitely an input /tool and tech/ output question. Knowing that in general inputs are documents, look for an answer that is not a document.

In this example, "a," "b" and "d" are all documents. Answer "c" is a system; it is the only tool and technique here, making it the right answer.

Input /Tool and Technique/ Output Question #2
Which of the following is *not* a tool and technique of scope definition?

    a.   product analysis
    b.   alternative identification
    c.   expert judgment
    d.   scope management plan

Again, we have not covered scope definition yet, but let's give this a try.

Step one: We know we are in the planning process group because the question says "scope definition." In fact, we are in the scope knowledge area, more specifically, the scope definition process step. Scope definition deals with creating the scope statement.

Step two: The qualifier word here is *not*. We want the one that *does not belong*.

Step three: This is definitely an input/tool and tech/output question. Tools and techniques are things we do to documents to create other documents.

In this example, answers "a," "b" and "c" are all tools and techniques. Answer "d" is a document and, therefore, not a tool and technique of anything, which makes "d" the right answer. I do not even need to know that "a," "b" and "c" are tools and techniques of scope definition to get this question right.

Input /Tool and Technique/ Output Question #3

Which of the following is an input of develop project management plan?

    a.   preliminary project scope statement
    b.   project management information system
    c.   project planning methodology
    d.   project management plan

Step one: We are in the planning process group, the integration knowledge area, as well as in the step of develop project management plan. (You may not have known the process group or the knowledge area here, but hopefully you can see the process step of develop project management plan, which focuses on integrating and coordinating all project plans to create a consistent, coherent project plan.)

Step two: There are no qualifying words here.

Step three: This is an input/ tool and tech /output question.

In this example question, answer "a" is a document, so it may be an input. You might put a question mark on this one. Answers "b" and "c" are both tools and techniques, meaning they cannot be documents. Let's eliminate "b" and "c." Answer "d" is also a document, so it may be an input.

We have eliminated all but answers "a" and "d." Let's see if definitions or common sense can help now. The step is called develop project management plan, which is about integrating and coordinating all project plans to create a consistent, coherent project plan. Answer "d" is project management plan. This is probably an output of develop project management plan, not an input. This leaves us with answer "a" as the right answer (and it is correct).

Questions That Ask, *What Would You Do First?*

The *PMBOK Guide* has defined the interaction of the process steps in Chapter 3. Study figures 3-5, 3-6, 3-7, 3-8, 3-9, and 3-10. It is more important to understand these charts in great detail than to memorize them.

When reading these questions, ask yourself what step is associated with each answer and use that information to help you answer the question.

What would you do first? Question #1.

You are just starting your project. Which document needs to be created first?
   a.   contract management plan
   b.   procurement management plan
   c.   work breakdown structure
   d.   project charter

Answer "a," the contract management plan, is an output of select sellers, which is a procurement step of the executing process group. Answer "b," the procurement management plan, is an output of plan purchase and acquisitions, which is a procurement step of the planning process group. Answer "c," the work breakdown structure, is an output of create WBS, which is a scope step of the planning process group. Finally, answer "d," the project charter is an output of develop project charter, which is an integration step of the initiating process group.

Based on Figure 3-5, the initiating process group comes before the planning process group and the executing process group, making answer "d" the correct answer.

What would you do first? Question #2.

You are thinking of subcontracting out part of your project work. Which document needs to be created first?
   a.   contract management plan
   b.   procurement management plan
   c.   proposal
   d.   contract

In answer "a," the contract management plan is an output of select sellers, which is a procurement step of the executing process group. Answer "b," the procurement management plan, is an output of plan purchase and acquisitions, which is a procurement step of the planning process group. In answer "c," the proposal is an output of the request sellers' responses, which is a procurement step of the executing process group. Finally, answer "d," the contract, is an output of select sellers, which is a procurement step of the executing process group.

Answer "b" is the only output of a planning step. Answers "a," "c" and "d" are all outputs of executing steps. Planning comes before executing, making answer "b" the correct answer.

Definitional type questions
Expect many definitional type questions especially in the quality knowledge area. At a minimum, make sure you know the definitions of all 44 process steps. In this area, you may want to use the strategy of eliminating the wrong answers. In many cases the wrong answers will be definitions of other words from the same knowledge area.

Definitional type question #1.

1. Perform quality assurance is most concerned with:
   a. identifying which quality standards are relevant to the project and determining how to satisfy them
   b. applying the planned, systematic quality activates to ensure that the project employs all processes needed to meet requirements
   c. monitoring specific project results to determine whether they comply with relevant quality standards and identifying ways to eliminate causes of unsatisfactory performance
   d. consistency that the value of repeated measurements are clustered and have little scatter.

Answer "a" gives the definition of quality planning and is incorrect. Answer "b" provides the definition of perform quality assurance, making it the correct answer. Answer "c" is the definition of perform quality control, which is incorrect. Finally, answer "d" offers the definition of precision, which is also incorrect.

In the example above, if you do not know the right answer, try to eliminate all the answers that you know are wrong.

Professional responsibility type questions

With these questions, we are looking for answers that are both legal and ethical. Remember to do the right thing.

Professional responsibility type question #1.

1. You are preparing a cost estimate for management review. Your staff warns you that management always cuts estimates by 10%. What would you do?

   a. give your manager an estimate 10% higher than you really need and hope she will cut it by the historical 10 %.
   b. give your manager an estimate 15% higher than you really need, and hope she will cut it by the historic 10%, thus leaving you 5% extra, just in case.
   c. search for ways to justify the 10% buffer before you present it to management, knowing if you can't justify it, it will be cut.
   d. present your realistic estimate and be prepared to defend it.

Answers "a", "b" and "c" all present numbers that you know are not realistic. As Project Managers, we must only present numbers we believe. Therefore, answer "d" can be the only correct answer.

Part Three: Sample Questions and Solutions

Each section in part three is set up in the same format:

- What you should know about the section
- At least 40 questions per section that are followed by the solutions
- References
  - Most questions have a reference, many referring back to the *PMBOK® Guide*
  - Solutions without references often are general knowledge. The author suggests a WEB search on these topics instead of sending students to specific books. The only reference book that need to be purchased for this exam is the ***PMBOK® Guide Third Edition.***
- Solutions:

  - ☺ the smiley face designates the right answer
  - ☹ the sad face designates wrong answers

- Exam Directions:
  Remember that the exam will direct you to "choose the best answer." More than one answer may be a true statement. You are being tested specifically on your ability to find the right (best) answer. Review Part One and Part Two of this book as often as you need, so that you stay focused on eliminating the wrong answers and determining the best answer.

Author suggestions:

- Take 10 questions, score yourself, and review your answers.
- With each answer, whether you scored correctly or incorrectly, read through the detailed solutions provided.
- Go to the *PMBOK® Guide* and read all you can on the topic.
- Do a web search on any new terms that are not in the *PMBOK® Guide*.
- After you have conquered 10 questions, move onto the next 10.
- Be sure you are answering questions correctly because you know the material, not because you are guessing well. Continue studying each topic until you are very sure of the material and questions.

Table of Contents

PROJECT MANAGEMENT FRAMEWORK

Sample Questions

Read Chapter One and Two of the *PMBOK® Guide* before answering the questions in this section.

Big Picture Things to Know:

Chapter 1 of *PMBOK® Guide*

- Definition of a project
- Difference between a Project/Program /Operations/Portfolio/Strategic plan
- Definition of project management and PMO
- Nine knowledge areas and processes of each knowledge area
- The project environment

Chapter 2 of *PMBOK® Guide*

- Project life cycle versus product life cycle versus project management life cycle
- Trends in project life cycle
- Everything about stakeholders
- Organizational Structures
  - functional
  - matrix
  - expediter versus coordinator
  - projectized
  - composite

1. Progressive elaboration is associated with all of the following *except*:

a. project scope
b. scope creep
c. product scope
d. assumptions

2. You have just been hired by the federal government of your country. Your title is electronics systems engineer. It seems though that your primary role is to go to the different functional groups such as electrical engineering, mechanical engineering and structural engineering and ensure they are communicating with each other. For the projects of this organization you really are operating as the:

a. project manager
b. project coordinator
c. project expeditor
d. functional manager

3. Projects and operations share which of the following characteristics?

a. planned, executed, and controlled
b. temporary
c. unique products
d. progressive elaboration

4. After a long day of work, you are socializing with other project managers in your organization. It seems that most of the other project managers are managing one large project. You on the other hand are managing a large group of related projects and the maintenance and operations to support the products coming from these projects. In reality you:

a. should be paid more than the other project managers since you have more responsibility
b. are a portfolio manager since you are managing not just projects but maintenance and operations
c. should be promoted to senior management since you have so much responsibility
d. are a program manager since you are managing a group of related projects

5. The three elements of the triple constraint include which of the following?

a. cost, time, quality
b. quality, cost, scope
c. cost, time, scope
d. scope, time, quality

6. Your organization has gone through a huge realignment with a focus on core competencies. It seems that much of the work that used to be done internally will now be done externally. People are furious and jobs are being lost. Based on this current situation you are more likely to see more of what in the future?

a. projects
b. programs
c. subprojects
d. subprograms

7. The knowledge area concerned with assuring that the project includes all the work required and only the work required to complete the project successfully is:

a. project integration management
b. project scope management
c. project quality management
d. project procurement management

8. Based on your years of success as a project manager, you have just been hired by a non-profit organization. You will be managing such projects as the yearly membership drive, art auction, as well as other cyclical undertakings. In reality you are now a:

a. project manager
b. program manager
c. project expeditor
d. project coordinator

9. The knowledge described in the *PMBOK® Guide* includes all of the following *except*:

a. project life cycle definition
b. application area knowledge, standards and regulations
c. project management process groups
d. knowledge areas

10. Your organization has a long and successful history as a manufacturing company. Project management is just being introduced and it is your responsibility to make sure everyone is clear on what project management is and is not. You explain that managing a project includes all the following except:

a. identifying requirements
b. establishing clear objectives
c. balancing the competing needs of the triple constraint
d. sustaining the business

11. The project team should consider the local ecology as part of the project's:

a. cultural environment
b. social environment
c. international and political environment
d. physical environment

12. You have spent years managing small and midsize projects for your organization. Based on your success you are managing your first large scale project with what seems like an unending list of project stakeholders. The number of change requests is so large it is hard to make progress. The most likely reason for this is:

a. not enough money in the budget
b. not enough time in the schedule
c. not enough focus on stakeholder identification and analysis
d. no quality assurance department assigned to the project

13. Leadership, management, motivation, and effective communication are all part of:

a. general management knowledge and skills
b. interpersonal skills
c. the project environment
d. Project Management Body of Knowledge

14. You began your career as a project manager in the construction industry. From there you moved to IT and now you are a project manager working for a large pharmaceutical company. Which statement represents what you have learned about life cycles as you move from application to application?

a. project life cycles are often application specific
b. project management life cycles are often application specific
c. project life cycles should be applied uniformly regardless of the application
d. project management processes should be applied uniformly regardless of the application

15. A portfolio is a:

a. group of related projects
b. group of related programs
c. group of related projects and programs that are managed together
d. group of projects or programs that may not necessarily be related

16. For years your organization has believed that project management is all about schedules and budgets. Based on many failed projects, stakeholder management is now being viewed as much more important. Management wants you to focus on the positive stakeholders who can aid in the success of the project. You remind management that a primary reason you must also focus on negative stakeholders is:

a. stakeholder classification can be very difficult
b. overlooking negative stakeholders can decrease the probability of project success
c. stakeholders must be identified and their requirements determined
d. society at large may be a stakeholder on your project

17. Which of the following is **not** a process of project scope management?

a. scope planning
b. develop preliminary project scope statement
c. scope definition
d. create WBS

18. You are managing an internal Information Technology (IT) project for your organization. During planning, the WBS, schedule and cost estimates your team developed were approved and set as the project baselines. You should be able to meet all of your baselines but it seems that your critical resources keep getting pulled to support other projects and programs. Setting priorities across projects and programs is often the responsibility of:

a. the customer
b. the project sponsor
c. senior management
d. the project managers

19. Which of the following should you do first?

a. plan contracting
b. plan purchase and acquisitions
c. contract administration
d. select sellers

20. Phase one of your project is almost completed. As the project manager you are ensuring that all deliverables are completed. All of the following statements about deliverables are true except:

a. a deliverable is a measurable verifiable work product
b. completion and approval of project deliverables define the end of project phases
c. deliverables should only be the end product or components of the end product of the project
d. deliverables are part of the generally sequential process to ensure the desired product

21. The project life cycle generally defines all of the following *except*:

a. what technical work is to be accomplished in each phase
b. how the product will be divested
c. who is involved in each phase
d. how to control and approve each phase

22. As a program manager, you have seventeen project managers reporting to you. Some are members of PMI® and some are not. All the junior project managers are CAPM® certified, while all the senior project managers are PMP® certified. A few new project managers have joined your group in the last few months and have submitted their application for PMP® certification. Based on the fact that all of your staff are either certified through PMI® or have submitted applications to be certified, which document must all of your staff adhere to?

a. *PMBOK® Guide* 3rd Edition
b. All PMI® published materials
c. PMI® Code of Ethics and Professional Conduct
d. all PMI® standards

23. The level of uncertainty is which of the following?

a. highest at the start of the project and drops off
b. gets progressively higher throughout the life of the project
c. low at the start and peaks during the intermediate phases
d. remains the same throughout the life of the project

24. As a project manager for a large international organization, you often run projects in many parts of the world. Business practices are often different, depending on where you are in the world. As a Project Management Professional (PMP®) the PMI® Code of Ethics and Professional Conduct guides your actions. Which of the following is not one of the four core values described in the PMI® Code of Ethics and Professional Conduct?

a. loyalty
b. honesty
c. respect
d. responsibility

25. A deliverable can be described as which of the following?

a. related to project management processes only
b. related to the end product or components of the end product for which the project was created only
c. related to the project management processes and/or the end product of the project
d. an input into schedule development

26.   Your organization is new to project management and has decided to try the matrix approach. Your background is mechanical engineering and you have already managed three small projects. As a project manager you will be managing one large project with resources coming from engineering, marketing, finance, and manufacturing. What can you say about this new environment, compared to the old way of managing projects?

a. communication will be less complex
b. you are likely to have a better understanding of the work content of your team members
c. your teams members will only have one boss
d. you as the project manager have more control over the resources

27. The transitional actions included and not included in the project life cycle definition help link which of the following?

a. the project to the product
b. the project to the ongoing operations of the performing organization
c. the product to the project
d. the project to the suppliers

28. The technology transfer project was scheduled for eighteen months. It is now month twenty-one and your team members are past ready to start something new. There is heated debate about the definition of "project completion". Projects are considered complete when:

a. the final product has been delivered
b. the deliverables all pass quality control
c. the project objectives have been met
d. all contracts with suppliers have been closed

29. The type of organization in which each employee has one clear superior is which of the following?

a. strong matrix
b. composite structure
c. weak matrix
d. functional structure

30. As a project manager in the electronics field, it is clear that your projects are not top priority. After speaking with your management it is clear that the real issue is that your projects are not aligned with the corporate objectives. You convince your organization that one approach to help with alignment is to adopt the Management by Objectives (MBO) concept developed by Peter Drucker. All of the following are ideas associated with the objectives except:

a. focused on activities
b. specific
c. related to time
d. attainable

31. Co-location is most often associated with the:

a. strong matrix
b. projectized structure
c. weak matrix
d. composite structure

32. You have been managing projects very successfully for the last twenty years. You always hit the requirements, on time and on budget. You credit your success with being able to manage the triple constraint very well. Over the last few years though, it has become clear that the view of the triple constraint of project management has expanded and you must catch up to stay successful. One concept that has been added to the "new" definition of the triple constraint is:

a. time
b. cost
c. scope
d. risk

33. A PMO is most likely to be seen in a:

a. balanced matrix
b. projectized structure
c. weak matrix
d. functional structure

34. The performance measurements on your project are good and holding steady but your project seems completely out of control. The project CPI is 1.04 and the project SPI is 1.03. You have 405 team members in 30 different countries. You know that your focus should be on communications yet all of your time is spent on managing changes. All of the changes are catching you by surprise. Your team is closing out phase four of an eight phase project. One likely lesson learned is that more effort should have been placed on:

a. identifying a project manager for every country
b. planning for delays related to the number of countries involved
c. planning for cost overruns related to the number of countries involved
d. identifying stakeholders

35. Organizational cultures are often reflected in all of the following *except*:

a. regulations
b. shared values, norms, and beliefs
c. policies and procedures
d. work ethics and work hours

36. A project manager has been managing a long term training project. The training is over and she is trying to close out her project. The situation is not good. All of the requirements have been met but the customer is not satisfied. The customer is stating that the results of the training are not what they expected. One likely cause of this is:

a. the instructors were not qualified
b. the customer's expectations were not turned into requirements
c. the customer is trying to exploit the contract
d. the training did not go into enough detail

37. When an organization identifies an opportunity to which it would like to respond, it often initiates a:

a. preliminary project scope statement
b. feasibility study
c. work breakdown structure
d. project management plan

38. You work for a large company that has existed for over 100 years. Your business is building and maintaining the railroad systems for the country. Projects have always been managed using a functional structure and you, as a new project manager are pushing to move to a projectized structure. What disadvantage of a projectized structure might this functional manager use to support staying in a functional structure:

a. higher potential for conflict
b. more complex to manage
c. extra administration required
d. less efficient use of resources

39. You have been working in the road construction industry in a large city for many years as a project manager. Most of your projects span 18 to 36 months and have a minimum budget of $20 Million dollars (US). You have decided to switch positions and want to move to being a project manager building small hospitals in developing countries. During your interview for this new position, one strong statement you might use to show your qualifications is:

a. the project life cycle is basically the same for all projects
b. the project environment is the basically the same for all projects
c. the project management life cycle is the basically the same for all projects
d. the information in the *PMBOK® Guide* is 100 % applicable for all projects

40. Your company is responsible for publishing thousands of books a year. A reorganization is planned and the role of product managers and the role of project managers are being redefined. To do this there needs to be a clear definition of a product life cycle and a project life cycle. In general:

a. the project life cycle is often a subset of the product life cycle
b. the product life cycle is often a subset of the project life cycle
c. the product and the project life cycle usually are the same
d. the project life cycle and the product life cycle both end when the objectives have been met

41. As a project manager in a global company, you realize that you need not only project management skills but also interpersonal skills. Problem solving is an example of an interpersonal skill. Which of the following is *not* an element of problem solving?

a. risk management
b. problem identification
c. alternative identification
d. decision-making

42. In your PMO, the terms project leader and project manager are often used interchangeably. Which of the following statements is *false* about leadership and management?

a. leadership involves developing a vision and strategy
b. management is overseeing the day-to-day work of people
c. leadership involves motivating others
d. leadership and management are basically the same thing

43. Your manager has just come back from a training course on project management and immediately purchased the *PMBOK® Guide* 3rd Edition for every project manager in the organization. He states that all the answers to managing projects can be found in the book. You explain that the *PMBOK® Guide* 3rd Edition contains:

a. the entire project management body of knowledge
b. a subset of the project management body of knowledge
c. the application specific knowledge, strategies and regulations needed to manage every type of project
d. the general management knowledge and skills needed to manage every type of project

44. As a project manager in the software industry, it seems your projects are overridden with requested changes. You try to explain to your customers the effect changes have on the triple constraint. One simple way to explain the idea is that if one element of the triple constraint changes:

a. the project cost will increase
b. the project schedule will get longer
c. at least one other factor is likely to be affected
d. both of the other factors will be affected

45. In your organization, the terms *projects, programs* and *portfolios* are often used interchangeably. You explain to management the difference between these words. Which of the following is a true statement?

a. projects and portfolios are often a subset of programs
b. senior management or senior management teams often manage portfolios
c. programs are a group of projects that may or may not be related
d. projects are usually bigger than programs

46. The projects of your organization are getting so large and hard to manage that they are now being divided into phases. These phases represent:

a. the project life cycle
b. the project management life cycle
c. the product life cycle
d. the process groups

47. You are a consultant who has been brought into a medical device company to advise on both project and product management. Based on your work with this group to date, it seems that there is a tremendous amount of disconnect between research, development, and manufacturing. One of your first recommendations is for the organization to consider:

a. fast-tracking
b. crashing
c. concurrent engineering
d. resource leveling

48. You are a cost estimator for all major projects in your organization. In your position you try to convince project managers that early scope definition is critical. The main reason behind this is:

a. scope definition drives cost estimating
b. the ability to influence cost is greatest at the early stages of the project
c. cost estimating drives scope definition
d. your organization must complete scope definition before any cost estimating can begin

49. Your company is really a mix of multiple organizational structures. It seems you are always in the part of the organization that gives the project manager the least amount of authority. You most likely work in a:

a. weak matrix
b. tight matrix
c. functional organization
d. strong matrix

50. You know through your outside reading that functional organizations are very different from matrix organizations. Which of the following is *not* true of a typical project in a functional organization?

a. the organization looks like a hierarchy
b. the workers are grouped by specialty and report to the project manager
c. the scope of the project is usually bound by the work of the functional group
d. if questions arise that are outside the function, the questions are passed up and down the hierarchy

© May 2007 AME Group, Inc.

PROJECT MANAGEMENT FRAMEWORK

Learning Solutions

1.   b.   *PMBOK® Guide* 1.2.1.3
☺   b. *Scope creep* is adding features and functionality (project scope) without addressing the effects on time, costs, and resources, or without customer approval. Scope creep is undesirable.
☹   a., c and d. Progressive elaboration is associated with project scope, product scope, and assumptions. Progressive elaboration is continuously improving and detailing a plan as more detailed and specific information, as well as more accurate estimates, become available. This ensures that plans produced are more accurate and complete because of successive iterations of the planning process.

2.   c.   *PMBOK® Guide* 2.3.3
☺   c. The project expeditor's role on a project is to serve as a communications link.
☹   a. The project manager's role is to manage the project, not just serve as a communications link.
☹   b. The project coordinator is similar to a project expeditor but has some minimal authority.
☹   d. The functional manager directs the work of the individuals in his function.

3.   a.   *PMBOK® Guide* 1.2.2
☺   a. Projects and operations are performed by people, constrained by limited resources, and planned, executed, and controlled.
☹   b. Projects are temporary; operations are ongoing.
☹   c. Projects produce unique products; operations produce multiple units of the same product.
☹   d. Progressive elaboration is associated with project scope, product scope, and assumptions, not with operations in general.

4.   d.   PMBOK® Guide 1.6.1
☺   d. Program managers manage groups of projects and their related work.
☹   a. There is not enough information to know who should be paid more money. This kind of answer is not likely to be correct on the exam.
☹   b. Portfolio managers manage groups of projects and programs that may not necessarily be interdependent or directly related. Look for a better answer.
☹   c. Senior management manages portfolios. This question is about managing programs, not portfolios.

5   c.   *PMBOK® Guide* 1.3
☺   c. The elements of the triple constraint are cost, time, and scope.
☹   a, b and d. Project quality is affected by balancing cost, time, and scope. Quality is not one of the three elements of the triple constraint.

6.   c.   PMBOK® Guide 1.6.3
☺   c. Subprojects are components of projects that are often contracted to an external organization or another part of the organization. Since your organization is now focused on core competencies, you are likely to see more work being subcontracted out.
☹   a and b. An organization's focus on core competencies will not lead to an increase in projects or programs. In fact, this may drive to a decrease of internal projects and programs.
☹   d. Subprograms is a made up term.

7. b. *PMBOK® Guide* 1.4.3
☺ b. Project scope management includes the processes required to ensure that the project includes all the work required, and only the work required, to complete the project successfully.
☹ a. Project integration management includes the processes and activities needed to identify, define, combine, unify, and coordinate the various processes and project management activities within the Project Management Process Groups.
☹ c. Project quality management includes the processes and activities of the performing organization that determine quality policies, objectives, and responsibilities so that the project will satisfy the needs for which it was undertaken.
☹ d. Project procurement management includes the processes to purchase or acquire the products, services, or results needed from outside the project team to perform the work.

8. b. *PMBOK® Guide* 1.6.1
☺ b. Programs may involve a series of repetitive undertakings. In this example, cyclical undertakings imply that you are a program manager.
☹ a. Cyclical undertakings are associated with programs not projects.
☹ c and d. There is nothing in this question on authority or communications so project expeditor or coordinator are not likely to be the right answer.

9. b. *PMBOK® Guide* 1.5.1 and 1.5.2
☺ b. Application areas are categories of projects that have common elements significant in such projects, but are not needed or present in all projects. The knowledge, standards, and regulations associated with specific applications would be found in publications related to that application. The knowledge and practices described in the *PMBOK® Guide* are applicable to most projects most of the time.
☹ a. The project life cycle definition is described in Chapter Two of the *PMBOK® Guide*.
☹ c. The project management process groups are described in Chapter Three of the *PMBOK® Guide*.
☹ d. The nine knowledge areas are described in Chapters Four through Twelve of the *PMBOK® Guide*.

10. d. *PMBOK® Guide* 1.2.2
☺ d. Sustaining the business is the objective of ongoing operations, not projects.
☹ a. Identifying requirements is an early part of managing a project.
☹ b. Establishing clear objectives is an early part of managing a project.
☹ c. Balancing the competing needs of the triple constraint can be a very difficult part of project management.

11. d. *PMBOK® Guide* 1.5.3
☺ d. The physical environment includes such items as the local ecology and the physical geography.
☹ a and b. The cultural and social environments include the economic, demographic, educational ethical, ethnic, religious, and other characteristics of the people. The organizational culture and the view of project management is also part of the cultural and social environments.
☹ c. The international and political environments include international, national, regional and local laws, and customs as well as the political climate. Time zone differences, national and regional holidays, travel requirements, etc., must also be considered as part of this environment.

12.   c.   *PMBOK® Guide* 2.2

☹   c. Change requests are often initiated by stakeholders who were not involved in early project planning.

☹   a. There is nothing in the question that states the project is in trouble from a cost standpoint. Don't draw conclusions that are not in the question.

☹   b. There is nothing in the question that states the project is in trouble from a schedule standpoint. Don't draw conclusions that are not in the question.

☹   d. Quality assurance is the application of quality activities to ensure the project will meet requirements. Quality assurance is about applying processes. This answer is not related to the question.

13.   b.   *PMBOK® Guide* 1.5.5

☺   b. Leadership, management, motivation, and effective communication are all part of interpersonal skills.

☹   a. General management knowledge and skills include such items as financial management, accounting, purchasing, procurement, sales, and marketing, etc.

☹   c. The project environment includes the cultural and social environment, the international and political environment, and the physical environment.

☹   d. The project management body of knowledge includes the project life cycle and organization, the five process groups and the nine knowledge areas.

14.   a.   *PMBOK® Guide* Chapter 3 Introduction

☺   a. Project life cycles often define the product oriented processes. These processes often vary by application. An IT organization may have one lifecycle while a pharmaceutical organization may use a different life cycle.

☹   b. The project management life cycle is another name for the project management processes. These processes are common to most projects most of the time.

☹   c. Project life cycles often define the product oriented processes. These processes often vary by application. An IT organization may have one lifecycle while a pharmaceutical organization may use a different life cycle.

☹   d. Even though the project management processes are common to most projects most of the time, the appropriate use and rigor of each process should be determined by the project manager and the project management team.

15.   d.   *PMBOK® Guide* 1.6.2

☺   d. A portfolio is a collection of projects or programs and other work that are grouped together to facilitate effective management of that work to meet strategic business objectives. The projects or programs of the portfolio may not necessarily be interdependent or directly related.

☹   a. A program is a group of related projects managed in a coordinated way to obtain benefits and control not available from managing them individually. Programs may include elements of related work outside of the scope of the discrete projects in the program.

☹   b and c. The projects and programs in a portfolio may not necessarily be interdependent or directly related.

16.   b.   *PMBOK® Guide* 2.2

☺   b. There must be a focus on negative stakeholders because ignoring these stakeholders can increase the risk of not achieving project success.

☹   a. Stakeholder classification can be difficult but this does not explain why we need to put a focus on negative stakeholders.

☹   c. The statement that stakeholders must be identified and their requirements determined is true. This does not explain why we need to focus on negative stakeholders.

☹   d. Society at large may be a stakeholder on our project yet this does not explain why we need to put a focus on negative stakeholders.

17.   b.   *PMBOK® Guide* 1.4.3

☺   b. The processes of project scope management include: scope planning, scope definition, creating WBS, scope verification, and scope control. Developing a preliminary project scope statement is part of Project Integration Management.

☹   a, c and d. Scope planning is process one of scope; scope definition is process two of scope; and create WBS is process three of scope.

18.   c.   *PMBOK® Guide* 1.6.2

☺   c. Senior management is responsible for setting priorities across projects and programs. Senior management manages the portfolios.

☹   a. The customer may not be the best choice since each project or program may have a different customer.

☹   b. The project sponsor may not be the best choice since each project or program may have a different sponsor.

☹   d. The project managers have authority to manage to the objectives set for their own project but not the authority to set priorities across projects.

19.   b.   *PMBOK® Guide* 1.4.3

☺   b. The steps of project procurement management are, in order: plan purchase and acquisition, plan contracting, request seller responses, select seller, contract administration, and contract closure.

☹   a. Plan contracting is step two of procurement, and plan purchase and acquisitions is step one.

☹   c. Contract administration is step five of procurement and plan purchase and acquisitions is step one.

☹   d. Selecting sellers is step four of procurement and plan purchase and acquisitions is step one.

20.   c.   *PMBOK® Guide* 2.1.2

☺   c. Deliverables can be associated with the end product or the project management processes.

☹   a. A deliverable is a measurable verifiable work product such as a plan, a report, a computer program, etc.

☹   b. The completion of one or more deliverables often signifies the end of a project phase.

☹   d. Deliverables often are sequential to ensure control and that the objectives of the project are met.

21.   b.   *PMBOK® Guide* 2.1.1 and 2.1.3

☺   b. The product life cycle, not the project life cycle, often includes the business plan, the project life cycle, operations, and product divestment.

☹   a, c and d. The project life cycle defines what technical work to do, when the deliverables are to be generated, who is involved, and how to control and approve each phase.

22.   c.   PMI® Code of Ethics and Professional Conduct

☺   c. The PMI® Code of Ethics and Professional Conduct is applicable for both PMI® members and individuals who have applied for or received certification through PMI® regardless of their membership in PMI®.

☹   a. The *PMBOK*® *Guide* 3rd Edition is a standard, not a regulation. It does not have to be followed. It is suggested that the project management team tailor the information in the *PMBOK*® *Guide* to their specific project.

☹   b. PMI® publishes a tremendous amount of information. It is the responsibility of the project management team to determine what is appropriate for any given project.

☹   d. PMI® standards are standards, not regulations. They do not have to be followed.

23.   a.   *PMBOK*® *Guide* 2.1.1

☺   a. The level of uncertainty is highest at the start of the project and continues to get lower throughout the life of the project.

☹   b. The cost of changes gets progressively higher throughout the life of the project.

☹   c. Cost and staffing levels are low at the start and peak during the intermediate phases.

☹   d. It is hard to imagine anything that stays constant throughout the life of the project.

24.   a.   PMI® Code of Ethics and Professional Conduct

☺   a. The four core values described in the PMI® Code of Ethics and Professional Conduct are: responsibility, respect, fairness and honesty. A conflict of interest occurs when we are in a position to influence an outcome when such outcomes could affect one or more parties with which we have competing loyalties.

☹   b, c and d. The four core values described in the PMI® Code of Ethics and Professional Conduct are: responsibility, respect, fairness and honesty.

25.   c.   *PMBOK*® *Guide* 2.1.2

☺   c. A deliverable is a measurable, verifiable work product such as a spec, feasibility study report, etc. Some deliverables relate to the project management processes whereas others are the end products or components of the end products.

☹   a and b. Be careful of the word *only*. Deliverables can relate to the project or product.

☹   d. Schedule development has many inputs, none being a "deliverable."

26.   d.   *PMBOK*® *Guide* Figure 2-6.

☺   d. If the question does not tell you what structure to compare to, then you need to compare to the functional structure. In a matrix you have more control (though how much depends on the matrix) than in a functional structure.

☹   a. In a matrix, the communication is more complex than in a functional structure.

☹   b. In a matrix, you will have people on the team coming from other functions, not just your own. As a mechanical engineer you are likely to have less of an understanding of accounting, marketing etc, than if you were in a functional group and all your team members were other mechanical engineers.

☹   c. In a matrix, your team members have two bosses, you and their functional manager. In a functional organization, your team members only have one boss, the functional manager.

27.   b.   *PMBOK® Guide* 2.1.3
☺   b. Transitional actions in the project life cycle help link the project to the ongoing operations.
☹   a and c. The project life cycle is often a series of phases to create a product. Sometimes the project life cycle is considered a subset of the product life cycle.
☹   d. Contracts help relate the project to the suppliers.

28.   c.   *PMBOK® Guide* 8.3
☺   c. The definition of project completion is meeting objectives.
☹   a. Just because the final product is delivered does not mean that all objectives have been met. Delivery is not enough.
☹   b. Quality control is about correctness. All the project deliverables may be "correct" yet the project may not meet the objectives.
☹   d. All contracts with vendors should be closed before we close the project. Completion of the project though is not just about the project's vendors. Completion is measured against the project objectives.

29.   d.   *PMBOK® Guide* 2.3.3
☺   d. In a functional organization the worker has one and only one supervisor. Every person in a functional organization works in their function. As an example; engineers work in a engineering group, sales people work in a sales group.
☹   b. A composite organization involves multiple structures at various levels. In the functional part of the composite, the worker has only one supervisor; in the matrix part, the worker may have more than one supervisor.
☹   a and c. In a matrix (weak, balanced, or strong) the worker has a functional manager and at least one project manager.

30.   a. Web Search on Management by Objectives- Peter Drucker
☺   a. Objectives should be focused on results, not on activities.
☹   b, c and d. Objectives should be SMART (specific, measurable, attainable, relevant, time bounded).

31.   b.   *PMBOK® Guide* 2.3.3
☺   b. Co-location is a strategy to place team members physically close together to improve communication and productivity. In a projectized organization, the PM often has a lot of independence and authority. Placing the team members in one place makes it easier for the team to work together. One objective of projectizing is to move the loyalty from the functional groups to the project team, which is one benefit of collocation.
☹   a and c. In a matrix the workers are borrowed from the functional groups and support one or more projects. In general the workers are still physically located within their functional groups.
☹   d. A composite is made up of all structures, which may allow for some collocation.

32.   d.   *PMBOK® Guide* 1.3
☺   d. The "old" view of the triple constraint included: time, cost and scope. The expanded view also includes: quality, risk and customer satisfaction.
☹   a, b and c. The "old" view of the triple constraint included: time, cost and scope. The expanded view also includes: quality, risk and customer satisfaction.

33.   b.   *PMBOK® Guide* 2.3.4

☺   b. You may find a PMO is any of the organizational structures but the greater the authority of the project manager the more likely you are to see a PMO. From the list given, answer *projectized* (answer b) is where the PM has the most authority. From this list, the functional organization is where you are least likely to see a PMO.

☹   a, c and d. It is possible to see a PMO in any of these organizations. To answer the question, pick the answer where the project manager has the most authority because that is the most likely situation in which to see a PMO.

34.   d.   *PMBOK® Guide* 2.2

☺   d. Often the underlying reason for "too many" change requests is the lack of identification of all stakeholders. If we do not identify a stakeholder, we do not identify their requirements and therefore we are likely to experience many change requests.

☹   a. There is nothing in the question to lead up to believe that the issue of too many change requests is because of a lack of a project manager in each country. Do not read information that is not in the question.

☹   b. The SPI is 1.03. The project is ahead of schedule.

☹   c. The CPI is 1.04. The project is running under budget.

35.   a.   *PMBOK® Guide* 1.5.2 and 2.3.2

☺   a. A regulation is a government imposed requirement and thus no reflection of the organizational culture.

☹   b, c and d. Shared values, policies, procedures, views of authority relationships, work ethic, and work hours are all representative of organizational cultures and styles.

36.   b.   *PMBOK® Guide* 5.2.2.4

☺   b. Stakeholders needs, wants and expectations must be analyzed and converted into requirements. Often unidentified expectations or unquantifiable expectations can put customer satisfaction at risk.

☹   a. There is nothing in the question to tell us that the instructors were not qualified. In fact, the requirements were met, so this is not the likely explanation.

☹   c. There is nothing in the question to make us believe that the customer is trying to exploit the contract. In fact, this is not a likely "type" of right answer on the test.

☹   d. There is nothing in the question to tell us that the training did not go into enough detail. In fact, the requirements were met, so this is not the likely explanation.

37.   b.   *PMBOK® Guide* 2.1.1

☺   b. A feasibility study is often initiated to help an organization decide whether is should undertake a project.

☹   a. A preliminary project scope statement is developed after a project has been chartered but not to help decide if a project should be undertaken.

☹   c. The work breakdown structure defines the total scope of the project. It is developed long after a project has been chartered.

☹   d. The project management plan is a formal approved document that describes how the project will be executed, monitored, and controlled. It is developed long after the project is chartered.

38.　d.　　*PMBOK® Guide* 2.3.3
☺　d. In a projectized structure the is often less efficient us of resources. As an example, the project may require an accounting person for half time, yet if the organization is projectized, the accounting person will be full time on the project.
☹　a. A higher potential for conflict is a negative of the matrix structure not the projectized structure.
☹　b. A matrix structure is more complex to manage, not a projectized structure.
☹　c. A matrix structure requires extra administration, not a projectized structure.

39.　c.　　*PMBOK® Guide* 3.2
☺　c. The five process groups are performed in the same sequence on each project. Another name for the five process groups is the project management life cycle. This life cycle describes the processes for managing the project.
☹　a. The project life cycle tells you the work of the project and is different from project to project. (*PMBOK® Guide* 2.1.3)
☹　b. Each project exists in its own cultural and social, international and political, and physical environment. (*PMBOK® Guide* 1.5.3)
☹　d. The project management team is responsible for determining what is appropriate from the *PMBOK® Guide* for each project (*PMBOK® Guide* 1.1).

40.　a.　　*PMBOK® Guide* 2.2
☺　a. The project life cycle is often a subset of the product life cycle. The product is going to last much longer than the project.
☹　b. This statement is reversed. The project life cycle is the subset, not the product life cycle.
☹　c. and d. The project life cycle lasts until the objectives have been met, then terminates. The product life cycle may include operations and lasts until divestment.

41.　a.　　*PMBOK® Guide* 1.5.5
☺　a. Problem solving is a combination of problem identification, alternative identification and decision making. Risk management is not one of the three elements.
☹　b, c and d. Problem solving is a combination of problem identification, alternative identification and decision making

42.　d.　　*PMBOK® Guide* 1.5.5
☺　d. Leadership is related to setting a vision and motivating others to achieve that vision. Management is overseeing the day-to-day work of people. There are very different ideas.
☹　a, b and c. These statements are all true. The question is looking for the false statement.

43.　b.　　*PMBOK® Guide* Figure 1-2
☺　b. The *PMBOK® Guide* is a guide to the project management body of knowledge. Therefore, it is a subset of the project management body of knowledge.
☹　a. It would not be possible to put the entire project management body of knowledge in one book. The knowledge resides in the minds and work of the practitioners.
☹　c. Each application often has it own standards and regulations that are not detailed in the *PMBOK® Guide*.

☹ d. General management skills are required of the project manager but not detailed in the *PMBOK® Guide*. There is a tremendous amount of literature on general management skills and it was decided not to repeat the details of that information in the *PMBOK® Guide*.

44.   c.   *PMBOK® Guide* 1.3

☺ c. As one element of the triple constraint changes (cost, time, scope) at least one other element is likely to change. As an example, if we add scope, generally we will need to either add cost or add time or add both.

☹ a. A change is not always a growth. If we de-scope the project, the cost may go up or down, based on the de-scope.

☹ b. A change is not always a growth. If we de-scope the project, the schedule may get shorter or longer, depending on the de-scope.

☹ d. If we change one element (cost, time, scope) of the triple constraint, at least one other element is likely to change. Both other elements may change but that depends on the details of the first change.

45.   b.   *PMBOK® Guide* 1.6

☺ b. Portfolios are groups of projects or programs that may or may not be related. It is the responsibility of senior management to oversee the management of portfolios.

☹ a. Projects are a subset of programs. Projects and programs are a subset of portfolios.

☹ c. Portfolios are a group of projects or programs that may or may not be related. All projects in a program are related.

☹ d. Projects are a subset of programs and are usually smaller than programs.

46.   a.   *PMBOK® Guide* 2.1.1

☺ a. The phases of a project, such as initiation, planning, implementation and closeout, represent the project life cycle.

☹ b and d. The project management life cycle and the process groups are the same. They are initiating, planning, executing, monitoring and controlling, and closing.

☹ c. The product life cycle is the cycle the product will go through. The project life cycle may be a subset of the product life cycle. The product life cycle often includes the business plan, the project life cycle, operations and divestment.

47.   c.   *PMBOK® Guide* Chapter 2— Introduction

☺ c. Concurrent engineering is a process that allows the implementers to be involved with requirements and design. One idea behind concurrent engineering is to do research and development with manufacturing in mind.

☹ a. Fast-tracking allows you to overlap activities that you would prefer to be done in series. This helps to pull in the schedule but will not help fix the disconnect described in the question.

☹ b. Crashing allows you to add resources to activities on the critical path. This helps to pull in the schedule but will not help fix the disconnect described in the question.

☹ d. Resource leveling is a network technique that allows us to base schedule decisions on availability of resources. This often extends the schedule and will not solve the disconnect described in the question.

48.   b.   *PMBOK® Guide* Chapter 7— Cost Introduction

☺   b. The question is asking why early scope definition is critical. It is important to define the scope early since early in the project is when we can have the greatest influence in cost.

☹   a. Scope definition does drive cost estimating but this is not a strong enough answer to define why we need to do scope definition early. Look for an answer that addresses the word *early*.

☹   c. Usually scope definition drives cost estimating, not the other way around.

☹   d. There are two trigger words in this statement. One is *complete* and the other is *any*. Some cost estimating can begin before scope definition is complete. Remember that planning is iterative.

49.   c.   *PMBOK® Guide* Figure 2-6

☺   c. The functional organization is the structure where the project manager has the least amount of authority.

☹   a. This is a good answer but not the best answer. In a weak matrix the project manager has less authority than the functional manager. There is still a structure though where the project manager has even less authority than in a weak matrix.

☹   b. The tight matrix is not an organizational structure. It is another name for co-location. If your team is co-located, you probably have some level of authority.

☹   d. In a strong matrix the project manager has more authority than the functional mangers.

50   b.   *PMBOK® Guide* 2.3.3

☺   b. The workers are grouped by specialty in a functional organization but they do not report to the project manager. The workers report to their functional manager.

☹   a. The organization looks like a hierarchy with the functional manager, not the project manager at the top.

☹   c. The project is bound by the work of the functional group. The project is not cross-functional.

☹   d. Questions outside of the function go up and down the hierarchy. This can take time and slow projects down.

PROJECT MANAGEMENT PROCESSES

Sample Questions

Big Picture Things to Know

Read Chapter Three of the *PMBOK® Guide* before answering the questions in this section.

- Plan-Do-Check-Act

- Know the five process groups:
    - Initiating process group—defines and authorizes the project or a project phase
    - Planning process group—defines and refines objectives and plans the course of action required to attain the objectives and scope that the project was undertaken to address
    - Executing process group—integrates people and other resources to carry out the project management plan for the project
    - Monitoring and controlling process group—regularly measures and monitors progress to identify variances from the project management plan so that corrective action can be taken when necessary to meet project objectives
    - Closing process group—formalizes acceptance of the product, service or result and brings the project or a project phase to an orderly end

- Focus on the five process groups
    - Know what steps occur in each process group
    - Know sequence of steps in each process group
    - Know Figures 3-5, 3-6, 3-7, 3-8, 3-9 and 3-10 cold

1. The project life cycle defines:

a. product oriented processes
b. project oriented processes
c. both product and project oriented processes
d. neither product or project oriented processes

2. The five project management process groups include:

a. initiating, planning, executing, monitoring and controlling
b. integration, scope, time, cost, and quality
c. initiating, planning, executing, monitoring and controlling, and closing
d. concept, planning, execution, controlling, and closeout

3. Shewhart and Deming are famous for what cycle?

a. concept-development-execution-closeout
b. plan-do-check-act
c. forming-storming-norming-performing
d. initiating-planning-executing-monitoring and controlling-closing

4. The monitoring and controlling process group corresponds to what component of the plan-do-check-act cycle?

a. do-check
b. check-act
c. act-plan
d. plan-do

5. Large and complex projects are often separated into distinct phases. The five process groups are:

a. the same as these project phases
b. normally repeated in each of these phases
c. related to the product and, therefore, not related to the project phases
d. related to project management and, therefore, not related to the project phases

6. The processes of which process group are normally performed external to the project's scope of control?

a. initiating
b. planning
c. executing
d. monitoring and controlling

7. In multi-phase projects, the initiating processes occur:

a. only during the concept phase
b. in every phase
c. only in the early phases
d. only when the sponsor requests them

8. The project becomes officially authorized through the:

a. approval of the concept phase gate
b. approval of the project charter
c. approval of the WBS
d. approval of the scope statement

9. The document that provides a high-level definition of the project is:

a. project charter
b. preliminary scope statement
c. scope management plan
d. WBS

10. The process group that must provide feedback to implement corrective or preventative action is:

a. planning
b. executing
c. monitoring and controlling
d. implementation

11. The project scope statement is the primary output of:

a. scope definition
b. scope planning
c. develop project management plan
d. create WBS

12. The scope baseline is an output of:

a. create WBS
b. scope planning
c. scope definition
d. activity definition

13. The project schedule network diagrams are an output of:

a. activity definition
b. develop project management plan
c. schedule development
d. activity duration estimating

14. The cost baseline is an output of:

a. cost estimating
b. cost budgeting
c. cost control
d. schedule development

15. The quality baseline is an output of:

a. perform quality assurance
b. cost budgeting
c. quality planning
d. schedule development

16. The contract SOW is an output of:

a. scope planning
b. plan purchases and acquisitions
c. develop project management plan
d. scope definition

17. Which are you likely to create first?

a. WBS
b. scope management plan
c. project charter
d. preliminary project scope statement

18. Which are you likely to create first?

a. cost baseline
b. WBS
c. schedule baseline
d. quality baseline

19. Which are you likely to create first?

a. activity list
b. WBS
c. scope statement
d. schedule

20. Which are you likely to create last?

a. activity list
b. WBS
c. scope statement
d. schedule

21. The vast majority of the project budget is spent during which process group?

a. initiating
b. planning
c. executing
d. monitoring and controlling

22. The five process groups are:

a. often performed in a random sequence
b. always performed in the same sequence
c. performed in a different sequence based on the project phase
d. performed in a sequence determined by the project management team

23. The scope management plan is the primary output of:

a. scope definition
b. scope planning
c. develop project management plan
d. create WBS

24. What must be documented before the beginning of the initiating process group activities?

a. project charter
b. name of project manager
c. project schedule
d. organization's business need

25.   Approval and funding for the project are handled:

a. external to the project boundaries
b. internal to the project boundaries
c. by the project manager
d. by the project management team

26. The initiating processes are:

a. performed only at the start of the project
b. performed/reviewed at the start of every phase
c. performed/reviewed at the start and end of every phase
d. performed/reviewed as needed, based on the project management team

27. The preliminary project scope statement includes all of the following *except:*

a. project scope baseline
b. project and product objectives
c. project boundaries
d. approval requirements

28.   Which statement below best describes the relationship between create WBS and activity definition?

a. the output of create WBS is the activity list, and the output of activity definition is the WBS
b. the output of create WBS is in the form of deliverables; the output of activity definition is in the form of schedule activities
c. activity definition that defines the activity list is usually done before create WBS, which defines the WBS
d. create WBS must always be completed before activity definition can begin

29. Bottoms-up estimating is a tool and technique of which step?

a. activity duration estimating
b. activity resource estimating
c. activity sequencing
d. create WBS

30. Contract administration includes:

a. managing the relationship with your external seller only
b. managing the relationship with your external buyer only
c. managing the relationship with your external seller and external buyer as appropriate
d. managing the relationship with your internal seller and the internal buyer as appropriate

30

31. The process necessary for formalizing acceptance of the completed project deliverables is known as:

a. close project
b. contract closure
c. perform quality control
d. scope verification

32. The process for controlling factors that create change to ensure those changes are beneficial is?

a. scope control
b. perform quality control
c. integrated change control
d. monitor and control project work

33. The process necessary for monitoring specific project results to determine whether they comply with relevant quality standards and identifying ways to eliminate causes of unsatisfactory performance is:

a. perform quality control
b. perform quality assurance
c. quality planning
d. scope verification

34. Which step are you most likely to do first?

a. plan purchase and acquisitions
b. scope definition
c. create WBS
d. plan contracting

35. Contracts and projects are:

a. both legally binding relationships
b. a contract is a legally binding relationship; a project is not
c. a project is a legally binding relationship; a contract is not
d. not legally binding

36. The code of accounts and the chart of accounts are:

a. different names for the same thing
b. the code of accounts is a numbering system used to identify each component of the WBS; the chart of accounts is a numbering system used to monitor project costs by category
c. the chart of accounts is a numbering system to identify each component of the WBS; the code of accounts is a numbering system used to monitor project costs by category
d. the code of accounts helps relate the project to the financial accounts of the performing organization; the chart of accounts helps relate each unique element of the WBS

37. Configuration management is a tool of:

a. scope control
b. schedule control
c. cost control
d. perform quality control

38. The summary budget first appears in the:

a. project charter
b. activity cost estimates
c. cost baseline
d project management plan

39. Based on an approved change in scope, you are now updating your cost baseline. You are most likely in which process?

a. cost budgeting
b. cost estimating
c. cost control
d. scope control

40. Cost estimating policies are often part of what?

a. organizational process assets
b. enterprise environmental factors
c. cost management plan
d. cost baseline

41. As the most experienced project manager in the company, you have been assigned the project of developing a project management methodology that can be applied to most projects most of the time. At the first meeting of your core team you get into a heated discussion of project phases and project management process groups. You explain that all of the following are true concerning the process groups *except*:

a. they are performed in the same sequence on each project
b. they have clear dependencies
c. they are dependent on the application area or industry focus
d. they are often iterated multiple times on each project

42. At the first meeting of the core project management methodology team you explain that the project has just completed the initiation phase. All of the following are true concerning initiation *except*:

a. initiating processes are often done external to the project's scope of control
b. the primary output of the initiating process group is the project's scope statement
c. before the initiating steps the project's business needs or requirements are documented
d. approval and funding for the project are handled external to the project boundaries

43. For months everyone in your organization has been talking as if the project management methodology project has been approved. You realize that the project is officially approved when:

a. the initiating process steps begin
b. the project charter is approved
c. the project manager is assigned
d. the project baselines have been established

44. Project planning has begun with your core team and there is conflict on the sequence of the planning activities. From the list below, which sequence is *least* likely to occur?

a. create WBS before activity definition
b. create WBS before scope definition
c. create WBS before cost estimating
d. create WBS before plan purchase and acquisitions

45. Project planning has begun with your core team and there is conflict on the sequence of the planning activities. From the list below which sequence is *least* likely to occur?

a. cost budgeting before cost estimating
b. qualitative risk analysis before quantitative risk analysis
c. plan purchase and acquisitions before plan contracting
d. quality planning before schedule development

46. You have spent months with your core team planning your project and it is finally time to begin the executing work. You realize that executing involves all of the following *except*:

a. approving changes
b. coordinating people and resources
c. integrating and performing the activities of the project
d. implementing approved changes

47. You have been working as a project manager for six years and have never really had to manage a project budget before. This is changing now that money has become tighter. Based on your experience and your outside reading, which of the following statements about costs and budgets is *not* true?

a. a majority of the project's budget will be spent during the executing process group
b. cost and price always mean the same thing
c. cost estimates should be developed before cost budgets
d. the ability to influence costs is highest early in the project

48. It seems that your team does a great job of planning projects but somehow losses insight into the project during executing. Based on this you have decided to put more effort into the monitoring and controlling of the project. You realize that monitoring and controlling involves all of the following *except*:

a. collecting, measuring, and disseminating performance information
b. risk monitoring and control
c. source selection
d. controlling factors that create change to ensure those changes are beneficial

49. Change control has been a big issue for you on past projects. It seems that some changes get put into the project baselines without approvals and other approved changes never make it to the baseline. Which of the following is *not* one of the three elements of integrated change control?

a. immediately implementing all government mandated changes
b. controlling factors that create changes to make sure those changes are beneficial
c. determining when a change has occurred
d. managing the approved changes

50. You have been managing projects very successfully for 20 years. Now you are trying to relate accepted project management terminology to your world. You understand the project life cycle and are beginning to even understand the project management life cycle. You are familiar with the phrase: *project management domains*. All of the following statements about project domains are true *except*:

a. there are six domains in project management
b. the project life cycle is a subset of the project management domains
c. the project management life cycle is a subset of the project management domains
d. the project process groups are a subset of the project management domains

PROJECT MANAGEMENT PROCESSES

Learning Solutions

1.   a.   *PMBOK® Guide* Chapter 3 Introduction

☺   a. Product oriented processes are typically defined by the project life cycle and vary by application area.

☹   b and c. The project oriented processes have the purpose to initiate, plan, execute, monitor and control, and close the project, and are not defined by the project lifecycle (*PMBOK® Guide* 3.4). They are defined in the five process groups.

☹   d. Product oriented processes are typically defined by the project life cycle and vary by application area.

2.   c.   *PMBOK® Guide* Chapter 3 Introduction

☺   c. The five project management process groups are initiating, planning, executing, monitoring and controlling, and closing.

☹   a. Monitoring and controlling together are the fourth process group; they are not two separate groups. Closing is *not* on this list.

☹   b. Integration, scope, time, cost, and quality are knowledge areas, *not* process groups.

☹   d. Concept, execution, and closeout are often names for phases of a project life cycle, *not* the five project management process groups.

3.   b.   *PMBOK® Guide* 3.1

☺   b. Shewhart and Deming are famous for the plan-do-check-act cycle.

☹   a. Concept-development-execution-closeout is one example of a project life cycle.

☹   c. Forming-storming-norming-performing are four stages of team development, as defined by Bruce Tuchman.

☹   d. Initiating-planning-executing-monitoring and controlling-closing are the five project management process groups.

4.   b.   *PMBOK® Guide* 3.1

☺   b. The monitoring and controlling process group corresponds to the "check and act" components.

☹   a. The executing process group corresponds to the "do" component.

☹   c and d. The planning process group corresponds to the "plan" component.

5.   b.   *PMBOK® Guide* 3.2

☺   b. The five process groups are normally repeated in each project phase. The process groups are not the project phases themselves.

☹   a. The project life cycle typically defines the product oriented processes.

☹   c. The five project management process groups are related to the project, not the product.

☹   d. Projects are managed through the five process groups, and the five process groups are repeated in each of the project phases.

6.   a.   *PMBOK® Guide* 3.2.1

☺   a. Initiating is about the formal authorization to start a new project or project phase. Initiating processes are often performed outside of the project's scope of control. This at times may blur the project boundaries.

☹   b, c and d. The planning, executing, and monitoring and controlling processes are all done internal to the project's scope of control.

7.   b.   *PMBOK® Guide* 3.2.1

☺   b. The initiating processes are repeated at the start of every phase. Reviewing the initiating processes at the beginning of every phase helps to keep the project focused.

☹   a, c and d. The initiating processes are repeated at the start of every phase. Reviewing the initiating processes at the beginning of every phase helps to keep the project focused.

8.   b.   *PMBOK® Guide* 3.2.1.1

☺   b. The project charter authorizes the project or the project phase.

☹   a. The approval of the concept phase gate signifies that the work of the concept phase is complete.

☹   c. The approval of the WBS, and the scope statement before it, signifies that we have a scope baseline, which is completed after the project is authorized.

☹   d. The scope statement is the definition of the project, which is completed after the project is authorized (*PMBOK® Guide* 5.2.3.1).

9.   b.   *PMBOK® Guide* 3.2.1.2

☺   b. The preliminary scope project scope statement provides a high-level definition of the project.

☹   a. The project charter authorizes the project and documents the business need.

☹   c. The scope management plan describes how the project scope will be defined, documented, verified, managed, and controlled.

☹   d. The work breakdown structure defines the total scope of the project.

10.   c.   *PMBOK® Guide* 3.2

☺   c. The monitoring and controlling process group provides feedback to implement corrective or preventative actions to bring the project into compliance with the project management plan or to appropriately modify the project management plan.

☹   a. The planning process group defines the course of action required to attain the objectives and scope the project was undertaken to address.

☹   b. The executing process group integrates people and other resources to carry out the project management plan for the project.

☹   d. There is no such thing as an implementation process group.

11.   a.   *PMBOK® Guide* Table 3-5

☺   a. Scope definition has the project scope statement as its primary output.

☹   b. Scope planning has the project scope management plan as its primary output (*PMBOK® Guide* Table 3-4).

☹   c. Develop project management plan has the project management plan as its only output (*PMBOK® Guide* Table 3-3).

☹   d. Create WBS has the WBS as one of its outputs (*PMBOK® Guide* Table 3-6).

12.   a.   *PMBOK® Guide* 5.3.3.4

☺   a. Create WBS has the scope baseline as an output.

☹   b. Scope planning has the project scope management plan as its primary output (*PMBOK® Guide* 5.1.3.1).

☹   c. Scope definition has the project scope statement as an output, which is part of the scope baseline (*PMBOK® Guide* 5.2.3.1).

☹   d. Activity definition has the activity list has its output (*PMBOK® Guide* 6.1.3.1).

13.   c.   *PMBOK® Guide* 6.5.3.1

☺   c. Schedule development has the project schedule as an output. One form of a project schedule is a network diagram.

☹   a. Activity definition has the activity list as its output (*PMBOK® Guide* 6.1.3.1).

☹   b. Develop project management plan has the project management plan as its only output. The schedule network diagram is part of the project plan but we should look to see if there is a more specific answer (*PMBOK® Guide* 4.3.3.1).

☹   d. Activity duration estimating has activity duration estimates as its primary output (*PMBOK® Guide* 6.4.3.1).

14.   b.   *PMBOK® Guide* 7.2.3.1

☺   b. Cost budgeting has the cost baseline as an output.

☹   a. Cost estimating has activity cost estimates as an output (*PMBOK® Guide* 7.1.3.1).

☹   c. Cost control has cost baseline updates as an output (*PMBOK® Guide* 7.3.3.1).

☹   d. Schedule development has the project schedule as an output (*PMBOK® Guide* 6.5.3.1).

15.   c.   *PMBOK® Guide* 8.1.3.5

☺   c. Quality planning has the quality baseline as an output.

☹   a. Perform quality assurance has many outputs but not the quality baseline.

☹   b. Cost budgeting has the cost baseline not the quality baseline as an output (*PMBOK® Guide* 7.2.3.1).

☹   d. Schedule development has the schedule baseline not the quality baseline as an output (*PMBOK® Guide* 6.5.3.3).

16.   b.   *PMBOK® Guide* 12.1.3.2

☺   b. Plan purchases and acquisitions has the contract statement of work as an output.

☹   a. Scope planning has the project scope management plan as its primary output (*PMBOK® Guide* 5.1.3.1).

☹   c. Develop project management plan has the project management plan as its only output (*PMBOK® Guide* 4.3.3).

☹   d. Scope definition has the project scope statement as an output (*PMBOK® Guide* 5.2.3.1).

17.   c.   *PMBOK® Guide* Figure 3-6

☺   c. The project charter is an output of develop project charter, which is the first process of the 44 processes.

☹   a. WBS is an output of create WBS, which is in the planning process group. Look to see what process from this list comes before create WBS (*PMBOK® Guide* Figure 3-7).

© May 2007 AME Group, Inc.

☹ b. Scope management plan is an output of scope planning, which is in the planning process group. Look to see what process from this list comes before scope planning (*PMBOK® Guide* Figure 3-7).

☹ d. Preliminary project scope statement is an output of develop preliminary project scope statement, which is in the initiating process group. Look to see what step from this list comes before develop preliminary project scope statement (*PMBOK® Guide* Figure 3-6).

18. b. *PMBOK® Guide* Figure 3-7

☺ b. The WBS is an output of create WBS, which comes first sequentially from the items on the list.

☹ a. The cost baseline is an output of cost budgeting which comes after create WBS.

☹ c. The schedule baseline is an output of schedule development which comes after create WBS.

☹ d. The quality baseline is an output of quality planning which comes after create WBS.

19. c. *PMBOK® Guide* Figure 3-7

☺ c. The scope statement is an output of scope definition, which comes first sequentially from the items on the list.

☹ a. The activity list is an output of activity definition, which comes after scope definition.

☹ b. The WBS is an output of create WBS, which comes after scope definition.

☹ d. The schedule is an output of schedule development.

20. d. *PMBOK® Guide* Figure 3-7

☺ d. The schedule is an output of schedule development; it would be the last completed step on the list.

☹ a. The activity list is an output of activity definition and completed before you can create a schedule.

☹ b. The WBS is an output of Create WBS and completed before you can create a schedule.

☹ c. The scope statement is an output of scope definition, completed before you can create a schedule.

21. c. *PMBOK® Guide* 3.2.3

☺ c. The executing process group is where a vast majority of the project budget is spent.

☹ a. The initiating process group's steps are often done external to the project's scope of control.

☹ b. The planning processes develop the project plan. More money is spent executing the project plan then developing the project plan.

☹ d. The monitoring and controlling processes observe project execution. Potential problems are analyzed and corrective action taken. More money is spent in general on executing than monitoring and controlling.

22. b. *PMBOK® Guide* 3.2

☺ b. The project management processes are always performed in the same sequence because they have clear dependencies.

☹ a, c and d. The project management processes are always performed in the same sequence because they have clear dependencies.

23.   b.   *PMBOK® Guide* 5.1.3.1
☺   b. The scope management plan is the primary output of scope planning.
☹   a. The project scope statement is an output of scope definition (*PMBOK® Guide* 5.2.3.1).
☹   c. The project management plan is the only output of develop project management plan (*PMBOK® Guide* 4.3.3.1).
☹   d. The work breakdown structure as well as project scope statement updates are two of several outputs of create WBS (*PMBOK® Guide* 5.3.3).

24.   d.   *PMBOK® Guide* 3.2.1
☺   d. The organization's business need or requirements must be documented before beginning the initiating processing group processes.
☹   a. The project charter is an output of develop project charter, a step of the initiating process group; therefore, the project charter cannot be documented before the start of the initiating process group (*PMBOK® Guide* 3.2.1.1).
☹   b. The name of the project manager is included in the project charter, which is an output of develop project charter, a step of the initiating process group. Therefore, the name of the project manager will not be documented before the start of the initiating process group (*PMBOK® Guide* 4.1).
☹   c. The project schedule is an output of schedule development, a planning process step. Because the planning steps occur after the initiating steps, the project schedule cannot be documented before the initiating process group steps. (*PMBOK® Guide* 6.5.3.1).

25.   a.   *PMBOK® Guide* 3.2.1
☺   a. Approval and funding for the project are handled external to the project boundaries.
☹   b. Approval is done external, not internal, to the project.
☹   c. Approval for the project is handled external to the project and cannot be completed by the project manager.
☹   d. Approval for the project is handled external to the project and cannot be completed by the project management team.

26.   b.   *PMBOK® Guide* 3.2.1
☺   b. The initiating processes are performed/reviewed at the start of every phase.
☹   a. The initiating processes are performed not only at the start of the project but at the start of every phase.
☹   c. The initiating processes are performed/reviewed at the start of every phase but never at the end of any phase.
☹   d. The initiating processes are performed/reviewed at the start of every phase, not only as needed.

27.   a.   *PMBOK® Guide* 5.3.3.4
☺   a. The project scope baseline is an output of create WBS and not part of the preliminary project scope statement.
☹   b, c and d. The project and product objectives, the project boundaries and the approval requirements are all part of the preliminary project scope statement (*PMBOK Guide* 4.2).

28.   b.   *PMBOK® Guide* 5.3.3 and 6.13

☺   b. The output of create WBS is in the form of deliverables; the output of activity definition is in the form of schedule activities.

☹   a. This statement is reversed; the output of create WBS is the WBS and the output of activity definition is the activity list.

☹   c. This statement is reversed; create WBS is usually performed before activity definition (*PMBOK® Guide* Figure 3-7).

☹   d. Be careful of the word *always* in an answer. Activity definition is usually completed after create WBS, but they can be executed concurrently (*PMBOK® Guide* 6.1.2.1).

29.   b.   *PMBOK® Guide* 6.3.2.5

☺   b. Activity resource estimating has bottoms-up estimating as a tool and technique.

☹   a, c and d. Bottoms-up estimating is not a tool and technique of activity duration estimating, activity sequencing or create WBS.

30.   c.   *PMBOK® Guide* 3.2.4.12

☺   c. Contract administration includes managing the relationship with your external seller and external buyer as appropriate.

☹   a and b. Be careful of answers with the word *only*. Contract administration is managing the relationship with the external sellers and external buyers when appropriate.

☹   d. Contract administration is about dealing with outside parties, not inside parties.

31.   d.   *PMBOK® Guide* 3.2.4.3

☺   d. Scope verification is the process for formalizing acceptance of the completed project deliverables.

☹   a. Close project is the process necessary to finalize all activities across all of the process groups to formally close the project or project phase (*PMBOK® Guide* 3.2.5.1).

☹   b. Contract closure is the process for completing and settling each contract (*PMBOK® Guide* 3.2.5.2).

☹   c. Perform quality control is about correctness, not acceptance.

32.   c.   *PMBOK® Guide* 3.2.4.2

☺   c. Integrated change control is the process necessary for controlling factors that create change to make sure those changes are beneficial, determining whether a change has occurred, and managing the approved changes.

☹   a. Scope control is the process necessary for controlling changes to the project scope (*PMBOK® Guide* 3.2.4.4).

☹   b. Perform quality control is the process necessary for monitoring specific project results to determine whether they comply with relevant quality standards and identifying ways to eliminate causes of unsatisfactory performance (*PMBOK® Guide* 3.2.4.7).

☹   d. Monitor and control project work is the process necessary for collecting, measuring, and disseminating performance information, and assessing measurements and trends to effect process improvements (*PMBOK® Guide* 3.2.4.1).

33.   a.   *PMBOK® Guide* 3.2.4.7

☺   a. Perform quality control is the process necessary for monitoring specific project results to determine whether they comply with relevant quality standards and identifying ways to eliminate causes of unsatisfactory performance.

☹   b. Perform quality assurance is the process necessary for applying the planned, systematic quality activities to ensure that the project employs all processes needed to meet requirements (*PMBOK® Guide* 3.2.3.2).

☹   c. Quality planning is the process necessary for identifying which quality standards are relevant to the project and determining how to satisfy them (*PMBOK® Guide* 3.2.2.12).

☹   d. Scope verification is the process for formalizing acceptance of the completed project deliverables (*PMBOK® Guide* 3.2.4.3).

34.   b.   *PMBOK® Guide* Figure 3-7

☺   b. Scope definition is the step in which the scope statement is created. This step is completed before the other steps listed.

☹   a. Plan purchase and acquisitions occurs after scope definition.

☹   c. Create WBS occurs immediately after scope definition.

☺   d. Plan contracting occurs after all the other steps on the list.

35.   b.   *PMBOK® Guide* Glossary

☺   b. A contract is a legally binding relationship, a project is not.

☹   a. A project is not a legally binding relationship.

☹   c. This answer is reversed.

☹   d. A contract is legally binding.

36.   b.   *PMBOK® Guide* Glossary

☺   b. The code of accounts is a numbering system used to identify each component of the WBS; the chart of accounts is a numbering system used to monitor project costs by category.

☹   a. The chart of accounts and the code of accounts are very different things.

☹   c. This answer is reversed.

☹   d. This answer is also reversed.

37.   a.   *PMBOK® Guide* 5.5.2.4

☺   a. Scope control has configuration management as a tool and technique.

☹   b, c and d. Configuration management is not a tool and technique of these processes.

38.   a.   *PMBOK® Guide* 4.1

☺   a. The project charter is the first document created from the items on this list. There is a summary budget in the project charter and, therefore, it is the first instance on the list where a summary budget is identified.

☹   b. The activity cost estimates are a quantitative assessment of the likely costs of the resources required to complete schedule activities.

☹   c. The cost baseline is the time-phased budget that is used as a basis against which to measure, monitor, and control overall cost performance (*PMBOK® Guide* 7.2.3.1). This budget comes long after the summary budget that appears in the project charter.

☹   d. The project management plan includes the cost baseline (*PMBOK® Guide* 4.3). The project management plan is developed after the project charter.

39.   c.   *PMBOK® Guide* 7.3

☺   c. Cost control has an input of approved change requests and an output of cost baseline updates. Therefore, based on the scenario, we are in cost control.

☹   a. Cost budgeting does not have approved change requests as an input and the output is the cost baseline, not cost baseline updates. We are not in cost budgeting. (*PMBOK® Guide* 7.2).

☹   b. Cost estimating does not have approved change requests as an input and has cost estimates, not cost baseline updates, as an output. We are not in cost estimating (*PMBOK® Guide* 7.1).

☹   d. Scope control has approved change requests as an input but has scope baseline updates as an output, not cost baseline updates (*PMBOK® Guide* 5.5).

40.   a.   *PMBOK® Guide* 7.1.1.2

☺   a. Organizational process assets will contain existing formal and informal cost estimating-related policies, procedures, and guidelines for an organization.

☹   b. Enterprise environmental factors are any and all external and internal environmental factors that influence a project, including culture, structure, infrastructure, etc.

☹   c. The cost management plan for a project will have the organizational policies as an input; the plan itself will not contain the policies.

☹   d. The cost baseline is the time-phased budget for a project; it does not include the organizational policies.

41.   c.   *PMBOK® Guide* 3.2

☺   c. The five process groups of project management are initiating, planning, executing, monitoring and controlling, and closing. There are the same, regardless of the application area.

☹   a and b. The five process groups of project management are performed in the same sequence on every project due to their clear dependencies.

☹   d. If a project is divided into phases the process groups are repeated in each phase (*PMBOK® Guide* 3.3)

42.   b.   *PMBOK® Guide* 3.2.1

☺   b. The primary outputs of the initiating process group are the project charter and the preliminary project scope statement. The project scope statement is part of planning, not initiating.

☹   a and d. Approval and funding are examples of initiating work done external to the project.

☹   c. The project's business needs and requirements are documented before the project charter is created.

43   b.   *PMBOK® Guide* 3.2.1

☺   b. The project charter is the official document through which the project is authorized.

☹   a. It is the completion of the project charter, not the start of the initiating process that authorizes the project.

☹   c. The project manager is often assigned to a project in the project charter. It is the signing of the project charter though, not the assigning of a project manager that officially means we have an approved project.

☹ d. The project baselines are often established at the end of the planning phase. The planning phase ends long after the project has been authorized.

44. b.   *PMBOK® Guide* Figure 3-7
☺ b. The project scope statement is the output of the scope definition step. The project scope statement is an input of the create WBS step. Therefore, create WBS is going to occur after not before scope definition.
☹ a. The WBS is an output of create WBS. The WBS is an input of activity definition. Therefore, create WBS is going to occur before activity definition.
☹ c. The WBS is an output of create WBS. The WBS is an input of cost estimating. Therefore, create WBS is going to occur before cost estimating.
☹ d. The WBS is an output of create WBS. The WBS is an input of plan purchase and acquisitions. Therefore, create WBS is going to occur before plan purchase and acquisitions.

45. a.   *PMBOK® Guide* Figure 3-7
☺ a. The cost estimates are an output of cost estimating and an input of cost budgeting. Therefore, cost estimating is likely to occur before cost budgeting.
☹ b. Qualitative risk analysis is the process of prioritizing risk for quantitative analysis. It makes sense that qualitative risk analysis would come before quantitative risk analysis.
☹ c. Three of the outputs of plan purchase and acquisitions (procurement management plan, contract statement of work, and make-or-buy analysis) are all inputs to plan contracting.
☹ d. There is a simple trick for this one. Schedule development is the last step of the planning process group. Therefore, any other planning step is going to occur before it.

46. a.   *PMBOK® Guide* 3.2.3
☺ a. Approving changes is part of the monitoring and controlling process group, not the executing process group.
☹ b, c and d. These ideas are all part of the executing process group. Note that implementing approved changes, not approving the changes is part of executing.

47. b   *PMBOK® Guide* Chapter 7 and Chapter 12
☺ b. Cost is the amount spent to deliver a product or service. Price is the amount charged to a customer. The price may or may not be related to the cost. Often the price is market driven.
☹ a, c and d. These statements are all true.

48. c.   *PMBOK® Guide* Figure 3-8 and Figure 3-9
☺ c. Source selection is the step in which the buyer selects a source for goods or services. This is an executing step, not a monitoring and controlling step.
☹ a. This is a description of the performance reporting step of monitoring and controlling.
☹ b. Risk monitoring and control is a step of the monitoring and controlling process group.
☹ d. This statement is one of three parts to the integrated change control step of the monitoring and controlling process group.

49.   a.   *PMBOK® Guide* 3.2.4.2
☺   a. Every change should go through the change control process. In this example we may decide to cancel the project versus implement the change.
☹   b, c and d. The three elements of integrated change control are: controlling factors that create changes to make sure those changes are beneficial; determining when a change has occurred; and managing the approved changes.

50.   b.   PMI®, *Project Management Professional Role Delineation Study*
☺   b. The project life cycle is not a subset of the project management domains. The six domains are initiating, planning, executing, monitoring and controlling, closing and professional responsibility.
☹   a, c and d. These statements are all true. The six domains are initiating, planning, executing, monitoring and controlling, closing and professional responsibility. The project management life cycle is made up of initiating, planning, executing, monitoring and controlling and closing. The five process groups are the same as the project management life cycle.

PROJECT INTEGRATION MANAGEMENT

Sample Questions

Big Picture Things to Know

Read Chapter Four of the *PMBOK® Guide* before answering the questions in this section.

Integration Management has seven steps. Know how these steps provide for the integration of the project.

- Develop Project Charter—developing the project charter that formally authorizes a project or a project phase
- Develop Preliminary Project Scope Statement—developing the preliminary project scope statement that provides a high-level scope narrative
- Develop Project Management Plan—documenting the actions necessary to define, prepare, integrate, and coordinate all subsidiary plans into a project management plan
- Direct and Manage Project Execution—executing the work defined in the project management plan to achieve the project's requirement defined in the project scope statement
- Monitor and Control Project Work—monitoring and controlling processes used to initiate, plan, execute, and close a project to meet the performance objectives defined in the project management plan
- Integrated Change Control—reviewing all change requests, approving changes, and controlling changes to the deliverables and organizational process assets
- Close Project—finalizing all activities across all the Project Management Process Groups to formally close the project or a project phase

1. The process steps of Integration that are part of the initiating process group include:

a. develop project charter, develop preliminary project scope statement, develop project management plan
b. develop project charter, develop project management plan
c. develop preliminary scope statement, develop project management plan
d. develop project charter, develop preliminary project scope statement

2. Your customer seems pleased with project progress, yet they are constantly coming to you with change requests to add scope. Requested changes are an output of what step?

a. develop project management plan
b. monitor and control project work
c. integrated change control
d. close project

3. The stimuli for chartering and authorizing projects include all the following *except:*

a. problems
b. opportunities
c. business needs
d. project selection

4. A nongovernmental organization in a developing country authorizing a project to provide potable water systems, latrines, and sanitation education to communities suffering from high rates of cholera is an example of a:

a. market demand
b. social need
c. legal requirement
d. technology advance

5. Examples of mathematical models used for project selection include:

a. benefit contribution
b. linear programming algorithms
c. comparative approaches
d. economic models

6. The tool and technique that identifies and documents the functional and physical characteristics of a product or component is called:

a. change control system
b. configuration management system
c. project management methodology
d. expert judgment

7. It is hard to imagine a project without change requests. Change requests on projects may be either rejected or approved. Approved changes are processed through which step for implementation?

a. develop project management plan
b. direct and manage project execution
c. monitor and control project work
d. integrated change control

8. During the life of your project it seems that requested changes are coming at you from all directions. In fact, requested changes are an output of all the following steps except:

a. integrated change control
b. scope control
c. create WBS
d. schedule control

9. Your project is in the process of being formally authorized. What is the name given to the document indicating that you have been assigned as the project manager?

a. project management plan
b. project charter
c. preliminary project scope statement
d. work breakdown structure

10. Project selection is not only about what projects to authorize and *not* authorize but also which of the following?

a. choosing the project manager
b. choosing the project management information system
c. choosing alternative ways of executing the project
d. choosing the project management team

11. You are finally wrapping up your project. It seems that it has been going on for years and now it is just about complete. From the list below what are you most likely to do last?

a. turn the product over to the customer
b. gain formal acceptance of the project's product
c. update your lessons learned
d. release resources

12.   Your management is going through their quarterly process of project selection. In the past the organization has always used benefit measurement methods to select projects. It seems now they want to use constrained optimization methods. Which method below is your organization most likely to use now?

a. comparative approaches
b. scoring model
c. linear programming algorithm
d. murder board

13. During quality control it has been determined that several of the deliverables due today do not meet the technical specifications. A change request has been generated and will be approved or rejected in what step?

a. monitor and control project work
b. integrated change control
c. scope verification
d. direct and manage project execution

14. Organizational process assets include:

a. historical information, lessons learned
b. organization's culture
c. project management information system
d. human resource pool

15. It has been determined that several of the deliverables due today do not meet the technical specifications. A change request has been generated and approved. The defect is repaired, or so it seems. During what step is defect repair validated?

a. scope verification
b. perform quality control
c. direct and manage project execution
d. monitor and control project work

16. Receipt from customer that the terms of the contract have been met is done during:

a. close project
b. contract administration
c. scope verification
d. perform quality control

17. After your last status meeting, your customer has come to you with a change request. What should you do first?

a. meet with your management
b. meet with the project sponsor
c. evaluate the change request
d. make the change since it is the customer making the request

18. Project success is most often defined by:

a. customer satisfaction
b. meeting requirements
c. meeting budget
d. customer acceptance

19. Your management is heavily involved in making choices of where to concentrate resources on your project, anticipating potential project issues and dealing with these issues before they become critical. You remind your manager that on a project these type roles are handled by:
a. the sponsor
b. the project manager
c. the team
d. the functional managers

20. Your organization has just won a large contract. Management says start work immediately. For you this means to get a project charter approved. Management tells you there is no time for this. What should you do first?

a. explain the risks of proceeding without a charter
b. begin work on planning and at the same time push until you get the charter defined and approved
c. say you will skip the charter but demand that management allows you time to create a WBS
d. assume the contract is the charter and begin work

21. As a new project manager you are trying to understand the purpose of all the management plans. You begin by developing a list of management plans. All of the following are on your list except?

a. communications management plan
b. staffing management plan
c. risk management plan
d. integration management plan

22. Typical items found in the project management plan include all of the following *except*:

a. the contract
b. the schedule
c. the procurement management plan
d. the process improvement plan

23. History tells you that projects in your organization have been troubled by the lack of a system to submit, track, and validate changes.   A configuration management system is certainly what is needed. The configuration management system is considered a subset of the:

a. project management methodology
b. project management information system
c. change control system
d. expert judgment

24. It has been determined that several of the deliverables due today do not meet the technical specifications. A change request has been generated and approved. The defects are repaired. Defect repair is really another name for:

a. corrective action
b. preventive action
c. rework
d. scope updates

25. You have spent months planning your project and you and your team are ready to start execution. Direct and management project execution is really about implementing the project management plan as well as implementing all of the following except:

a. approved corrective action
b. approved preventative action
c. approved defect repair
d. approved contract changes

26. Forecasts are updated and reissued as an output of:

a. develop preliminary project scope statement
b. develop project management plan
c. monitor and control project work
d. integrated change control

27. The procedures to transfer the project products or services to production and/or operations are included in the:

a. administrative closure procedures
b. contract closure procedures
c. organizational process assets
d. enterprise environmental factors

28. Everything else being equal, which represents the best project?

a. project A with a payback period of 8 months
b. project B with a payback period of 10 months
c. project C with a payback period of 12 months
d. project D with a payback period of 22 months

29. When selecting projects you should take into account all of the following *except*:

a. sunk costs
b. opportunity costs
c. net present value
d. payback period

30. The government has created a new regulation that may affect your project. Based on this government mandate, what should you do first?

a. meet with your management
b. meet with the project sponsor
c. evaluate the change request
d. make the change since it is government mandated

31. In general you want your project's net present value to be:

a. as low as possible
b. $ 0
c. $ 1
d. as high as possible

32. You are working on your first large scale project. Your CPI is .90. You are running two weeks behind schedule and you have over 30 stakeholders. Where should you increase your focus?

a. schedule
b. cost
c. stakeholder management
d. conflict management

33. You are choosing between Project A with a NPV of $100 and Project B with a NPV of $300. If you choose Project B the opportunity cost is:

a. $ 100
b. $ 200
c. $ 300
d. -$ 200

34. You are working on your first large scale project. You are running $50, 000 over budget. Your SPI is .95. You have over 30 stakeholders. Where should you put your focus first?

a. schedule
b. cost
c. stakeholder management
d. conflict management

35. Which of the following should be considered during project selection?

a. schedule baseline
b. cost baseline
c. strategic plan
d. project management plan

36. You are managing a technology transfer project with over 400 engineers on your team. Your customer comes to you with another change request. Your first look tells you that this will delay your schedule at least 2 weeks. What should you do next?

a. talk to the customer
b. talk to your management
c. evaluate how the change request effects cost, scope, quality and risk
d. meet with your team to determine alternatives

37. It seems that on your projects you spend most of your time managing change requests. With each request, you first begin by evaluating the impact of the request on the triple constraint of project management. It is important that the triple constraint remains balanced. Balanced in this example means:

a. the three elements always have the same priority
b. you spend equal amounts of time focusing on each element
c. if one element changes, you evaluate the impact on the other two elements
d. all three elements should not change during the life of your project

© May 2007 AME Group, Inc.

38. Your company has just been awarded a very large contract. Your first thought is protecting your resources. In reality your main focus should be on:

a. how this project affects your project
b. how to get appointed the project manager on this effort
c. will your project management assistant be pulled to support this project
d. will your key technical lead be pulled to support this project

39. The project management methodology is used:

a. during every step of project integration management
b. during develop project charter and develop preliminary project scope statement of project integration
c. during develop project management plan, direct and manage project execution, and monitor and control project work of project integration management
d. during the processes of project scope management and *not* the processes of project integration management

40. In general you want your internal rate of return (IRR) to be—

a. 0 %
b. 1 %
c. as low as possible
d. as high as possible

41. Management is going through the annual review of projects to decide on what projects to continue and what projects to kill. You should provide management with all the following information *except*:

a. cost-performance trends on each project
b. schedule-performance trends on each project
c. sunk costs on each project
d. risk trends on each project

42. As always your project is under an extreme schedule crunch. Your manager recommends that you skip the step "develop preliminary project scope statement", You let your manager know that it is important to create this document since the document:

a. gives you authority as the project manager
b. sanctions that we have an approved and funded project
c. breaks down the detailed deliverable of the project
d. confirms that you and the sponsor are in agreement on the high level definition of the project

43. Planning on your technology transfer project has been going on for months. Finally all the planning documents are ready and the performance measurement baselines have been approved. What are you most likely to do next?

a. plan purchase and acquisitions
b. hold a kick-off meeting
c. hold a bidder conference
d. plan contracts

44. Deliverables are an outcome of:

a. direct and manage project execution
b. monitor and control project work
c. direct and manage project execution, and monitor and control project work
d. direct and manage project execution, and integrated change control

45. You are managing a technology transfer project moving technology from a development line into a manufacturing line. The manufacturing manager has requested yet another change. As you evaluate this change it seems to have a major affect on the high level project objectives. If a decision is made to accept this change, what document must be changed first?

a. project management plan
b. WBS
c. scope statement
d. project charter

46. You have joined a new organization and will be involved in map-making projects. Your new manager tells you that project managers have utmost authority as long as they stay within the project constraints. A typical financial constraint is:

a. available funding
b. lessons learned
c. mandated deadlines
d. product scope description

47. You have taken over a project from another project manager. The project seems to be running very smoothly. As the project gets closer to completion several team members feel they are ready to move on to another project. Based on your experience you know that there is often a lot more work involved in closeout than most people realize. From your view there is still much work to be done and conflict is starting to arise about release criteria. Release criteria should have been addressed in what document?

a. the project management plan
b. the staffing management plan
c. the project organizational chart
d. communication management plan

48. As a project manager you are used to having full support of top management. It seems with your new project that resources are being directed elsewhere and management has higher priority projects. What important input might have been overlooked?

a. contract
b. product scope description
c. commercial databases
d. strategic plan

49. Your organization has struggled in the past with too many projects and no clear priority. Based on a program management course, your management will now start reviewing project selection once a quarter. It has been decided to use mathematical models and not benefit measurement to drive project selection. One example of a mathematical model is:

a. scoring model
b. economic model
c. benefit contribution
d. linear algorithm

50. Based on lessons learned you realize that maintaining the integrity of project baselines has been a real challenge. It seems that some non-approved changes get released for incorporation into the project product and that some approved changes never make it into the project products. To better manage this in the future tighter control will need to occur in:

a. develop project management plan
b. direct and manage project execution
c. monitor and control project work
d. integrated change control

PROJECT INTEGRATION MANAGEMENT

Learning Solutions

1. d. *PMBOK® Guide* Figure 3-6 and Table 3-45

☺ d. Develop project charter and develop preliminary project scope statement are both steps of Integration and of the initiating process group.

☹ a, b and c. Develop project management plan is a step of Integration but it belongs to the planning process group, not the initiating process group (*PMBOK Guide* Figure 3-7).

2. b. *PMBOK® Guide* Figure 4-1

☺ b. Requested changes are an output of monitor and control project work.

☹ a. The project management plan is an output of develop project management plan.

☹ c. Approved and rejected changes are outputs of integrated change control.

☹ d. All requested changes should be approved or rejected, and approved changes implemented before close project.

3. d. *PMBOK® Guide* 4.1.2.1

☺ d. Project selection is used to determine which projects the organization will select. These methods generally fall in to one of two broad categories: benefit measurement methods and constrained optimization methods.

☹ a, b and c. The stimuli to charter or authorize a project are often called problems, opportunities, or business needs (*PMBOK® Guide* 4.1).

4. b. *PMBOK® Guide* 4.1

☺ b. This is an example of a social need.

☹ a. An example of a market need is a car company authorizing a project to build more fuel-efficient cars in response to gasoline shortages.

☹ c. An example of a legal requirement is a paint manufacturer authorizing a project to establish guidelines for handling toxic materials.

☹ d. An example of a technological advance is an electronics firm authorizing a new project to develop a faster, cheaper, and smaller laptop after advances in computer memory and electronics technology.

5. b. *PMBOK® Guide* 4.1.2.1

☺ b. Mathematical models that use linear, nonlinear, dynamic, integer, or multi-objective programming algorithms are used in project selection.

☹ a , c and d. Benefit contribution, comparative approaches, and economic models are all examples of benefit measurement methods used in project selection.

6. b. *PMBOK® Guide* 4.6

☺ b. The configuration management system is a subsystem of the overall project management system. It is a collection of formal documented procedures used to apply technical and administrative direction and surveillance to: identify and document the functional and physical characteristics of a product, result, service or component; control any changes to such characteristics; record and report each change and its implementation status; and support the audit of the products, results, or components to verify conformance to requirements.

☹ a. The change control system is a collection of formal documented procedures that define how project deliverables and documentation will be controlled, changed, and approved. In most application areas the change control system is a subset of the configuration management system.

☹   c. The project management methodology defines a set of project management process groups, their related processes and the related control functions that are consolidated and combined into a functioning unified whole (*PMBOK® Guide* 4.1.2.2

☹   d. The project team uses stakeholders with expert judgment on the change control board to control and approve all requested changes to any aspect of the project (*PMBOK® Guide* 4.6.1.3).

7.   b.   *PMBOK® Guide* Figure 4-1

☺   b. Direct and manage project execution has approved change requests as an input and implemented changes as an output.

☹   a. Change requests are not an input or output of develop project management plan.

☹   c. Requested changes are an output of monitor and control project work.

☹   d. Integrated change control has requested changes as an input and approved and rejected changes as an output.

8.   a.   *PMBOK® Guide* Figure 4-1 and Figure 5-1

☺   a. Integrated change control has requested changes as an input and approved and rejected changes as outputs.

☹   b. The results of project scope control may generate requested changes as an output.

☹   c. The results of create WBS may generate requested changes to the project scope statement.

☹   d. The results of schedule control may generate requested changes to the project schedule baseline.

9.   b.   *PMBOK® Guide* 4.1

☺   b. The project charter lists the assigned project manager and authority level.

☹   a. The project management plan defines how the project is executed, monitored and controlled, and closed. It does not name the project manager (*PMBOK® Guide* 4.3).

☹   c. The preliminary project scope statement is the definition of the project: what needs to be accomplished. It does not name the project manager.

☹   d. The WBS is a deliverable-oriented hierarchical decomposition of the work to be accomplished by the project team to accomplish the objectives and create the required deliverables. It does not name the project manager (*PMBOK® Guide* 5.3).

10.   c.   *PMBOK® Guide* 4.1

☺   c. Project selection is about deciding what projects to authorize and charter. Project selection also applies to choosing alternative ways of executing the project.

☹   a. The project manager should always be assigned prior to the start of planning, and preferably while the project charter is being developed (*PMBOK® Guide* 4.1).

☹   b. The project management information system is a standardized set of automated tools available within the organization and integrated into a system.

☹   d. Human resource planning determines project roles, responsibilities, and reporting relationships, and creates the staffing management plan (*PMBOK® Guide* 9.1). Acquire project team is the process of obtaining the human resources needed to complete the project (*PMBOK® Guide* 9.2).

11.   d. *PMBOK® Guide* 4.7

☺   d. In general release resources in the last thing we do on the project. All of the other items on the list take resources to accomplish them and therefore we need to release the resources last. Releasing resources as the last thing we do is not specifically called out in the *PMBOK® Guide*.

☹   a. Turning the product over to the customer takes resources, so this item would not be last.

☹   b. Gaining formal acceptance must occur before we can turn the product over to the customer, so this step cannot be last.

☹   c. Updating your lessons learned should be done by the project resources, so this step cannot be last.

12.   c.   *PMBOK® Guide* 4.1.2

☺   c. The linear programming algorithm is an example of a constrained optimization method, often called a mathematical model.

☹   a, b and d. Comparative approaches, scoring model and murder board are all examples of benefit measurement methods.

13.   b.   *PMBOK® Guide* Figure 4-1

☺   b. Integrated change control has requested changes as an input and approved and rejected changes as an output.

☹   a. Requested changes are an output of monitor and control project work

☹   c. Scope verification is the process step in which the customer inspects the deliverables for acceptance.

☹   d. Direct and manage project execution has approved change requests as an input and implemented changes as an output.

14.   a.   *PMBOK® Guide* 4.1.1.4

☺   a. Organizational process assets include any or all process related assets, from any or all of the organizations involved in the project that are or can be used to influence the projects success. These process assets include formal and informal plans, policies, procedures, and guidelines. The process assets also include the organizations' knowledge bases such as lessons learned and historical information.

☹   b, c and d. Enterprise environmental factors are from any or all of the enterprises involved in the project and include the human resource pool, organizational culture and structure, infrastructure, existing resources, commercial databases, market conditions, and project management software (*PMBOK® Guide* 4.1.1.3).

15.   b.   *PMBOK® Guide* Figure 8-1

☺   b. Perform quality control is the step in which specific project results are monitored. In this step the defect repair that has been done is validated.

☹   a. Scope verification is the step in which the customer accepts or rejects the project deliverables. Scope verification is about acceptance, not correctness.

☹   c. Direct and manage project execution has validated defect repair as an input, not an output.

☹   d. Monitor and control project work has recommended, not validated defect repair as an output.

16.   a.   *PMBOK® Guide* 4.7.7.3

☺   a. Formal acceptance and handover of the final product or service to the customer should include receipt of a formal statement that the terms of the contract have been met and be part of close project.

☹   b. During contract administration each party makes sure that the other party meets their obligations. Final receipt that the all the work is complete does not happen here (*PMBOK® Guide* 12.5).

☹   c. Formal acceptance of the project scope and deliverables is achieved through scope verification. Scope verification would occur before close project (*PMBOK® Guide* 5.4).

☹   d. Quality control involves monitoring specific project results to determine whether they comply with relevant quality standards, and identifying ways to eliminate causes of unsatisfactory results. Quality control is more about correctness than acceptance (*PMBOK® Guide* 8.3).

17.   c.   *PMBOK® Guide* 4.6

☺   c. Evaluate the change request is the first thing we do when a change request comes to us, regardless from whom the change request came.

☹   a and b. We don't want to meet with our management or sponsor until we have information about the impact of the requested change and we are able to recommend alternatives.

☹   d. Every change request must be evaluated, even if it comes from the customer. We do not make any changes unless an evaluation has been completed.

18.   a. *PMBOK® Guide* 3.2.1

☺   a. Customer satisfaction is the true measure of project success.

☹   b. Meeting requirements is a measure of quality management.

☹   c. Meeting budget is a measure of cost management.

☹   d. Customer acceptance is required to close the project. Remember: We may achieve customer acceptance without customer satisfaction.

19.   b.   *PMBOK® Guide* Integration-Introduction

☺   b. The items listed are all project integration activities and thus the responsibility of the Project Manager.

☹   a. The sponsor provides the financial resources for the project (*PMBOK® Guide* 2.2).

☹   c. The team is responsible to analyze and understand the project scope, document specific criteria of the product requirements, prepare the WBS, etc.

☹   d. The functional managers provide the people we need in a matrix organization.

20.   a. *PMBOK® Guide* 4.1

☺   a. The charter is the document that states we have an approved project and assigns the project manager. We do not want to proceed without this document as the probability of project success goes down.

☹   b. Starting work on planning without a charter raises the risk on project failure.

☹   c. As a project manager we cannot demand anything of our management. In general, the word demand will not be found in the right answers on the test unless the question is asking what not to do.

☹   d. The contract is not the charter. The contract is an input to building the charter.

21.   d.   *PMBOK® Guide* Figure 4.1

☺   d. There is no such thing as an integration management plan. There is a project management plan.

☹   a. The communications management plan describes how we will manage communication.

☹   b. The staffing management plan describes how resources will be brought on and taken off of the project.

☹   c. The risk management plan describes the approach to risk management that will be taken on the project.

22.   a.   *PMBOK® Guide* Glossary

☺   a. The contract is a mutually binding agreement that obligates the seller to provide the specified product or service or result and obligates the buyer to pay for it. The project management plan defines how the project is executed, monitored and controlled, and closed. The project management plan is an internal document.

☹   b, c and d. The project management plan defines how the project is executed, monitored and controlled, and closed. It should include the schedule, the procurement management plan, the process improvement plan, as well as many other documents.

23.   b.   *PMBOK® Guide* 4.3.2

☺   b. The configuration management system is a subset of the entire project management information system used to generate, facilitate feedback, control changes to and release the approved documents.

☹   a. The project management methodology defines a process which aids the team in developing and managing the project management plan.

☹   c. The change control system is a subset of the configuration management system.

☹   d. Expert judgment is used to help create the project management plan as well as to help throughout the project.

24.   c.   *PMBOK® Guide* Glossary

☺   c. Defect repair is the step in which we rework or replace the component so the defect no long exists.

☹   a. Corrective action is the action taken to bring us back on plan,

☹   b. Preventative action is the action taken to reduce the probability of negative results from risks.

☹   d. Scope updates are updates to the Scope statement, WBS and/or WBS dictionary.

25.   d.   *PMBOK® Guide* 12.5

☺   d. Contract changes are handled in the contract administration step, not the direct and manage project execution step.

☹   a. Approved corrective actions are implemented during direct and manage project execution.

☹   b. Approved preventative actions are implemented during direct and manage project execution.

☹   c. Approved defect repairs are implemented during direct and manage project execution.

26.   c.   *PMBOK® Guide* Figure 4-1

☺   c. Forecasts include estimates or predictions of conditions and events in the project's future. Forecasts are updated and reissued based on work performance information provided as the project is executed.

☹   a and b. These steps are planning steps. We need work performance information to update and reissue forecasts.

☹   d. Approved and requested change requests, *not* forecasts are an output of integrated change control.

27.   a.   *PMBOK® Guide* 4.7.3.1

☺   a. Administrative closure procedures include the procedures to transfer the projects products or services to production and/or operations.

☹   b. Contract closeout procedures are developed to address the terms and conditions of the contract (*PMBOK® Guide* 4.7.3.2).

☹   c. Organization process assets (updates) include the development of the index and location of project documentation using configuration management (*PMBOK® Guide* 4.7.3.4).

☹   d. Enterprise environmental factors are not an output of close project and thus would not include information about transferring the product.

28.   a.   Meredith et al. *Project Management: A Managerial Approach*

☺   a. Project A with a payback period of 8 months has the shortest payback period, everything else being equal than, this is the best project.

☹   b, c and d. Project A has a shorter payback period than the others. Payback period for a project is the number of years it takes a project to pay back its initial investment. Everything else being equal, the shorter the better.

29.   a.   Any Accounting Textbook or Web Search

☺   a. Sunk costs are costs that have already been expended but cannot be recouped. We should not take these into account during project selection.

☹   b. Opportunity costs represent the opportunity we pass over when selecting one project instead of another. We should take these into account during project selection.

☹   c. In general we want the present value of inflows to be greater than the present value of outflows (a positive net present value) when selecting projects. Thus, we should take into account net present value.

☹   d. In general we want the payback period (the time required for the project to repay its initial investments) to be as short as possible. Thus, we should take into account payback period.

30.   c.   *PMBOK® Guide* 4.6

☺   c. Evaluate the change request is the first thing we do when a change request comes to us, regardless from whom the change request came.

☹   a and b. We don't want to meet with our management or sponsor until we have information about the impact of the requested change and are able to recommend alternatives.

☹   d. Every change request must be evaluated, even if it is mandated by the government. We may decide to cancel the project instead of making the change on the project. We do not make any changes unless an evaluation has been done.

31.   d.   Meredith et al. *Project Management: A Managerial Approach*

☺   d. Net present value is the value of inflows minus the value of outflows. We want this number to be as high as possible.

☹   a. The lower the NPV, the weaker the project is from a financial standpoint.

☹   b. For the NPV to be equal to 0, the present value of the inflow would need to be equal to the present value of the outflow (breakeven project).

☹   c. For the NPV to be equal to 1, it means the present value of the money coming in is $1 more than the present value of the money going out. We would want this number to be as high as possible.

32.   b.   *PMBOK® Guide* 7.3.2.2

☺   b. You have a CPI that is less than one. You are therefore running over budget and need to put your focus there first.

☹   a. The question says you are two weeks behind schedule. This is noise. You do not know if it is a two week or ten year project. You need to know your SPI before deciding to put your focus on schedule.

☹   c. Stakeholder management is the step responsible to manage communication, satisfy the needs and resolve issues of stakeholders. There is nothing in the question that states we need to put more focus on stakeholder management. 30 stakeholders is noise.

☹   d. There is no information in the question to lead us to believe we need a larger focus on conflict management. 30 stakeholders is noise.

33.   a.   Any Accounting Textbook or Web Search

☺   a. $100 opportunity costs represent the opportunity we pass over when selecting one project instead of another. Since we choose project B, the opportunity cost is the NPV of project A.

☹   c. $300 would be the opportunity cost if we chose Project A because it is the NPV of Project B.

☹   b. and d. These are distracter numbers. The opportunity cost is the NPV of the opportunity not chosen.

34.   a.   *PMBOK® Guide* 7.3.2.2

☺   a. Your have an SPI that is less than one. You are therefore running behind schedule and need to put your focus there first.

☺   b. You are running $50, 000 over budget. This is noise. You do not know if this is a $50,000 or $50 Mil project. You need to know the CPI to know the status of cost and if cost needs more focus.

☹   c. Stakeholder management is the step responsible to manage communication, satisfy the needs and resolve issues of stakeholders. There is nothing in the question that states we need to put more focus on stakeholder management. 30 stakeholders is noise.

☹   d. There is no information in the question to lead us to believe we need a larger focus on conflict management. 30 stakeholders is noise.

35.   c.   *PMBOK® Guide* 4.1.1.2

☺   c. The strategic plan is an input (try to find it) to develop project charter and considered during project selection. All projects should support the organizations strategic goals.

☹   a, b and d. The schedule baseline, the cost baseline and the project management plan are all created during the planning process group and, therefore, do not exist during project selection (completed during the initiating process group) (*PMBOK® Guide* Figure 3-7).

36.   c.

☺   c. When a change is requested, the first step is usually to evaluate how the change affects the triple constraint.

☹   a. Talking to the customer is often the last thing we would do from this list.

☹   b. We want to talk to management but not until we understand the impact of the change and have looked at alternatives.

☹   d. We want to meet with the team to discuss alternatives after we understand the impact of the requested change on the triple constraint.

37.   c.   *PMBOK® Guide* 1.3

☺   c. If one element of the triple constraint changes we need to evaluate the impact on the other elements. As an example, if scope is added we need to evaluation how the schedule or budget or both will be affected.

☹   a. On certain projects one element of the triple constraint may have a higher priority than the other two. This should be clear in the project charter.

☹   b. We should spend the amount of time required on each element of the triple constraint.

☹   d. It is unrealistic to expect no changes during the life of the project. What is important is to evaluate the change requests and make sure we have enough time and money to complete the scope of the project.

38.   a.   *PMBOK® Guide* 1.6.2

☺   a. As a new project is added to the organization, the focus should be on how this project affects current projects.

☹   b. We may be thinking about getting appointed the project manager but our responsibility right now is to look after our correct project and our current team.

☹   c. This answer is too specific. We need to be thinking about our project in total.

☹   d. This answer is too specific. We need to be thinking about our project in total.

39.   a.   *PMBOK® Guide* Figure 4-1

☺   a. The project management methodology is used during every step of project integration management.

☹   b and c. Both of these statements are true. Look for an answer that is even more complete.

☹   d. This statement is half true. The project management methodology is used during both of these steps.

40.   d.   Meredith et al. *Project Management: A Managerial Approach*

☺   d. In general we want our internal rate of return (IRR) to be as high as possible.

☹   a, b and c. These answers are completely wrong. Everything else being equal, we want our IRR to be as high as possible.

41.   c.   Any Accounting Textbook or Web Search

☺   c. Sunk costs are costs that cannot be altered by current or future actions. Sunk costs should not be considered when making decisions about what projects to continue and what projects to kill.

☹   a, b and d. Cost performance, schedule performance, and risk trends should all be considered when making decisions about what projects to continue and what projects to kill.

42.   d.   *PMBOK® Guide* 4.2
☺   d. The preliminary scope statement is created by the project manager based on information from the sponsor. It is high level definition of the sponsor's and the project manager's view of the project.
☹   a. The project charter gives you authority as the project manager.
☹   b. The project charter sanctions that we have an approved and funded project.
☹   c. The WBS breaks down the deliverables on the project

43.   b.   Common Practice in Project Management
☺   b. We are at the end of planning and just about to start executing. We want to hold a kick-off meeting for the executing portion of the project.
☹   a. Plan purchase and acquisitions should have been completed before we have our baselines approved.
☹   c. A bidder conference is a tool of request seller responses and is held during the executing process group. This comes after planning.
☹   d. Plan contracts should have been completed before we have our baselines approved.

44.   d.   *PMBOK® Guide* Figure 4-1
☺   d. Deliverables are an output of direct and manage project execution and integrated change control.
☹   a. Deliverables are an output of direct and manage project execution but check to see if there is a more complete answer.
☹   b and c. Monitor and control project work does not have deliverables as an output.

45.   d.   *PMBOK® Guide* 4.1
☺   d. In this question we need to look at the list given. First determine which documents on this list will be updated based on a change in objectives then put those documents in sequence. The project charter is the first document in sequence that will be updated based on a change in objectives.
☹   a. The project management plan may be updated, but it will not be updated first. What document comes before it in sequence?
☹   b. The WBS most likely will be updated but it will not be updated first.
☹   c. The scope statement most likely will be updated but it will not be updated first.

46.   a.   *PMBOK® Guide* 7.2.1.1
☺   a. Available funding is a financial constraint and may be related to annual funding authorizations.
☹   b. Lessons learned are the lessons gained from this or previous projects. They guide us in decision making, not constrain us.
☹   c. Mandatory deadlines are examples of a schedule constraint not a *financial* constraint.
☹   d. The product scope description may be a scope constraint, but is not a *financial* constraint.

47.   b.   *PMBOK® Guide* 9.1.3.3
☺   b. The staffing management plan should include items such as staff acquisition, timetables, release criteria, training needs, recognition and rewards, compliance and safety.

☹   a. The project management plan is a true statement but look for an answer that is a little more specific.

☹   c. The project organization chart is a visual display of the project team members and their reporting relationships.

☹   d. The communication management plan documents the project communication needs and how those needs will be addressed.

48.   d.   *PMBOK® Guide* 4.1.1.2

☺   d. The strategic plan defines the direction an organization wants to go in the future. The question describes an issue with priorities. The answer to priorities should be found in the strategic plan.

☹   a and b. The contract and the product scope description are specific to your project and may not contain information about other projects in the organization. These documents will not contain information about the priorities of the organization.

☹   c. Commercial data bases may provide information about costs and duration estimates. It will not provide information about priorities across projects.

49.   d.   *PMBOK® Guide* 4.1.2.1

☺   d. Linear and nonlinear algorithms are examples of mathematical models used in project selection.

☹   a, b and c. Scoring models, economic models and benefit contribution are all examples of benefit measurement methods.

50.   d.   *PMBOK® Guide* 4.2

☺   d. Integrated change control is the process that maintains baseline integrity. This is where we need to address the approved changes and assure that all the approved changes get into the baseline.

☹   a. Develop project management plan is the process of documenting the actions required to plan and manage the project. This answer is true but not the best answer. Look for a more specific answer.

☺   b. Direct and manage project execution is about implementing the work of the project plan.

☹   c. Monitor and control project work is the process of measuring the work against the project plan and initiating corrective action. Requested changes, not approved or rejected changes, come out of this step.

PROJECT SCOPE MANAGEMENT

Sample Questions

Big Picture Things to Know

Read Chapter Five of the *PMBOK® Guide* before answering the questions in this section.

Scope Management has five steps. Know how these steps ensure that the project includes all the work required, and only the work required, to complete the project successfully.

- Scope Planning—creating a project scope management plan that documents how the project scope will be defined, verified, controlled, and how the work breakdown structure will be created and defined.
- Scope Definition—developing a detailed project scope statement as the basis for future project decisions.
- Create WBS—subdividing the major project deliverables and project work into smaller, more manageable components.
- Scope Verification—formalizing acceptance of the completed project deliverables.
- Scope Control—controlling changes to the project scope.

Also of importance:
- Contrast project scope and product scope
- WBS details
  - o Decomposition
  - o Types
- Scope baseline

1. Scope Definition is the process of:

a. creating the project scope management plan
b. creating the project scope statement
c. creating the work breakdown structure
d. creating the project management plan

2. The relationship between the scope management plan and the project management plan is described by which of the following?

a. the scope management plan is a subset of the project management plan
b. the project management plan is a subset of the scope management plan
c. the plans are not related
d. the plans are exactly the same

3. You have just received your PMP® and are now a mentor for new project managers. They all are arguing that a WBS is really a long list of items to complete. You explain that a WBS is all of the following except:

a. a deliverable oriented hierarchy of the work to be done
b. a document that shows the sequence of work
c. a team building tool
d. an input to many other planning processes

4. A predefined budget is an example of a:

a. project constraint
b. project assumption
c. project deliverable
d. project requirements

5. The WBS is:

a. task oriented
b. deliverable oriented
c. both task and deliverable oriented
d. neither task or deliverable oriented

6. After months of planning, you are at the point of having your baselines approved. All of the following documents are part of the scope baseline except:

a. scope management plan
b. scope statement
c. WBS
d. WBS dictionary

7. If a project is done through a legal relationship, the constraints are defined:

a. by the customer
b. in the contract provisions
c. by the performing organization
d. by the project manager

8. An example of an alternative identification technique is:

a. value engineering
b. lateral thinking
c. systems analysis
d. functional analysis

9. Your technology transfer project is wrapping up and you are determining where you stand as far as scope. Completion of project scope is measured against all of the following except:

a. project management plan
b. scope statement
c. WBS
d. product requirements

10. The project manager has been busy with the core team developing all of the baselines required to manage the project. A status meeting is being held and the customer is reviewing all of the baselines. One reason to review the Scope Baseline is to see:

a. the planning dates for each of the work packages
b. the sequencing of the activities of the project
c. the estimated cost broken down by deliverable
d. all the deliverables of the project

11. Project scope creep is another name for:

a. uncontrolled changes
b. influencing the factors that create project scope changes
c. controlling the impact of those changes
d. use of the integrated change control system

12. Your product development project is wrapping up and your management asks where you stand as far as product scope. Completion of product scope is measured against the:

a. project management plan
b. scope statement
c. WBS
d. product requirements

　　　　　　　　　　© May 2007 AME Group, Inc.

13. Decomposition is a tool used to create the:

   a. project scope management plan
   b. work breakdown structure
   c. project scope statement
   d. project management plan

14. The document that states explicitly what is excluded from the project is the:

   a. WBS
   b. project scope statement
   c. scope management plan
   d. project management plan

15. Stakeholder analysis is used to document all of the following except?

a. stakeholder needs
b. stakeholder wants
c. stakeholder expectations
d. stakeholder requirements

16. Which document is often developed in response to a subproject WBS?

a. contract work breakdown structure
b. risk breakdown structure
c. bill of materials
d. organizational breakdown structure

17. Your manager asks you for hierarchical tabulations of the physical assemblies, etc., to build the project's product. What should you provide to him?

a. work breakdown structure
b. bill of materials
c. risk breakdown structure
d. resource breakdown structure

18. You work in a large mapmaking organization. Your project is really a new product development. At your first team meeting you are trying to help your team understand the difference between product scope and project scope. All of the following statements are true about products and projects except:

a. product scope is defined first, than project scope
b. all project deliverables should be related to the product scope
c. the project life cycle is a subset of the product life cycle
d. the configuration management system manages and controls changes to the product scope

19. When a project terminates early, what process should be followed to document the level and extent of completion?

a. perform quality control
b. scope verification
c. contract closure
d. scope control

20. You have been assigned to a project with major cost and schedule overruns, as well as a long list of uncontrolled changes, which are also known as:

a. cost growth
b. schedule growth
c. scope creep
d. scope changes

21. You have been managing a large mapmaking project for the federal government of your country. Your customer is asking for multiple scope changes. You are looking at these requested changes and trying to determine the true magnitude of these changes. You are most likely to review what document?

a. project management plan
b. WBS
c. project charter
d. integrated change control system

22. The WBS dictionary is developed during:

a. scope definition
b. create WBS
c. activity definition
d. develop project management plan

23. Requirements come from:

a. stakeholder needs
b. stakeholder wants
c. stakeholder needs and wants
d. stakeholder needs, wants, and expectations

24. Most projects within a given organization may have the following in common *except*:

a. similar project life cycles
b. the same or similar project deliverables
c. the same products
d. similar WBS templates

25. You are involved in the design/build of a large manufacturing facility. The project life cycle is expected to span several years. You are able to do a detailed WBS for the early phases but not for the later phases. Your management though feels all sections of the WBS should be decomposed to the same level. You need to explain what concept to them?

a. rolling wave planning
b. the use of templates
c. activity definition
d. product analysis

26. Your customer has requested that you accomplish a set of deliverables that may be outside of the project boundaries. To determine if this work is inside or outside of the project boundaries, you review which of the following?

a. the project scope statement
b. the project schedule
c. the scope management plan
d. the scope change control system

27. Your project team is new to project management. They are struggling with the idea of a WBS versus an activity list. You explain that:

a. the activity list is really the lowest level of the WBS
b. the WBS shows the sequence of activities
c. the activity list drives the creation of the WBS
d. the WBS is deliverable oriented whereas the activity list is action oriented

28. Proper decomposition of the WBS can lead to:

a. enhanced ability to plan, manage, and control the work
b. decreased efficiency in performing the work
c. non-productive management effort
d. inefficient use of resources

29. Your manager has just returned from an "advanced management" course. He states that during scope definition we need to focus more on alternative identification. He describes one such method as a way of approaching alternatives indirectly at diverse angles instead of concentrating on one approach at length. He really is describing:

a. SWOT analysis
b. value analysis
c. stakeholder analysis
d. lateral thinking

30. The code of accounts is:

a. a numbering system used to uniquely identify each component of the WBS
b. a numbering system used to monitor project costs by category
c. based on the corporate chart of accounts of the performing organization
d. the level of the WBS above the work package level

31. The project scope statement defines:

a. the project's deliverables and the work required to create those deliverables
b. the process that enables the creation of the WBS
c. the process that specifies how formal verification and acceptance of the completed project deliverables will be obtained
d. the process to control change requests to the scope statement

32. One of your internal stakeholders has requested information about the detailed content of the components contained in the WBS, including the details of the work packages and control accounts. This information can be found in the:

a. project management plan
b. WBS dictionary
c. activity list
d. scope statement

33. Your customer has requested a change that may have a major effect on the triple constraint of project management. What should your first step be?

a. meet with your management
b. meet with your sponsor
c. evaluate the change request
d. determine alternatives

34. Your customer has requested a change that will affect the project objectives. If the change is approved, what document will need to be changed first?

a. project management plan
b. scope statement
c. WBS
d. project charter

35. Project scope changes are:

a. also called scope creep
b. inevitable
c. detailed in the bill of materials
d. defined in the risk breakdown structure

36. Close project happens when?

a. at the end of the project
b. at the end of each phase of the project
c. at the end of each phase and the end of the project
d. at the end of each contract

37. Customer satisfaction is most often associated with which of the following?

a. proper needs analysis
b. perform quality control
c. schedule control
d. cost control

38. The triple constraint of project management includes what?

a. schedule, cost, and time
b. cost, schedule, and budget
c. scope, time, and quality
d. scope, time, and cost

39. The WBS should be decomposed to as detailed a level as:

a. possible based on the scope of the work
b. money allows in the project budget
c. time allows in the project schedule
d. can be assigned to a single organizational unit

40. You are planning a project to develop a new telephone system. The system will include hardware, software, training, and implementation. Since this project will result in a product with subsidiary components you should expect which of the following?

a. each component to have its own separate but interdependent product scope
b. each component to have its own separate and independent product scope
c. one product scope for the project but multiple project scopes
d. one product scope for the project and one project scope

41. During scope planning we are likely to use what?

a. product analysis
b. alternative identification
c. stakeholder analysis
d. expert judgment

42.   Scope defined in terms of features and functions is:

a. project scope
b. product scope
c. both project scope and product scope
d. neither project scope and product scope

43. Product breakdown analysis involves:

a. focusing on optimizing cost performance
b. generating different approaches to execute and perform the work of the project
c. developing a better understanding of the product by breaking it down into constituent parts
d. identifying the influence and interests of the various stakeholders

44. The 80-hour rules states that no work package should be:

a. more than 80 hours in duration
b. more than 80 hours in effort
c. less than 80 hours in duration
d. less than 80 hours in effort

45. Scope control is about all the following *except*:

a. influencing the factors that create scope changes
b. managing actual scope changes
c. controlling the impact of schedule changes
d. assuring requested changes are processed through integrated change control

46. Your organization has had product managers for years and is now introducing project managers. There is confusion between the two roles. You decide the best way to start defining the difference is to define the difference between product scope and project scope. Which of the following statements is false?

a. product scope describes the features that characterize the product or service
b. completion of the product scope is measured against the project management plan
c. project scope describes the work to be done to deliver the product
d. project scope management needs to be integrated with all of the other knowledge areas of project management

47. The PMO for your organization has just rolled out a project management methodology that has been tested and proven on a very large successful project. You manage multiple small projects and have been instructed to apply this detailed methodology to each of these small projects. In this case the best thing you should do is:

a. ask the PMO to review its mandate to use the methodology on all projects as you remind them that the project management effort should be reflective of the project's size, complexity and priority
b. follow the methodology explicitly since it has already been tested and proven on a successful project
c. ignore the methodology because you believe it does not make sense for your projects
d. follow the parts of the methodology that make sense for your projects

48. As you and your core team sit down with your customer it is clear that your customer is trying to define the product requirements. As you push back you explain to the customer the difference between functional and technical requirements. Which of the following statement is true about requirements?

a. functional requirements come before technical requirements
b. technical requirements come before functional requirements
c. technical requirements are written in a language for the customer
d. functional requirements are written in a language for the project team

49. Often the best way to define something is to define *what it is not*. Your organization has asked you to clearly state what will be excluded from the project. You are most likely to do this in what document?

a. project charter
b. project scope statement
c. work breakdown structure
d. project management plan

50. One big lesson learned from past projects is that different parts of the organizations will have different interpretations of the work packages. To decrease the probability of this in the future each project should now include:

a. WBS dictionary
b. detailed WBS
c. bill of materials
d. control accounts

PROJECT SCOPE MANAGEMENT

Learning Solutions

PROJECT SCOPE MANAGEMENT - *PMBOK® Guide* Chapter 5

1.   b.   *PMBOK® Guide* 5.2
☺   b. Creating the project scope statement is the purpose of the scope definition process.
☹   a. Creating the project scope management plan is the purpose of scope planning (*PMBOK Guide* 5.1).
☹   c. Creating the work breakdown structure is the purpose of create WBS (*PMBOK Guide* 5.3).
☹   d. Creating the project management plan is the purpose of develop project management plan (*PMBOK® Guide* 4.3).

2.   a.   *PMBOK® Guide* 5.1.3
☺   a. The scope management plan is a subset of the project management plan.
☹   b. The statement is backwards.
☹   c. The plans are related. The scope management plan is a subset of the project management plan.
☹   d. The plans are not exactly the same. The scope management plan is a subset of the project management plan and only addresses scope.

3.   b.   *PMBOK® Guide* 5.3
☺   b. A WBS shows the hierarchy of deliverables. It does not show sequence. A network diagram or schedule shows sequence.
☹   a. The WBS is deliverable oriented. Each level shows the progressive level of detail.
☹   c. The output of building the WBS is the WBS. A secondary effect is that they work it takes to build the WBS also builds the team.
☹   d. Review Figure 3.7. With more investigation you will find that the WBS is an input to most of the planning steps that follow it.

4.   a.   *PMBOK® Guide* 5.2.3
☺   a. Project constraints limit the team's options. Examples include a predefined budget or any imposed dates.
☹   b. Project assumptions are factors that are considered to be true without proof (*PMBOK® Guide* Glossary).
☹   c. Project deliverables include the outputs related to the product and the project (*PMBOK® Guide* 5.2.3).
☹   d. Project requirements describe the conditions or capabilities that must be met in order to satisfy a contract, standard, or specification (*PMBOK® Guide* Glossary).

5.   b.   *PMBOK® Guide* 5.3
☺   b. The WBS is deliverable oriented.
☹   a, c and d. The WBS is deliverable oriented only.

6.   a.   *PMBOK® Guide* 5.3.3.4
☺   a. The scope management plan describes how we will define and manage scope. The scope itself is not defined in the scope management plan.
☹   b. There are three documents that make up the scope baseline. The scope statement is one of them.
☹   c. There are three documents that make up the scope baseline. The WBS is one of them.
☹   d. There are three documents that make up the scope baseline. The WBS dictionary is one of them.

7.   b.   *PMBOK® Guide* 5.2.3

☺   b. The contract provisions will generally be the constraints when a project is done under contract.

☹   a and c. The customer and the performing organization may request constraints.

☹   d. The project manager must manage to the constraints but probably does not issue constraints.

8.   b.   *PMBOK® Guide* 5.2.2.2

☺   b. Lateral thinking is an unconventional approach to solving problems and an example of alternative identification.

☹   a , c and d. Value engineering, systems analysis, and functional analysis are all examples of product analysis.

9.   d.   *PMBOK® Guide* Chapter 5 Introduction

☺   d. Completion of the product scope, not the project scope is measured against the product requirements.

☹   a. Completion of the project scope is measured against several documents including the project management plan.

☹   b. Completion of the project scope is measured against several documents including the scope statement.

☹   c. Completion of the project scope is measured against several documents including the WBS.

10.   d.   *PMBOK® Guide* 5.3

☺   d. The WBS shows in a hierarchical form all the deliverables of the project

☹   a and b. The schedule, not the WBS shows the dates and the sequencing of the activities for the project

☹   c. The cost breakdown structure (CBS) shows the costs broken down by deliverable

11.   a.   *PMBOK® Guide* 5.5

☺   a. Uncontrolled changes are often called project scope creep.

☹   b. Influencing the factors that create project scope changes is a concern of project scope control.

☹   c. Controlling the impact of scope changes is a concern of project scope control.

☹   d. All requested changes should be processed through the integrated change control system. Good documentation and use of a change control system decreases the amount of scope creep.

12.   d.   *PMBOK® Guide* Chapter 5 Introduction

☺   d. Completion of the product scope is measured against the product requirements.

☹   a. Completion of the project scope is measured against several documents including the project management plan.

☹   b. Completion of the project scope is measured against several documents including the scope statement.

☹   c. Completion of the project scope is measured against several documents including the WBS.

13.   b.   *PMBOK® Guide* 5.3.2.2

☺   b. The work breakdown structure is created through the use of templates and decomposition. Decompose means to break down into parts.

☹   a. Expert judgment as well as templates are tools used to create the project scope management plan.

☹   c. Product analysis is used to create the project scope statement.

☹   d. Multiple tools such as the project management information system are used to create the project management plan.

14.   b.   *PMBOK® Guide* 5.2.3.1

☺   b. The project scope statement describes the project boundaries and states explicitly what is excluded from the project.

☹   a. The WBS defines the total scope of the project, but does not state what is excluded (*PMBOK® Guide* 5.3).

☹   c. The scope management plan provides guidance on how the project scope will be defined, documented, verified, managed, and controlled (*PMBOK® Guide* 5.1.3.1).

☹   d. The project management plan describes how the project will be executed, monitored and controlled, and closed (*PMBOK® Guide* 4.3).

15.   d.   *PMBOK® Guide* 5.2.2.4.

☺   d. We should not allow the project stakeholders to give us requirements. We should determine the stakeholders' needs, wants and expectations and then turn those needs, wants and expectations   into requirements. The stakeholders often do not have enough technical background to create requirements. That is often one reason they need the project team.

☹   a, b and c. Stakeholder analysis should be used to determine the stakeholders' needs, wants and expectations.

16.   a.   *PMBOK® Guide* Glossary

☺   a. The contract work breakdown structure is a part of the WBS for the project that is developed and maintained by a seller contracted to provide a subproject.

☹   b. The risk breakdown structure is a hierarchically organized depiction of the identified project risks.

☹   c. The bill of materials is a hierarchically organized depiction of the physical assemblies.

☹   d. The organizational breakdown structure is a hierarchically organized depiction of the project organization.

17.   b.   *PMBOK Guide* 5.3.3.2

☺   b. The bill of materials is a hierarchically organized depiction of the physical assemblies.

☹   a. The work breakdown structure is a deliverable-oriented hierarchical decomposition of the work to be executed by the project team, to accomplish the project objectives.

☹   c. The risk breakdown structure is a hierarchically organized depiction of the identified project risks.

☹   d. The resource breakdown structure is a hierarchically organized depiction of the resources by type to be used on the project.

18.   b.   *PMBOK® Guide* Figure 2-4

☺   b. Some project deliverables will be related to product scope and some will be related to project scope. An example of a deliverable related to project management would be the project management plan.

☹   a. Product scope is defined first. This is a driver or input into defined the project scope.

☹   c. The project life cycle is a subset of the product life cycle. Think of the product as a book and the project is to write the book. Writing the book is the subset. After we write the book we need to manufacture it, distribute it, do revisions on the book (more projects) and maybe eventually pull the book out of the market.

☹   d. The configuration management system helps us define, manage and control changes to the product. The change control system helps us do the same thing to the project.

19.   b.   *PMBOK® Guide* 5.4

☺   b. Scope verification is the next step after project termination. During scope verification we establish and document the level and extent of completion.

☹   a. Perform quality control is about correctness, not acceptance (*PMBOK® Guide* 5.3).

☹   c. Contract closure is about acceptance of the work of our suppliers, not about our customer accepting the work of the project (*PMBOK® Guide* 12.6).

☹   d. Scope control is the process step concerned with scope changes, not project terminations (*PMBOK® Guide* 5.5).

20.   c.   *PMBOK® Guide* 5.5

☺   c. Scope creep is another name for uncontrolled changes.

☹   a. Cost growth is a change to the cost of a project/contract because of an approved change in scope.

☹   b. Schedule growth is a change to the schedule of a project/contract because of an approved change in scope.

☹   d. Scope changes are approved changes to the project scope.

21.   b.   *PMBOK® Guide* 5.3

☺   b. The WBS is a deliverable oriented document. If something is in scope it is in the WBS. If something is out of scope it is not in the WBS.

☹   a. The project management plan is a true answer but not the best answer. We are not going to compare the change requests to the entire project management plan, only part of it. Look for a more specific answer.

☹   c The project charter is a document that states we have an approved document. It is not specific about the scope of the project. The scope of the project has not been defined yet.

☹   d. The integrated change control system contains the procedures for making changes. It does not contain the scope of the project.

22.   b.   *PMBOK® Guide* 5.3.3.3

☺   b. Create WBS has the WBS dictionary as an output.

☹   a. Scope definition has the scope statement as an output not the WBS dictionary (*PMBOK® Guide* 5.2.3.1).

☹   c. Activity definition has the activity list as an output not the WBS dictionary (*PMBOK® Guide* 6.1.3.1).

☹   d. Develop project management plan has the project management plan as an output (*PMBOK® Guide* 4.3.3.1).

23.   d.   *PMBOK® Guide* 5.2

☺   d. Stakeholder needs, wants, and expectations are converted into requirements.

☹   a, b and c. These answers are all true but not the best answer.

24.   c.   *PMBOK® Guide* 1.2.1.2 and 5.3.2.1

☺   c. A project creates unique products, services, or results. This is one of the ideas that separates projects from operations. Be careful of the word *except* in questions.

☹   a. Most projects within a given organization will have similar project life cycles.

☹   b. Most projects within a given organization will have the same or similar project deliverables by phase.

☹   d. Most projects within a given organization will have standard WBS templates.

25.   a.   PMBOK® Guide 5.3.2.2

☺   a. Rolling wave planning is a technique in which the project team waits for clarification before completely decomposing deliverables.

☹   b. Templates contain a defined structure for collecting, organizing and presenting information.

☹   c. Activity definition decomposes work packages into the activity list.

☹   d. Product analysis allows the project scope statement to be developed based on the scope of the product.

26.   a.   *PMBOK® Gui*de 5.2.3.1

☺   a. The project scope statement provides the baseline for evaluating whether requests for changes or additional work are contained within or outside the project's boundaries.

☹   b. The project schedule includes the planned start and end dates for each schedule activity. It is not the baseline for reviewing scope (*PMBOK® Guide* 6.5.3.1).

☹   c. The scope management plan provides guidance on how the project scope will be defined, documented, verified, managed, and controlled (*PMBOK® Guide* 5.1.3.1). The project scope is not defined in this plan.

☹   d. The scope change control system, documented in the project scope management plan, defines the procedures by which project scope and product scope can be changed (*PMBOK® Guide* 5.5.2.1).

27.   d.   *PMBOK® Guide* 5.3 and 6.1

☺   d. The WBS is a deliverable oriented hierarchy. The activity list is a list of all schedule activities for the project. The activity list is action oriented.

☹   a. The activity list is not part of the WBS. There is an activity list, but it is not part of the WBS.

☹   b. The network diagram shows the sequence of activities, not the WBS.

☹   c. The WBS drives the creation of the activity list, not the other way around.

28.   a.   *PMBOK® Guide* 5.3.2.2

☺   a. Enhanced ability to plan, manage, and control the work is the result of proper decomposition.

☹   b. Decreased efficiency in performing the work can be the result of excessive decomposition.

☹   c. Non-productive management effort can be the result of excessive decomposition..

☹   d. Inefficient use of resources can be the result of excessive decomposition.

29. d. *PMBOK® Guide* 5.2.2.2
☺ d. Lateral thinking is an alternative identification technique that approaches answers at diverse angles.
☹ a. SWOT analysis looks at the strengths, weaknesses, opportunities and threats of a project.
☹ b. Value analysis is a process whose goal is to increase value by reducing the cost/function relationship.
☹ c. Stakeholder analysis identifies the stakeholders of the project and determines their needs, wants and expectations.

30. a. *PMBOK® Guide* Glossary
☺ a. A numbering system used to uniquely identify each component of the WBS is the definition of the code of accounts.
☹ b. A numbering system used to monitor project costs by category is a definition of the chart of accounts.
☹ c. The project chart of accounts is usually based on the corporate chart of accounts of the performing organization.
☹ d. The level of the WBS above the work package level is the planning package.

31. a. *PMBOK® Guide* 5.2.3.1
☺ a. The project's deliverables and the work required to create those deliverables are in the project scope statement.
☹ b. The process that enables the creation of the WBS is included in the scope management plan (*PMBOK® Guide* 5.1.3.1).
☹ c. The process that specifies how formal verification and acceptance of the completed project deliverables will be obtained is included in the scope management plan (*PMBOK® Guide* 5.1.3.1).
☹ d. The process to control how requests for changes to the scope statement will be processed is included in the scope management plan (*PMBOK® Guide* 5.1.3.1).

32. b. *PMBOK® Guide* 5.3.3.3
☺ b. The WBS dictionary describes the detailed content of the components contained in the WBS, including the details of the work packages and control accounts.
☹ a. Many things are in the project management plan. Look for a more detailed answer.
☹ c. The activity list describes the activities, not the components of the WBS.
☹ d. The scope statement is created before the WBS and therefore would not describe the detailed content of the components of the WBS.

33. c. *PMBOK® Guide* 5.5
☺ c. Evaluate the change request is usually the first thing we do when a change request comes to us, regardless from whom the change request came.
☹ a and b. We don't want to meet with our management or sponsor until we have information about the impact of the requested change and be able to recommend alternatives.
☹ d. Determine alternatives is often what we do after we evaluate the change request and understand the impacts.

34. d. *PMBOK® Guide* 4.1
☺ d. The project charter is the first document created that contains the project objectives and the document that needs to be changed first.
☹ a. The project management plan may list the project objectives but this is not the first document to be changed. Look for an earlier document (*PMBOK® Guide* 4.3).
☹ b. The scope statement contains the project objectives but this is not the first document to be changed. Look for an earlier document (*PMBOK® Guide* 5.2.3.1).
☹ c. The WBS is deliverable oriented. It does not contain the project objectives.

35. b. *PMBOK® Guide* 5.5
☺ b. Change is inevitable.
☹ a. Uncontrolled changes are often called scope creep.
☹ c. Product details, not project scope changes, are in the bill of materials (*PMBOK® Guide* 5.3.3.2).
☹ d. Project risks, not project scope changes, are depicted in the risk breakdown structure.

36. c. *PMBOK® Guide* 4.7
☺ c. Close project occurs at the end of each phase and the end of the project.
☹ a. This statement is true but look for a better answer.
☹ b. This statement is true but look for a better answer.
☹ d. Contract closure occurs at the end of each contract (*PMBOK® Guide* 12.6).

37. a. Frame, *Managing Projects in Organizations*
☺ a. Proper needs analysis is closely linked to obtaining customer satisfaction.
☹ b. Perform quality control is related to measuring for correctness (*PMBOK® Guide* 8.3).
☹ c. Perform schedule control is related to schedule change management (*PMBOK® Guide* 6.5).
☹ d. Perform cost control is related to cost change management (*PMBOK® Guide* 4.3).

38. d. *PMBOK® Guide* 1.3
☺ d. Scope, time, and cost are the triple constraint of project management.
☹ a. Schedule and time are interchangeable in this list and not separate elements of the triple constraint.
☹ b. Cost and budget are interchangeable in this list and not separate elements of the triple constraint.
☹ c. Project quality is affected by balancing the three elements of the triple constraint. Quality is not one of the elements.

39. d. *PMBOK® Guide* 5.3.3.2
☺ d. The WBS should be decomposed until work can be assigned to a single organizational unit.
☹ a, b and c. The WBS should be decomposed to a level so that the items are both necessary and sufficient, *not* to the greatest level possible.

40. a. *PMBOK® Guide* Chapter 5- Scope Introduction
☺ a. Each product component will have its own separate but interdependent product scope.
☹ b. The products' scope will not be independent.

☹   c. This statement is reversed.

☹   d. This statement is partially correct. If there is one project, there is one project scope. If the product has subsidiary components, there will be more than one product scope.

41.   d.   *PMBOK® Guide* 5.1.2

☺   d. Expert judgment is a tool and technique of scope planning and, therefore, likely to be used.

☹   a. Product analysis is a tool and technique of scope definition not scope planning (*PMBOK® Guide* 5.2.2.1).

☹   b. Alternative identification is a tool and technique of scope definition not scope planning (*PMBOK® Guide* 5.2.2.2).

☹   c. Stakeholder analysis is a tool and technique of scope definition not scope planning (*PMBOK® Guide* 5.2.2.4).

42.   b.   *PMBOK® Guide* Chapter 5 - Scope Introduction

☺   b. Product scope includes the features and functions that characterize the product.

☹   a. Project scope is the work that needs to be done to deliver the product.

☹   c. This statement is only partially true. Project scope is the work that needs to be done to deliver the product.

☹   d. This statement is only partially true. Product scope includes the features and functions that characterize the product.

43.   c.   *PMBOK® Guide* 5.2.2

☺   c. Product breakdown analysis involves developing a better understanding of the product by breaking it down into constituent parts.

☹   a. Value analysis focuses on optimizing cost performance.

☹   b. Alternative generation involves generating different approaches to execute and perform the work of the project.

☹   d. Stakeholder analysis identifies the influence and interests of the various stakeholders.

44.   b.   Web Search

☺   b. The 80-hour rule states that no work packages should be more than 80 hours in effort.

☹   a. "Duration" is the word that makes this answer incorrect.

☹   c. "Should be less than" and "duration" make this statement incorrect.

☹   d. "Should be less than" makes this answer incorrect.

45.   c.   *PMBOK® Guide* 5.5

☺   c. The word "schedule" makes this the correct answer. Notice the work "except" in the question.

☹   a. Influencing the factors that create scope changes is one purpose of scope change.

☹   b. Manage actual scope changes is one purpose of scope change.

☹   d. Assure requested changes are processed through integrated change control is one purpose of scope change.

46.   b.   *PMBOK® Guide* Chapter 5 –Scope Introduction
☺   b. Completion of the product scope is measured against the product requirements not the project management plan.
☹   a, c and d. These statements are all true.

47.   a.   *PMBOK® Guide* 5.1
☺   a. The effort spent on project management should be appropriate based on the size, risk and importance of the project.
☹   b. As project managers, we should not follow this methodology explicitly. We need to work with the PMO to tailor the methodology for our project.
☹   c. The methodology should not be ignored. It should be tailored for our project.
☹   d. This answer is good but we need to work with the PMO since we have been instructed to follow the methodology.

48.   a.   Frame, *Managing Projects in Organizations,* p116
☺   a. The process begins with customer needs. From there we develop functional requirements. Functional requirements are turned into technical requirements.
☹   b. This statement is reversed. Functional requirements come before technical requirements.
☹   c. Technical requirements are written in a language for the project team.
☹   d. Functional requirements are written in a language for the customer.

49.   b.   *PMBOK® Guide* 5.2.3
☺   b. The project scope statement should describe the project boundaries. This section defines what is included in the project and what is excluded.
☹   a. The project charter describes many items such as the requirements, the business needs and the project purpose. The document that describes what is excluded comes later.
☹   c. The WBS is a deliverable-oriented hierarchical view of the work of the project. It does not state what is excluded from the project.
☹   d. The project management plan is a true answer but not the best answer. Find a more specific answer.

50.   a.   *PMBOK® Guide* 5.3.3.3
☺   a. The WBS dictionary describes the details of each work package. This detailed explanation should help lower the probability of different interpretations of the work packages.
☹   b. A detailed WBS means that you decompose the WBS to a tremendous amount of detail. This may help, but look for a better answer. The WBS lists the work packages but does not define them.
☹   c. A bill of materials is a hierarchical decomposition of the project's product. It does not contain a definition of the work packages.
☹   d. The control accounts are part of every WBS. Having control accounts will not help define the work packages because the control accounts are above the work packages.

PROJECT TIME MANAGEMENT

Sample Questions

Big Picture Things to Know

Read Chapter Six of the *PMBOK® Guide* before answering the questions in this section.

Time Management has six steps. Know how these steps ensure timely completion of the project.
- Activity Definition—identifying the specific schedule activities that need to be performed to produce the various project deliverables
- Activity Sequencing—identifying and documenting dependencies among schedule activities
- Activity Resource Estimating—estimating the type and quantities of resources to perform each schedule activity
- Activity Duration Estimating—estimating the number of work periods that will be needed to complete individual schedule activities
- Schedule Development—analyzing activity sequences, durations, resource requirements, and schedule constraints to create the project schedule
- Schedule Control—controlling changes to the project schedule

Also of importance:
- Contrast create WBS and activity definition
- Compare and contrast time and cost steps
- Know how to do a forward and backward pass
- Know total float, free float, project float

Time Questions #1- #4. Use the following diagram.

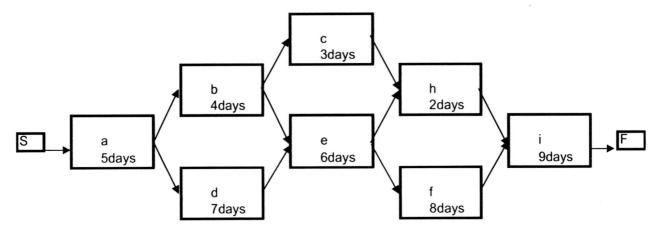

1. The duration of the project in the above diagram is:

a. 20 days
b. 26 days
c. 35 days
d. 37 days

2. The float of Activity C is:

a. 6 days
b. 9 days
c. 12 days
d. 24 days

3. The free float of Activity C is:

a. 6 days
b. 9 days
c. 12 days
d. 24 days

4. If management imposes an end time of 22 days the project float is:

a. 0 days
b. 4 days
c. -4 days
d. -13 days

Use the following table to asnwer questions 5-9.

Activity	Predecessor	Duration
a	start	3
b	start	7
c	a (start to start)	4
d	a,b	1
e	c,d	6
f	d	5
g	e,f	2
finish	g	

5. What is the project duration?

a. 15 days
b. 16 days
c. 17 days
d. 18 days

6. What activities are on the critical path?

a. b-d-f-g
b. d-e-g
c. a-c-e-g
d. b-d-e-g

7. What is the float of Activity d?

a. -1 days
b. 0 days
c. 1 days
d. 3 days

8. What is the free float of Activity d?

a. -1 days
b. 0 days
c. 1 days
d. 3 days

9. If management imposed an end date of 18 days, what is the project float?

a. -2 days
b. -1 day
c. 1 day
d. 2 days

Use the following table to answer questions 10-14.

	Predecessor	Successor	Duration
Task A	start	C, D	3 days
Task B	start	D, F	7 days
Task C	A	E, G	4 days
Task D	A,B	E, F	6 days
Task E	C, D	F, G	5 days
Task F	B,D, E	H	2 days
Task G	C, E	H	8 days
Task H	F, G	finish	9 days

10. What is the duration of the critical path?

a. 20 days
b. 26 days
c. 35 days
d. 42 days

11. What is the float of Task A?

a. 0 days
b. 3 days
c. 4 days
d. 7 days

12. What is the free float of Task A?

a. 0 days
b. 3 days
c. 4 days
d. 7 days

13. Management has imposed an end day of time 33. What is the project float?

a. 0 days
b. -2 days
c. 7 days
d. 9 days

14. Assuming managements imposed end day of time 33, what is the float of Task F?

a. 0 days
b. -2days
c. 4 days
d. 6 days

Time Questions #15-#18. Use the following Diagram.

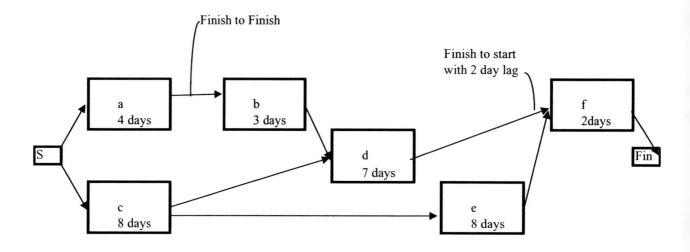

15. The project duration is:

a. 16 days
b. 17 days
c. 19 days
d. 21 days

16. What activities are on the critical path?

a. c-d-f
b. a-b-d-f
c. d-e-f
d. c-e-f

17. If it takes the engineers 6 days and not 8 to complete Activity E, what is the project duration?

a. 16 days
b. 17 days
c. 19 days
      d. 21 days

18. If the duration of Activity E is set back to 8 days, and management imposes an end time of 13 days, what is the new project float?

a. 2 days
b. 0 days
c. -2 days
d. -6 days

Use the following table to answer questions 19-23.

Activity	Predecessor	Duration
a	start	5 days
b	start	3 days
c	a +2day lag,b	7 days
d	b	8 days
e	c,d	6 days
finish	e	

19. What is the duration of the critical path?

a. 17 days
b. 18 days
c. 20 days
d. 24 days

20. What is the float of Activity B?

a. 0 days
b. 3 days
c. 4 days
d. 6 days

21. What is the free float of Activity B?

a. 0 days
b. 3 days
c. 4 days
d. 6 days

22. What activities are on the critical path?

a. c-e
b. a-c-e
c. b-c-e
d. b-d-e

23. If management imposes and end date of 18 days or less, what is the float of Activity E?

a. -4
b. -2
c. 0
d. 7

24. Your project has two activities: activity one is to paint the walls of a classroom and activity two is to hang whiteboards on the walls. It will take about 4 hours for the paint to dry between these activities. Paint drying is an example of:

a. float
b. free float
c. lead
d. lag

25. As a project scheduler you are trying to use statistics as part of project scheduling. If Activity A has a pessimistic estimate of 24 days and an optimistic estimate of 12 days, what is the variance of Activity A?

a. 12 days
b. 6 days
c. 4 days
d. 2 days

26. Management is reviewing your schedules and asks why all of the work packages are different sizes. They suggest that you consider the 80 hour rule. The 80 hour rule is an example of:

a. heuristic
b. a PMI regulation
c. a constraint
d. ground rules

27. You are managing the development of a new medical device. Hitting the market window is critical for project success. To analyze the amount of float each activity has you will most likely use what method?

a. bottom's up estimating
b. expert judgment
c. critical path method
d. resource leveling

28. When you first planned the development of your organizations new medical device, it seems that most of the activities contained float. You met with you team to develop the schedule and explained float to all the team members. Now you are running with several critical paths with more paths becoming critical each month. This is an example of:

a. Parkinson Theory
b. lazy team members
c. critical chain
d. critical path method

29. You are planning for a major customer review. Your customer has made it clear that their focus is on schedule. They want you to show plan versus actual during the presentation. You are most likely to use:

a. Monte Carlo Analysis
b. comparison bar chart
c. milestone chart
d. WBS

30. Your program manager has just returned for a class on program/project management and is filled with ideas. He seems to be using the terms fast tracking and concurrent engineering interchangeably. You try to explain high level the difference by stating:

a. fast tracking is about overlapping activities while concurrent engineering is moving implementers to an earlier phase of the project
b. fast tracking is about overlapping activities while concurrent engineering is adding resources to the critical path
c. fast tracking is about moving implementers to an earlier phase of the project while concurrent engineering is about adding resources to the critical path
d. fast tracking is overlapping phases while concurrent engineering is overlapping activities

31. You along with your project management team have spent a great amount of time developing the WBS, the schedule and the cost estimate. You work has finally been approved and you now have baselines for the triple constraint. The most likely thing you will do now before moving to executing is:

a. celebrate as a team
b. begin recommending preventative action
c. begin recommending corrective action
d. hold a kick-off meeting

32. Your map making project has been going very well. With great resistance from upper management you have been using the technique of rolling wave planning. You are at the point of planning the closing of the project. The last thing we often do on projects is:

a. deliver the product to the customer
b. conduct lessons learned
c. hold a celebration
d. release resources

33. You are working with your core team developing the network diagram for your map making project. Your management comes to you and tells you that they want you to set in your schedule that you will do a fly over of the area before researching the geography. You ask them why and they tell you it is a best practice. This is an example of a:

a. mandatory dependency
b. discretionary dependency
c. hard logic
d. external dependency

34. Your team is presently estimating the activity resources. You encourage the team to think of different alternative methods of accomplishing the work of the project. Examples of alternatives to accomplish the schedule activities include all of the following *except*:

a. make versus buy
b. hand versus automated tools
c. different size or type of machines
d. benefit measurement methods versus mathematical models

35. You are working on a medical device development project. Your organization embraced project management about a year ago and many of your team members now have their CAPM®. At this point you are developing your network diagrams. There is a heated discussion about the use of critical path method versus critical chain method. You explain the difference by stating:

a. critical path and critical chain are different names for the same method
b. the critical path is time constrained while the critical chain is resource constrained
c. the critical path assumes limited resources while the critical chain assumes unlimited resources
d. the critical path method is a newer idea while the critical chain idea has been around for many decades

36. You have added a new team member to your technology transfer project. He keeps using words like longest and shortest and is confusing your team. You explain that the critical path is:

a. the shortest path through the network and the shortest amount of time to complete the project
b. the longest path through the network and the longest amount of time to complete the project
c. the shortest path through the network and the longest amount of time to complete the project
d. the longest path through the network and the shortest amount of time to complete the project

37. As you are executing your project plan the total float and project float numbers continue to change. Management is very confused about these terms. You explain that:

a. total float and project float are different terms that mean the same thing
b. total float is related to an activity while project float is related to the entire project
c. total float is the amount of time an activity can slip before delaying the start of its successor while project float is the amount of time an activity can be delayed without delaying the entire project
d. total float is associated with an end date imposed by management while project float is associated with an individual activity.

38. Your manager has limited knowledge of project management but understands the basic idea that it is important to manage the critical path. You have one critical path on your project and seven near critical paths. Your manager has only had a basic course on project management and never heard of the idea of near critical path. You explain the more near critical paths you have the more:

a. float you have on your activities
b. cost you have on your project
c. risk you have on your project
d. people working on the project

39. One of the key resources on your project is being pulled to a higher priority project. Their activity has an early finish of 12 days and a late finish of 10 days. This means there is:

a. 2 days of total float
b. 2 days of free float
c. -2 days of free float
d. -2 days of total float

40. You have been managing projects very successfully using Activity On Node (AON) diagrams for years. Your company has hired you a project management mentor who wants you to move to Activity On Arrow (AOA) diagrams. You explain that one weakness of the activity on arrow diagrams is:

a. activity on arrow diagrams have the arrow represent the relationship and the activity
b. activity on arrow diagrams only use finish to start relationships
c. activity on arrow diagrams may be suited for the pharmaceutical industry when we need "if- then" statements
d. activity on arrow diagrams are most suited for the Information Technology industry when feedback loops are utilized

41. PERT stands for:

a. Project Evaluation Review Technique
b. Program Evaluation Review Technique
c. Project Estimating Review Tool
d. Program Evaluation Review Tool

42. As a project manager in the pharmaceutical industry your projects include running many drug trials. To accurately represent this on your network diagrams you need to include conditional statements. Most likely, what type of network diagramming technique will your project use?

a. arrow diagramming technique
b. precedence diagramming technique
c. graphical evaluation review technique
d. fast tracking technique

43. As a project management consultant, your main focus is to help organizations to obtain control over their schedules. Your present customer states that their workers never seem to finish anything early. The more time the organization gives people to complete the task, the more time they spend to complete the task. You explain that the organization is demonstrating:

a. student syndrome
b. Parkinson Law
c. resource leveling
d. crashing

44. Your team has just completed building a network diagram on the wall. The information is now being loaded into software. The software shows the theoretical early start and finish dates and theoretical late start and finish dates for each activity. Team members seem confused with all the numbers associated with each activity. You explain that the critical path method:

a. tells you the exact start and finish date of each activity
b. is a resource constrained schedule
c. indicates the time periods within which the schedule activity should be scheduled
d. analyzes the cost and schedule tradeoffs to determine the best schedule

45. The project sponsor has arrived unexpectedly at a team status meeting. He asks the team to status all of the critical activities. Your team looks around, not exactly sure what activities your sponsor deems to be critical. In general critical activities are defined as:

a. activities scheduled to start in the next 30 days
b. activities scheduled to finish in the next 30 days
c. all activities are critical
d. only activities on the critical path

46. You have been monitoring resource usage and a major difference is noticed between actual and plan. You have assumed in the past an even distribution as far as resource usage. In reality, people are available on a variable distribution day to day. To plan this into your schedule you should use:

a. what if scenario analysis
b. critical path method
c. crashing
d. resource contouring

47. Based on your success on small projects you now have been made the project manager of a large, complex, multi-year project. In the past, you have planned out all the detail of the WBS early in the project. For your current project you are more likely to do progressive elaboration through:

a. rolling wave planning
b. scope changes
c. WBS dictionary
d. templates

48. The growth of your product sales is leading to more and more calls for your call center operations center. A decision is made to move your call center group to a much larger location and you are now the project manager on the move. Many groups will be involved and dependencies are very important. Some dependencies are required while others are not. Dependencies based on knowledge of best practices are called:

a. external dependencies
b. mandatory dependencies
c. discretionary dependencies
d. hard logic

49. It is important on your software development project to accurately estimate the durations of activities. You suggest to management that PERT estimates be completed on each activity. You give them the following example. Your programmer estimates that most likely it will take 100 hours to complete the work. Optimistically it may only be 80 hours and pessimistically it could take as long as 150 hours. The PERT estimate is:

a. 100 hours
b. 105 hours
c. 110 hours
d. 150 hours

50. It is important on your software development project to accurately estimate the durations of activities. You suggest to management that three-point estimates be completed on each activity. You give them the following example. Your programmer estimates that most likely it will take 100 hours to complete the work. Optimistically it may only be 80 hours and pessimistically it could take as long as 150 hours. The three-point estimate is:

a. 100 hours
b. 105 hours
c. 110 hours
d. 150 hours

51. You are managing a large ship building project for a government customer. Due to proper planning the project has been running on schedule and budget. Now the customer has asked you to review pulling in the schedule without adding resources. Your most likely schedule compression method to accomplish this is:

a. crashing
b. fast-tracking
c. resource leveling
d. project management software

© May 2007 AME Group, Inc.

PROJECT TIME MANAGEMENT

Learning Solutions

Solution 1

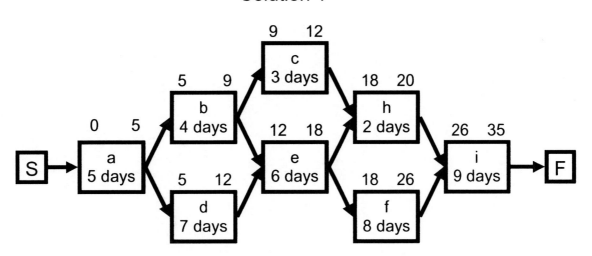

1. Do a forward pass through the network. The project duration is 35 days.
☺   c. 35 days is the correct answer.
☹   a,b and c. These are all distracter answers.

Solution 2

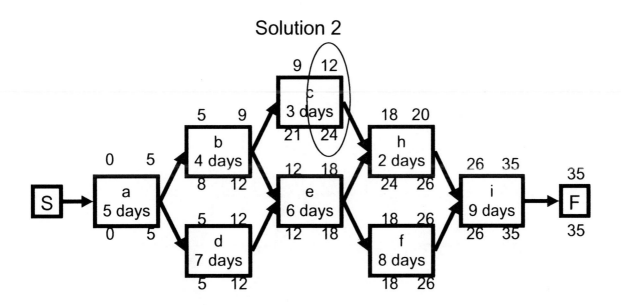

2. Now do a backward pass through the network.
Float = (late finish - early finish). The float of Activity C = (24 days - 12 days) = 12 days.
☺   c. 12 days is the correct answer.
☹   a, b and d. These are distracter answers.

Solution 3

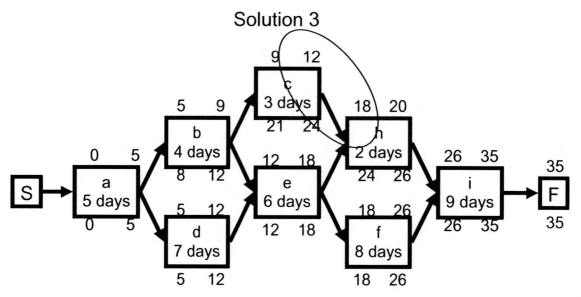

3. Free float is how much an activity can slip from its early finish before it affects the early start of its earliest successor. In this example, Activity H is the only successor to Activity C. Free float of Activity C = (18 days - 12 days) = 6 days.

☺   a. 6 days is correct.
☹   b, c and d. These are distracter answers.

Solution 4

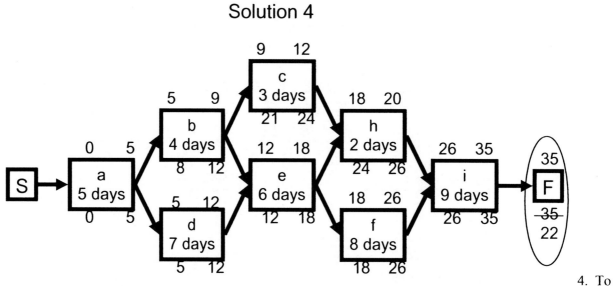

4. To determine project float, we take managements' imposed end date and make that our late finish for the project. Project float = (late finish - early finish) = (22 days - 35 days)
= - 13 days.

☺   d. -13 days is correct.
☹   a, b and c. These are distracter answers.

Solution 5

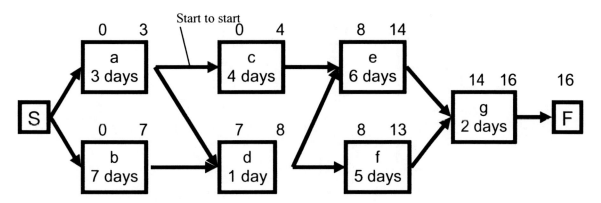

5. To determine project duration we must do a forward pass. The project duration is 16 days.

☺   b. 16 days is the correct answer.

☹   a, c and d. These are distracter answers.

Solution 6

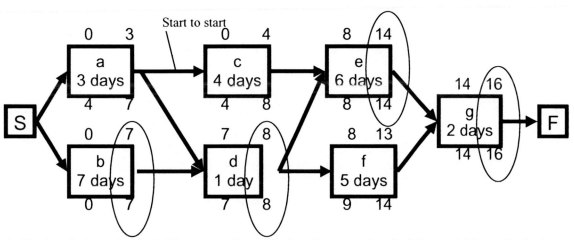

6. To deterimine what activities are on the critical path we need to find the activities with the least amounts of float (usually 0); therefore, we need to do a backwards pass.

☺   d.   b-d-e-g. These activities are on the critical path.

☹   a. Activity f has float and thus is not on the critical path.

☹   b. This path does not get us from start to finish.

☹   c. Activities a and c have float and are not on the critical path.

Solution 7

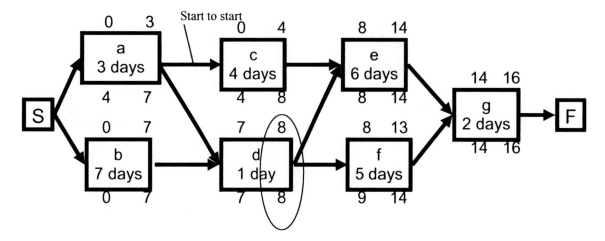

7. To find the float of an activity we need to have completed a forward and backward pass. Float=late finish–early finish. The float of Activity D = (8 days – 8 days) = 0 days.

☺   b. 0 days is correct.
☹   a, c and d. These are distracter answers.

Solution 8

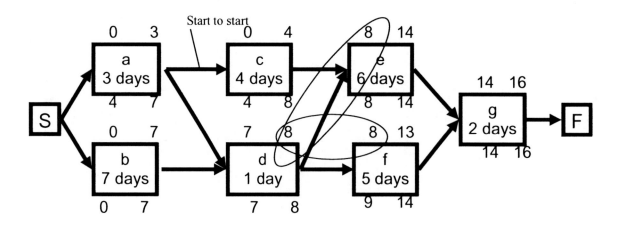

8. Free float is how much an activity can slip from its early finish before it affects the early start of its earliest successor. In this example, Activity F and Activity E are both successors that have the same early start and, therefore, we can look at either. Lets look at Activity F. Free float is how much Activity D can slip from its early finish of 8 days before it affects the early start of 8 days of Activity F. Therefore, the free float is 0.

☺   b. 0 days is the correct answer.
☹   a, c and d. These are distracter answers.

Solution 9

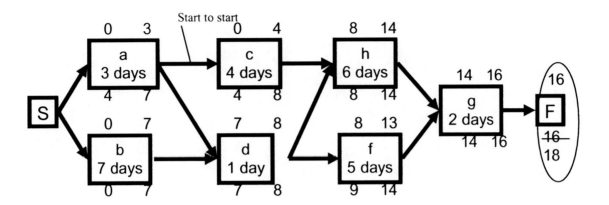

9. To calculate project float we take managements' imposed end date and make it our late finish for the project. Project float = (late finish - late start) = (18 days - 16 days) =
2 days

☺ d. 2 days is correct.
☹ a, b and c. These are distracter answers.

Solution 10

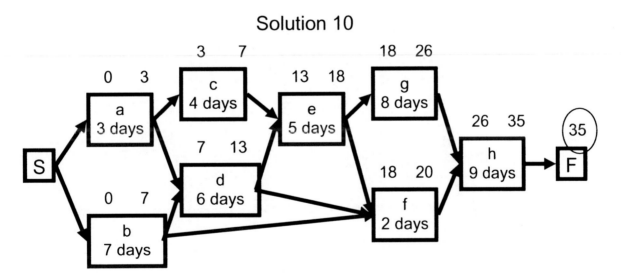

10. Ti determine the duration of the project or the critical path we do a forward pass. Duration = 35 days.

☺ c. 35 days is the correct answer.
☹ a, b and d. These are distracter answers.

Solution 11

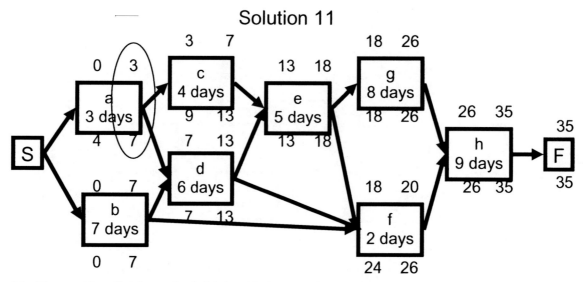

11. Float = (late finish - early finish) = (7 days - 3 days) = 4 days.

☺   c. 4 days is the correct answer.
☹   a, b and d. These are distracter answers.

Solution 12

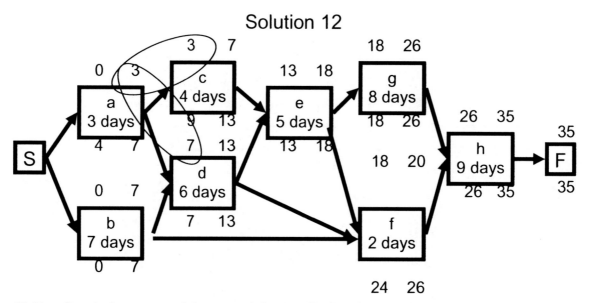

12. Free float is the amount of time an activity can slip from its early finish before it affects the early start of its earliest successor. In this example, Activity C and Activity D are both successors. Activity C has the earliest early start and so we look at the relationship between A and C. Activity A can slip 0 days from its early finish of 3 days before it would affect the early start of 3 days of C. Therefore, the free float is 0 days.

☺   a. 0 days is the correct answer.
☹   b, c and d. these are distracter answers.

Solution 13

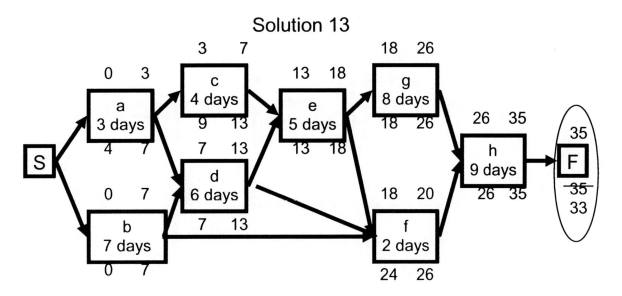

13. To calculate project float we take managements' imposed end date and make that our late finish.
 Project float = (late finish - early finish) = (33 days - 35 days) = - 2 days.

☺   b. -2 days is the correct answer.
☹   a., c., and d. These are distracter answers.

Solution 14

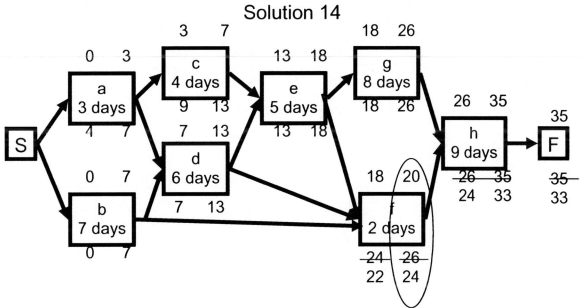

(NOTE: A backward pass was only done back to activity f... nothte whole diagram.)
14. Float = (late finish - early finish) = (24 days - 20 days) = 4 days.
☺   c. 4 days is the correct answer.
☹   a, b and d. These are distracter answers.

Solution 15

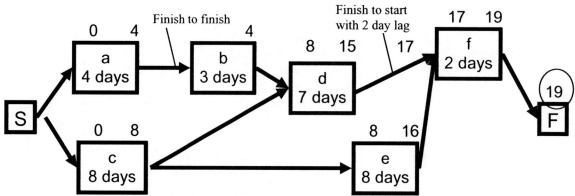

15. To determine duration we do a forward pass. Duration is 19 days.

☺   c. 19 days is the correct answer.
☹   a, b and d. These are distracter answers.

Solution 16

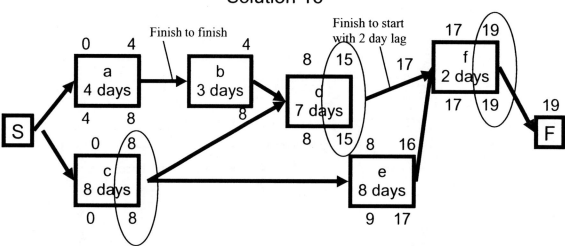

16. To determine what activities are on the critical path we need to find the activities with the least amount of float (usually 0); therefore, we need to do a backwards pass.

☺   a. c-d-f. these activities are on the critical path.
☹   b. Activity A and Activity B have float and are not on the critical path.
☹   c. This path does not get us from start to finish and, therefore, cannot be the critical path.
☹   d. Activity E has float and, therefore, cannot be on the critical path.

Solution 17

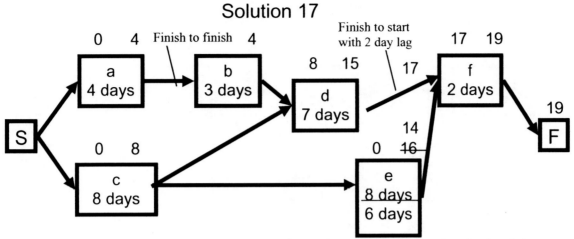

17. To determine project duration we must do a forward pass. The project duration is 19 days.

☺   c. 19 days is the correct answer.
☹   a,b and d. These are distracter answers.

Solution 18

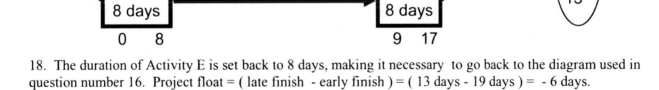

18. The duration of Activity E is set back to 8 days, making it necessary to go back to the diagram used in question number 16. Project float = (late finish - early finish) = (13 days - 19 days) = - 6 days.

☺   d. -6 days is the correct answer.
☹   a, b. and c. These are distracter answers.

Solution 19

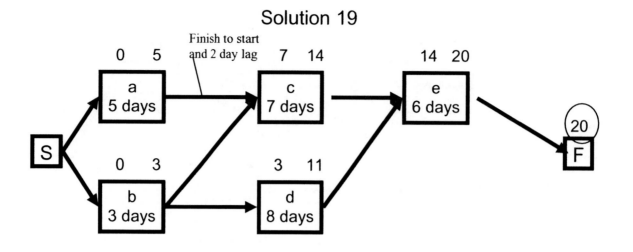

19. Based on the forward pass, the duration is 20 days.

☺   c. 20 days is the correct answer.
☹   a, b and d. These are distracter answers.

Solution 20

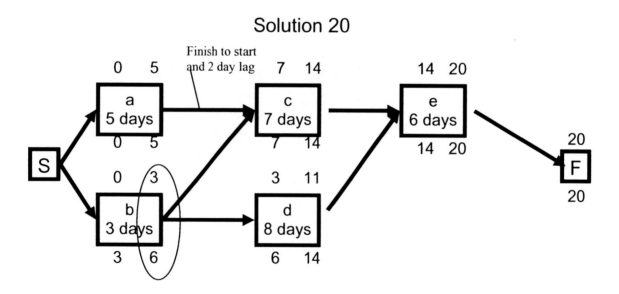

20. Float = (late finish - early finish) = (6 days - 3 days) = 3 days.

☺   b. 3 days is the correct answer.
☹   a, c and d. These are distracter answers.

Solution 21

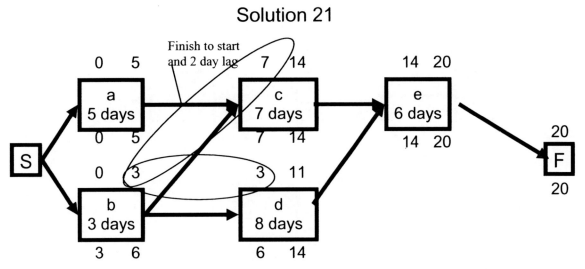

21. Free float is how much an activity can slip from its early finish before it affects the early start of its earliest successor. In this example, Activity C and Activity D are both successors of Activity B. Activity D has the earliest early start and so we look at the relationship between B and C. Activity B can slip 0 days from its early finish of 3 days before it would affect the early start of 3 days of C. Therefore, the free float is 0 days.

☺   a. 0 days is the correct answer.
☹   b, c and d. These are distracter answers.

Solution 22

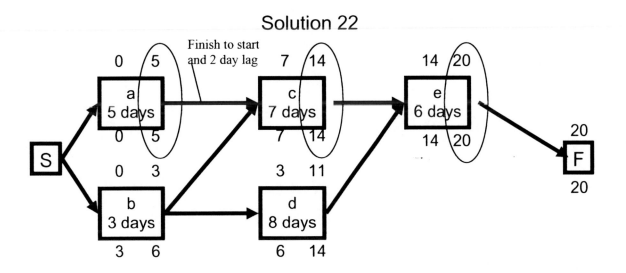

22. To deterimine what activities are on the critical path, we need to find the activities with the least amounts of float (usually 0). Therefore, we need to do a backwards pass.

☺   b. a-c-e These activities are on the critical path.
☹   a. This path does not get us from start to finish and, therefore, cannot be the critical path.
☹   c. Activity B has float and, therefore, is not on the critical path.
☹   d. Activity B and Activity D both have float and cannot be on the critical path.

Solution 23

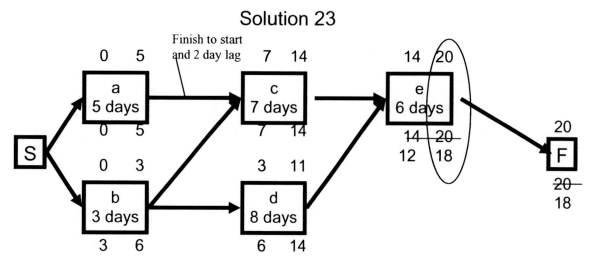

23. Note in this diagram a backward pass was only done to Activity E.
Float = (late finish - early finish) = - 2 days.

☺ b. -2 days is the correct answer.
☹ a, c and d. These are all distracter answers.

24. d. *PMBOK® Guide* 6.2.2.5
☺ d. Lag time is delay time; this is the time needed for the paint to dry.
☹ a. Total float is the total amount of time that a scheduled activity may be delayed from its early start without delaying the project finish date. This question has nothing to do with float.
☹ b. Free float is the amount of time that a schedule activity can be delayed without delaying the early start of any immediately following schedule activity. The question has nothing to do with free float.
☹ c. Lead is a modification of a logical relationship that allows an acceleration of the successor activity. This question it is the exact opposite of a lead.

25. c. Any statistics book
☺ c. The variance is defined as the square of the standard deviation. One standard deviation = (P-O)/6. = (24-12)/6= 2 days. The variance is (2 days) 2 = 4 days.
☹ a and b. These are distracter answers.
☹ d. 2 days is the standard deviation, not the variance.

26. a.
☺ a. The 80 hour rule is a heuristic. It is a rule of thumb that states that each work package should require 80 hours of effort or less.
☹ b. PMI has no regulations on the number of effort hours that should be required to complete a work package.
☹ c. A constraint limits the project team's options. Management made a suggestion. Suggestions are not constraints.
☹ d. Ground rules are often developed by teams to list acceptable and unacceptable behaviors to improve relationships.

27. c. *PMBOK® Guide* 6.5.2.2
☺ c. The critical path method is a schedule network analysis technique used to calculate theoretical start and finish dates as well as float.
☹ a. Bottom's up estimating is used to calculate the number of resources required for a project. It is not used to estimate float.
☹ b. Expert judgment is used in many planning processes, but a schedule network analysis technique is needed to determine float.
☹ d. Resource leveling is a schedule network analysis technique used after the float has been calculated to keep resource usage at a constant level.

28. a. Northcote Parkinson, Parkinson's Law: The Pursuit of Progress, London, John Murray (1958)
☺ a. Parkinson theory states that people will expand the work to fill the time allowed. In the question, more paths are becoming critical because people are expanding the work to fill the time and thus eating up the float.
☹ b. This could be lazy team members but lazy team members in not likely to be an answer on the exam.
☹ c. Critical chain is a network analysis technique that modifies the project schedule to account for limited resources. There is nothing in the question to lead us to critical chain.
☹ d. The critical path method calculates theoretical early and late start and finish dates. This is a network analysis technique. This answer does not address the issue in the question of additional critical paths.

29. b. *PMBOK® Guide* 6.6.2.6
☹ b. A comparison bar chart shows two bars, one for planned performance and one for actual performance.
☹ a. Monte Carlo analysis is a planning tool that shows what if scenarios. It does not show plan versus actual.
☹ c. A milestone chart shows scheduled start and finish dates of major deliverables and key external interfaces. Look for a better answer.
☹ d. The WBS is a planning tool for scope, not schedule.

30. a. *PMBOK® Guide* 2.1.1
☺ a. Fast tracking is about overlapping activities while concurrent engineering is moving implementers to an earlier phase of the project.
☹ b. Fast tracking is about overlapping activities. Crashing, not concurrent engineering is adding resources to the critical path.
☹ c. Concurrent engineering, not fast tracking, is about moving implementers to an earlier phase of the project. Crashing, not concurrent engineering, is about adding resources to the critical path.
☹ d. Fast tracking is overlapping phases as well as overlapping activities.

31 d. Standard practice of projects
☺ d. After we finish planning and before we move to executing we want to hold a kick-off meeting.
☹ a. Celebrate as a team should occur at the end of the project.
☹ b. Recommended preventative action is an output of monitor and control project work. We are still in planning, not monitoring and controlling.

☹   c. Recommended corrective action is an output of monitor and control project work. We are still in planning, not monitoring and controlling.

32.   d.   General Knowledge

☺   d. The last thing to do on a project is to release resources. All of the other answers take resources and thus must come before we release those resources.

☹   a. It takes resources to deliver the product to the customer, so this would not be the last thing to do.

☹   b. It takes resources to conduct lessons learned, so this would not be the last thing to do.

☹   c. It takes resources to hold a celebration, so this would not be the last thing to do.

33.   b.   *PMBOK® Guide* 6.2.2.4

☺   b. A discretionary dependency is based on best practice. The relationship is desired, though not mandatory.

☹   a and c. A mandatory dependency is inherent in the nature of the work being done. They involve physical limitations. Another name for a mandatory dependency is hard logic.

☹.   d. An external dependency involves the relationship between project and non-project activities.

34.   d.   *PMBOK® Guide* 6.3.2.2

☺   d. Benefit measurement methods and mathematical models are used in project selection, not in defining different methods to accomplish the work of the project.

☹   a, b and c. Make or buy, hand versus automated tools, and different size and type of machines are all examples of alternatives to accomplish the schedule activities (*PMBOK Guide* 6.3.2.2).

35   b.   *PMBOK® Guide* 6.5.2

☺   b. The critical path is time constrained. The critical chain is resource constrained.

☹   a. The critical path is time constrained. The critical chain is resource constrained. They are very different.

☹   c. The critical path assumes unlimited resources while the critical chain assumes limited resources.

☹   d. The critical path method has been around for decades while critical chain was coined in the 1990's.

36.   d.   *PMBOK® Guide* 6.5.2.2

☺   d. The critical path is the longest path through the network and the shortest amount of time to complete the project.

☹   a. The critical path is the longest, not the shortest, path through the network and the shortest amount of time to complete the project.

☹   b. The critical path is the longest path through the network and the shortest, not the longest, amount of time to complete the project.

☹   c. The critical path is the longest, not the shortest path through the network. It represents the shortest, not the longest, amount of time to complete the project.

37.   b.   *PMBOK® Guide* 6.5.2.2

☺   b. Total float is calculated by: total float= late finish –early finish. It is related to an activity. Project float is how much the project can float before it affects an imposed end date.

☹   a. Total float is for an activity. Project float is for the project.

☹   c. Free float, not total float, is the amount of time an activity can slip before delaying the start of its successor. Total float, not project float, is the amount of time an activity can be delayed without delaying the entire project.

☹   d. Project float, not total float is associated with an end date imposed by management. Total float is associated with an individual activity.

38.   c.

☺   c. The more near critical paths you have the more risk you have that you may miss your schedule.

☹   a. The more near critical paths you have the less float you have on your activities.

☹   b. There is no way to know from this question how schedule affects cost.

☹   d. Paths being critical or non-critical is not determined by the number of people working on the project.

39.   d.   *PMBOK® Guide*

☺   d. Total float = late finish –early finish= 10 -12 =-2 days

☹   a. Total float = late finish –early finish= 10 -12 =-2 days

☹   b. and c. To calculate free float we need to know the early start of all immediate successor activities. The question does not give us this information.

40.   b.   *PMBOK® Guide* 6.2.2.2

☺   b. One weakness of the Activity on Arrow diagram is that they only use finish to start relationships. They do not use finish to finish, start to start, or start to finish.

☹   a. This statement is not true. Activity on arrow diagrams have the arrow represent both the activity and relationship.

☹   c. GERT diagrams allow for "if-then" statements. Activity on arrow diagrams do not.

☹   d. GERT diagrams allow for feedback loops. Activity on arrow diagrams do not.

41.   b.   *PMBOK® Guide* 2000

☺   b. PERT stands for Program Evaluation Review Technique.

☹   a, c and d. These are made up terms. PERT stands for Program Evaluation Review Technique.

42.   c.   *PMBOK® Guide* 2000

☺   c. Graphical evaluation review technique allows for conditional statements.

☹   a. The arrow diagramming technique does not allow for conditional statements, such as "if-then".

☹   b. The precedence diagramming technique does not allow for conditional statements, such as "if-then".

☹   d. Fast tracking is a technique of overlapping activities or phases.

43.   b. Northcote Parkinson, Parkinson's Law: The Pursuit of Progress, London, John Murray (1958)

☺   b. Parkinson Law states that work expands so as to fill the time available for its completion.

☹   a. Student syndrome states that people will wait to the last minute to start tasks.

☹   c. Resource leveling is a schedule network analysis technique that addresses keeping selected resources at a constant level.

☹   d. Crashing is a schedule compression technique.

44.   c.   *PMBOK® Guide* 6.5.2.2

☺   c. The critical path method indicates the time periods within which the schedule activity should be scheduled.

☹   a. The critical path method indicates the time periods within which the schedule activity should be scheduled. It does not tell us the exact start and finish dates of for each activity.

☹   b. The critical path method leads to a time constrained schedule, not a resource constrained schedule.

☹   d. Crashing analyzes the cost and schedule tradeoffs to determine the best schedule.

45.   d.   *PMBOK® Guide* 6.5.2

☺   d. Critical path activities are those activities on the critical path.

☹   a., b and c. Critical path activities are those activities on the critical path.

46.   d.   Any Software Tool used for Scheduling

☺   d. Resource contouring allows you to schedule people on a variable distribution for a specific activity.

☹   a. What if scenario analysis using Monte Carlo allows the project manager to simulate different scenarios.

☹   b. The critical path method assumes unlimited resources.

☹   c. Crashing is a schedule compression technique in which resources are added to the critical path so a to pull in the schedule.

47.   a.   *PMBOK® Guide* 6.1.2.3

☺   a. Rolling wave planning allows for progressive elaboration planning. Near term work is planned in detail whereas long term work is planned at a higher level.

☹   b. Progressive elaboration means that over time we add detail. Progressive elaboration is not changing scope.

☹   c. A WBS dictionary is used to describe in detail the contents of the work packages. Whether we are doing a large part of our planning up front or throughout the project, a WBS dictionary may be used.

☹   d. Templates are documents in predefined formats that provide structure to develop other documents. Whether we are doing a large part of our planning up front or throughout the project, templates may be used.

48.   c.   *PMBOK® Guide* 6.2.2.4

☺   c. Discretionary dependencies are not required but based on knowledge of best practices. Discretionary dependencies are desired but other options are available.

☹   a. External dependencies are relationships between project and non-project activities.

☹   b and d. Mandatory dependencies, also called hard logic, are required dependencies, often involving physical limitations.

49.   b.   PMI, *PMBOK® Guide* 2000 (not in the Third Edition),

☺   b. PERT = (optimistic + 4* most likely + pessimistic)/6 = (80+(4*100)+150)/6 = 105 hours.

☹   a, c and d. Use the formula:

PERT = (optimistic + 4* most likely + pessimistic)/6 to find the correct answer.

50.   c.   *PMBOK® Guide* 6.4.2.4

☺   c. Three-point estimate = (optimistic + most likely + pessimistic)/3 = (80+100+150)/3 = 110 hours.

☹   a, b and d. Use the formula:

Three-point estimate = (optimistic + most likely + pessimistic)/3 to find the correct answer.

51.   b.   *PMBOK® Guide* 6.5.2.3

☺   b. Fast-tracking is a technique in which we allow activities to overlap or be completed in parallel that we would prefer to be done in series.

☹   a. Crashing is a schedule compression technique that involves adding resources to activities on the critical path. This is not the right answer since it involves adding resources.

☹   c. Resource leveling is not a schedule compression technique. In fact, the schedule often gets longer when resource leveling is done.

☹   d. Project management software certainly can help with schedule development but it is not a schedule compression technique.

PROJECT COST MANAGEMENT

Sample Questions

Big Picture Things to Know

Read Chapter Seven of the *PMBOK® Guide* before answering the questions in this section.

Cost management has three steps. Know how these steps ensure that the project can be completed within the approved budget.
- Cost Estimating—developing an approximation of the costs of the resources needed to complete project activities
- Cost Budgeting—aggregating the estimated costs of individual activities or work packages to establish a cost baseline
- Cost Control—influencing the factors that create cost variances and controlling changes to the project budget

Also of importance:
- Earned Value Management including EV, PV, AC, BAC, CV, SV, CPI, SPI, EAC, ETC, VAC
- Compare and contrast cost estimating and cost budgeting
- At this point, compare and contrast, integrated change control, scope control, schedule control and cost control
- Basic accounting ideas
    Direct and indirect costs *(PMBOK® Guide 12.1.2.3)*

Use the following scenario to answer questions 1-7.
Company A is working on a project. The project's budget is $1,000. The planned value as of today is $400. The project is 30% completed and 60% of the budget to date has been spent.

1. The Earned Value for this project is:

a. $ 240
b. $ 300
c. $ 400
d. $ 600

2. The actual cost to date for the project is:

a. $ 240
b. $ 300
c. $ 400
d. $ 600

3. According to the schedule, the project is:

a. ahead of schedule
b. behind schedule
c. on schedule
d. complete

4. According to the budget, the cost variance is:

a. $ 60
b. - $ 300
c. - $ 0
d. $ 400

5. If Company A continues to spend at the same rate the project will cost:

a. $ 1000
b. $ 800
c. $ 600
d. $ 400

6. What is the estimate to complete (ETC)?

a. $ 1040
b. $ 560
c. $ 300
d. $ 240

7. What is the variance at completion (VAC)?

a. $ 200
b. $ 560
c. $ 800
d. $ 1000

Use the following scenario for questions 8-15.

You are building a pen to keep animals. The pen will have four sides, all exactly the same. Your budget for the project is $400, or $100 per side. The schedule for the project is four days, one side per day. You started the project on Monday morning. It is now the end of the day on Tuesday. You have 25% of the total work done. You have spent $400 for the work that is complete.

8. What is the earned value for the project?

a. $ 100
b. $ 200
c. $ 400
d. $ 1600

9. What is the planned value as of today?

a. $ 100
b. $ 200
c. $ 400
d. $ 1600

10. What is the actual cost?

a. $ 100
b. $ 200
c. $ 400
d. $ 1600

11. The project cost variance is:

a. -$ 300
b. -$ 200
c. -$ 100
d. $ 0

12. The project schedule variance is:

a. -$ 300
b. -$ 200
c. -$ 100
d. $ 0

13. If the workers continue to spend at the same rate, what will the project cost?

a. $ 100
b. $ 200
c. $ 400
d. $ 1600

14. What is the expected variance at completion?

a. $ 1200
b. -$ 1200
c. $ 400
d. -$ 400

15. What is the estimate to complete?

a. $ 1200
b. -$ 1200
c. $ 400
d. -$ 400

16. Once again you are estimating the cost for your new project. Your estimates have not been good in the past and you want to make sure you are using reliable sources of information. The least reliable source of information is:

a. historical information
b. project files
c. project team knowledge
d. lessons learned

17. Once again you are estimating the cost for your new project. Your team members have expressed frustration in the past that you are unclear about the rounding you want in their estimates. Really they are asking you about the required:

a. precision level
b. control thresholds
c. earned value rules
d. report formats

18. Parametric estimates are most likely to be accurate when all the following statements are true *except:*

a. the historical information is accurate
b. the PM creates the model without inputs from other stakeholders
c. the parameters used in the model are readily quantifiable
d. the model is scalable

19. As you are planning your project, your team members are asking about the amount of variance that will be allowed. They are really asking you about:

a. precision level
b. control thresholds
c. earned value rules
d. report formats

20. The amount of cost variance allowed on a project usually:

a. increases over the life of the project
b. decreases over the life of the project
c. remains the same over the life of the project
d. starts low, gets much higher in the intermediate phases and drops off during the final phase

21. Your project is running so far over budget that you can no longer provide a realistic basis for performance measurement. Your next step is to:

a. update your cost management plan
b. create a revised project schedule
c. create a revised cost baseline
d. update your WBS

22. Your manager has rushed in and asked you for a ROM (rough order of magnitude) estimate for a potential project. You use your past experience and give your manager a ROM estimate of $100,000. This really means that you expect the project to complete in the range of:

a. $50,000 to $200,000
b. $75,000 to $175,000
c. $90,000 to $125,000
d. $95,000 to $110,000

23. On what contract type does the buyer typically have the lowest financial risk?

a. Time and materials
b. Cost plus percentage of cost
c. Cost plus fixed fee
d. Fixed price

24. When estimating project costs it is important to understand direct charges versus indirect charges. All of the following are typically considered direct charges except:

a. full time project staff
b. travel
c. material
d. fringe benefits

25. Your project has over 200 stakeholders. The stakeholders are located in 20 different countries and speak too many languages for you to name. In fact, your manager lives in another country and speaks a different language than you. Your SPI is running at .85. Your CPI is running at 1.2. Based on this scenario, what should you be most concerned about?

a. schedule
b. cost
c. stakeholder management
d. your management

26. The performance measure baseline is made up of what two categories:

a. distributed and undistributed
b. contingency reserve and management reserve
c. cost and profit
d. planning packages and work packages

27. The cost of quality is a tool and technique of:

a. cost estimating
b. cost budgeting
c. cost control
d. perform quality control

28. The 50-50 rule of progress reporting states that:

a. an activity gets credit when it is 50% complete and when it is 100% complete
b. an activity gets 50% credit for starting and the other 50% for completing
c. the contractor gets paid when the project is 50% complete and then again when the project is 100% complete
d. the contractor gets paid 50% when the project starts and the other 50% when the project completes

29. One of your team members just informed you that the project is about to experience a risk event. Your project costs:

a. will increase
b. will decrease
c. may increase or decrease
d. will not be affected

30. You project is running with a CPI of 1.2. The EAC is $100,000. What is the BAC?

a. $ 83,333
b. $100,000
c. $120,000
d. $150,000

31. Which of the following is not a cost estimating tool and technique?

a. funding limit reconciliation
b. analogous estimating
c. bottom-up estimating
d. parametric estimating

32. The BAC (budget at completion) for your project is $100,000. Your EAC is $120,000. What is your CPI??

a. .83
b. 1.0
c. 1.2
d. 1.5

33. Examining project performance over time to determine if performance is improving or deteriorating is called:

a. variance analysis
b. earned value technique
c. trend analysis
d. cost benefit analysis

34. As the project manager of a small start up company it is always important to understand your working capital. Working capital is defined as:

a. current assets minus current liabilities
b. present value of inflows minus present value of outflows
c. price-cost
d. price -profit

35. Your contractor is reporting to you on a monthly basis on cost performance using CPI. History has shown that the CPI on a project often becomes stable when what % of the work is complete?

a. 15%-20%
b. 25%-30%
c. 30%-45%
d. 30% -50%

36. A project manager should be rewarded on cost elements he can actually influence. Which of the following is hardest for the project manager to influence?

a. direct costs
b. indirect costs
c. variable costs
d. fixed costs

37. Management is going through an annual review of projects to decide on what projects to continue and what projects to kill. You should provide management with all the following information *except*:

a. cost performance trends on each project
b. schedule performance trends on each project
c. sunk costs on each project
d. risk trends on each project

38. Your project work is expected to be constant for the six month length of the project. During each month your budget is $200. At the end of month four you have 40% of the total work complete and you have spent 70% of your total budget. The budget at completion for the project is:

a. $ 80
b. $ 140
c. $ 840
d. $1,200

39. Your project work is expected to be constant for the six month length of the project. During each month your budget is $200. At the end of month four you have 40% of the total work complete and you have spent 70% of your total budget. The planned value for the project is:

a. $ 80
b. $ 140
c. $ 800
d. $1,200

40. Assuming an interest rate of 15%, the present value of $ 100 received two years from now will be:

a. $ 0
b. $ 100
c. less than $ 100
d. more than $ 100

41. During a project review meeting the project manager states that the project CPI is 1.11. This means:

a. for every dollar we spend we get 1.11 dollars of value
b. for every $1.11 we spend we get one dollar of value
c. for every day we work we get 1.11 days of work complete
d. for every 1.11 days we work we get one day of work complete

42. Factoring in the cost of operations and maintenance of the project's product is known as:

a. life-cycle costing
b. project cost estimating
c. project cost budgeting
d. opportunity cost

43. During a project review meeting the project manager states that the project SPI is 1.11. This means:

a. for every dollar we spend we get 1.11 dollars of value
b. for every $1.11 we spend we get one dollar of value
c. for every day we work we get 1.11 days of work complete
d. for every 1.11 days we work we get one day of work complete

44. The accuracy of cost estimates:

a. increases as the project progresses
b. stays the same as the project progresses
c. decreases as the project progresses
d. fluctuates as the project progresses

45. During cost estimating, market place conditions such as what products and services are available in the marketplace, from whom, and under what terms are part of:

a. organizational process assets
b. enterprise environmental factors
c. analogous estimating
d. parametric estimating

46. Your management has rushed into your office and requested that you develop a cost estimate for a potential customer project in the next 15 minutes. You have completed similar projects to the one management described and therefore you are most likely to use what type of cost estimating technique?

a. vendor bid analysis
b. parametric estimating
c. bottom-up estimating
d. analogous estimating

47. Management is concerned about the practice of cost estimators and project managers inflating cost estimates. To deal with this practice in a positive way, management has told you that you will be allowed a contingency reserve on your project if you can support the reserve with real data. From your project management training, you realize that all the following are true about a contingency reserve except:

a. they are set up for expected but not certain events
b. they are part of your project schedule and cost baselines
c. they are for unknown unknowns
d. they can be used at the good judgment of the project manager

48. Your management has approved a contingency reserve for the project. There seems to be some confusion between a contingency reserve and a management reserve. You explain that management reserve is:

a. the difference between the maximum funding and the top end of the cost baseline
b. the same as contingency reserve
c. part of the cost baseline
d. under the discretion of the project manager

49. As a project manager, you know it is important to link your project costs to the organization's accounting system. This is usually done at what level of the WBS?

a. work package level
b. activity level
c. control account level
d. planning package level

50. You are the cost estimator for your organization. The project manager working with you asked you to explain what types of costs are included in your estimates and what are not. An example of an item not included in your costs estimates is:

a. inflation allowance
b. contingency costs
c. management reserve
d. facility costs

PROJECT COST MANAGEMENT

Learning Solutions

1. -7. To answer these questions first determine: BAC, PV, EV, and AC.

BAC (budget at completion) represents the total project budget. The question states, "the project budget is $1000". Therefore BAC= $1000.

PV (planned value) is the budgeted cost of the work scheduled. The question states, "The planned value as of today is $400." This means that $400 worth of work should be done. Therefore, PV= $400.

EV (earned value) is the value of the work done. The question states, "30% of the total work is done." In other words, 30% of the BAC is done. Therefore, EV=30%(BAC) . EV=30% ($1000) = $300.

AC (actual cost) is the amount of money spent for the work completed. The question states,"60% of the budget to date has been spent." The budget to date is the same as the planned value (PV). Therefore, AC=60%(PV) = 60%($400)= $240. Be careful. Notice the question states 60% of the budget to date, not 60% of the total budget.

Now onto the questions:

1. b. *PMBOK® Guide* 7.3.2.2
☺ b. $300 is the EV. EV is the value of the work that is done.
☹ a. this is the AC, not the EV.
☹ c. this is the PV, not the EV.
☹ d. this number has no significance in relation to this problem.

2. a. *PMBOK® Guide* 7.3.2.2
☺ a. $ 240 is the AC. AC is a measure of the amount of money spent for the work completed.
☹ b. this is the EV, not the AC.
☹ c. this is the PV, not the AC.
☹ d. this number has no significance in relation to this problem.

3. b. *PMBOK® Guide* 7.3.2.2
☺ b. SV= (EV – PV). SV= ($300 - $400) = -$100. Since the answer is negative, the project is behind schedule.
☹ a. For the project to be ahead of schedule the SV would have to be a positive number.
☹ c. For the project to be on schedule the SV would have to equal $0.
☹ d. For the work to be complete the project EV would have to equal to the BAC. The work is not complete yet.

4. a. *PMBOK® Guide* 7.3.2.2
☺ a. CV= (EV – AC). CV= ($300 - $240) = $60.
☹ b, c and d. These numbers are distracter answers.

5. b. *PMBOK® Guide* 7.3.2
☺ b. EAC = (BAC/CPI). CPI = (EV/AC).
Calculate CPI First. CPI = ($300/$240) = (5/4) = 1.25.
EAC= (BAC/CPI). EAC= ($1000/1.25) = $ 800.

☹   a, c and d. These numbers are distracter answers.
6.   b.   *PMBOK® Guide* 7.3.2.3
☺   b. ETC is a measure of how much more money needs to be spent to complete the project. The team has spent $240 (the actual cost is $240) and the team now expects the project to cost $800 (the EAC is $800); therefore, the team expects to spend $560 more.
        ETC = (EAC - AC) = ($800 - $240)= $560.
☹   a, c and d. These numbers are distracter answers.

7.   a.   This term is not in the *PMBOK® Guide* but could be on exam.
☺   a. VAC (variance at completion) is a measure of how much the team expects to under run or overrun. The BAC = $1000. Now the team expects to finish for $800 (this is the EAC)… therefore the team expects to under run by $200. This is the VAC. Under runs are positive numbers; overruns are negative numbers.
        VAC= (BAC - EAC) = ($1000 - $800) = $200.
☹   b, c and d. These numbers are distracter answers.

8-15.
To answer these questions first determine:
BAC, PV, EV, and AC.

BAC (budget at completion) represents the total project budget. The question states, "The budget for the project is $400, or $100 per side." Therefore, BAC= $400.

PV (planned value) is the budgeted cost of the work scheduled. The question states, "You started the project on Monday. It is now the end of the day on Tuesday." Therefore, two days of work should be done. The schedule is one side per day. Therefore, we should have two sides completed. The budget for each side is $100; therefore, $200 worth of work should be completed. Therefore, PV= $200.

EV (earned value) is the value of the work done. The question states, "25% of the total work is done." In other words, 25% of the BAC is done. Therefore, EV=25% (BAC)= 25% ($400) =$100.

AC (actual cost) is the amount of money spent for the work completed. The question states, "You have spent $400 for the work that is complete." Therefore, AC= $400.

8.   a.   *PMBOK® Guide* 7.3.2.2
☺   a. $ 100 is your EV.
☹   b. $ 200 is your PV.
☹   c. $ 400 is your BAC.
☹   d. $ 1600 … you will see later what this number represents.

9.   b.   *PMBOK® Guide* 7.3.2.2
☺   b. $ 200 is your PV.
☹   a. $ 100 is your EV.
☹   c. $ 400 is your BAC.
☹   d. $ 1600 … You will see later what this number represents.

10.   c.   *PMBOK® Guide* 7.3.2.2
☺   c. $ 400 is your AC.

☹   a. $ 100 is your EV.

☹   b. $ 200 is your PV.

☹   d. $ 1600 … You will see later what this number represents.

11.   a.   *PMBOK® Guide* 7.3.2.3

☺   a. Cost variance = (EV-AC) = ($100 - $400) = -$300. The project is running over budget. You spent $400 to complete one side ($100 worth of work).

☹   b, c and d. These numbers are distracter answers.

12.   c.   *PMBOK® Guide* 7.3.2.3

☺   c. Schedule variance = (EV – PV) = ($100 - $200) = -$100. The project is running behind schedule. It took two days to complete one day's worth of work (one side). You are behind by one day's worth of work (one side).

☹   a, b. and d. These numbers are distracter answers.

13.   d.   *PMBOK® Guide* 7.3.2.3

☺   d. EAC = (BAC/CPI) = $400/(1/4)= $1600. We now expect the entire project to cost $1600.

☹   a. $ 100 is your EV.

☹   b. $ 200 is your PV.

☹   c. $ 400 is your BAC.

14.   b.   This term is not in the *PMBOK® Guide* but could be on the exam.

☺   b. VAC = (BAC – EAC) = ($400 - $1600)= -$1200.

☹   a. $ 1200. This is a distracter answer.

☹   c. $ 400. This is your BAC.

☹   d.-$ 400. This is a distracter answer.

15.   a.   *PMBOK® Guide* 7.3.2.3

☺   a. ETC= (EAC – AC) = ($1600 - $400) = $1200.

☹   b. -$ 1200. This is a distracter answer.

☹   c. $ 400. This is your BAC.

☹   d. -$ 400. This is a distracter answer.

16.   c.   *PMBOK® Guide* 7.1.1.2

☺   c. Project team knowledge is useful but far less reliable than documented performance.

☹   a. Historical information is documented information obtained from various parts of the organization.

☹   b. Project files are documented records of previous project performance.

☹   d. Lessons learned are documented lessons from previous projects. They may include cost estimates.

17. a. *PMBOK® Guide* Chapter 7 Introduction
☺   a. Cost estimates should be provided to a prescribed precision ($100, $1000) based on the activities and magnitude of the project.
☹   b. Control thresholds set the agreed amount of variance allowed over time on a project.
☹   c. Earned value rules define several items including the level of the work breakdown structure as which EV analysis will be performed.
☹   d. Report formats define the format of various cost reports.

18. b. *PMBOK® Guide* 7.2.2.3
☺   b. The PM should create the model **with** inputs from other stakeholders. The question is asking for the exception.
☹   a. The historical information going into the estimate should be accurate. We want this to be true.
☹   c. The parameters used in the model are readily quantifiable. We want this to be true.
☹   d. The model is scalable. We want this to be true.

19. b. *PMBOK® Guide* Chapter 7 Introduction
☺   b. Control thresholds set the agreed amount of variance allowed over time on a project.
☹   a. Cost estimates should be provided to a prescribed precision ($100, $1000) based on the activities and magnitude of the project.
☹   c. Earned value rules define several items including the level of the work breakdown structure as which EV analysis will be performed.
☹   d. Report formats define the format of various cost reports.

20. b. *PMBOK® Guide* 7.3.2.6
☺   b. The closer we get to completion the less cost variance we often will allow.
☹   a. This statement is just the opposite of what is true.
☹   c and d. At the beginning of a project we usually will allow a wide cost variance. As we get closer to completion, the amount of cost variance allowed tends to get smaller and smaller.

21. c. *PMBOK® Guide* 7.3.3.2
☺   c. A revised cost baseline may need to be created to provide a realistic basis for performance measurement.
☹   a. Your cost management plan is updated if approved changes impact the management of costs. This scenario does not affect the management of costs and therefore the cost management plan is not updated. (*PMBOK® Guide* 7.1.3.4).
☹   b. A revised project schedule is created when we can no longer measure schedule performance. The question relates to cost performance, not schedule performance (*PMBOK® Guide* 6.6..3.2).
☹   d. The WBS is updated when approved changes have an effect upon the project scope. This scenario does not imply a change in scope and therefore the WBS is not updated (*PMBOK® Guide* 5.5.3.2).

22. a. *PMBOK® Guide* Cost introduction
☺   a. A ROM estimate has a range of -50% to +100%. Therefore a ROM estimate of $100,000 would have a range of $50,000 (this is -50% of $100,000) to $200,000 (this is +100% of $100,000).

☹   b. An Order of Magnitude estimate has a range of -25% to +75%. Therefore an Order of magnitude estimate of $100,000 would have a range of $75,000 (this is -25% of $100,000) to $175,000 (this is +75% of $100,000).

☹   c. A Budget estimate has a range of 10% to +25%. Therefore a budget estimate of $100,000 would have a range of $90,000 (this is -10% of $100,000) to $125,000 (this is +25% of $100,000).

☹   d. A definitive estimate has a range of -5% to +10%. Therefore a definitive estimate of $100,000 would have a range of $95,000 (this is -5% of $100,000) to $110,000 (this is +10% of $100,000).

23.   d.   *PMBOK® Guide* 12.1.2.3

☺   d. Fixed price is the contract type in which the buyer has the lowest financial risk because the buyer knows exactly what the price of the contract will be if there are no approved change orders.

☹   a. Time and materials contracts in general are a higher risk for the buyer since this contract type is open ended. The full value of the agreement and the exact quantity of items to be delivered are not defined.

☹   b and c. Cost plus percentage of cost, and cost plus fixed fee, in general are a higher risk for the buyer because in these contract types the buyer must reimburse the seller for all allowable costs plus a fee. The buyer does not know the total price of the contract at the time of contract award.

24.   d.   *PMBOK® Guide* 12.1.2.3

☺   d. Fringe benefits are usually considered indirect charges. Indirect charges are costs allocated to the project by the project team as the cost of doing business. Indirect costs are usually calculated as a percentage of direct costs.

☹   a, b and c. Direct costs are incurred for the exclusive benefit of the project. Typical examples are full time project staff, travel and material.

25.   a.   *PMBOK® Guide* 7.3.2.2

☺   a. A SPI of less than one means that you are running behind schedule. You should put your focus on schedule.

☹   b. A CPI of 1.2 means that you are running under budget.

☹   c and d. We should always be concerned about our stakeholders and our management. There is nothing in the question though that states we need to focus more on our stakeholders or our manager. The question does state that we have an SPI that is less than we. This is measurable.

26.   a.   *Earned Value Management*, Fleming and Koppelaman

☺   a. The performance measurement baseline is split into the distributed budget and the undistributed budget.

☹   b. The contract budget is split into the performance measurement baseline and the management reserve. The contingency reserve is part of the performance measurement baseline.

☹   c. The contract price is split into the cost and profit.

☹   d. The cost accounts are split into the planning packages and the work packages.

27.   a.   *PMBOK® Guide* 7.1.2.8

☺   a. The cost of quality can be used to prepare the cost estimate.

☹   b. Cost budgeting involves applying the estimating costs of individual activities to establish a cost baseline. The cost of quality is not a tool (PMBOK® *Guide* 7.2).

☹   c. Cost control is the process of controlling changes to the project budget. The cost of quality is not a tool (*PMBOK® Guide* 7.3).

☹   d. Perform quality control is the process of monitoring specific project results to determine whether they comply with relevant quality standards and identifying ways to eliminate causes of unsatisfactory performance. The cost of quality is not a tool (*PMBOK® Guide* 8.3). The cost of quality is a tool of quality planning.

28.   *Earned Value Management*, Fleming and Koppelaman
☺   b. The 50-50 rule states that an activity will receive 50% of its PV (planned value) as earned value (EV) when it starts and 50% of its PV as earned value when it completes.
☹   a. With the 50-50 rule an activity gets credit for starting, not being 50% complete. It gets the rest of the credit when it finishes.
☹   c and d. The 50-50 rule is used at the activity level not the project level.

29.   c.   *PMBOK® Guide* Chapter 11 Cost Introduction
☺   c. Remember that risks events may have either a positive or a negative effect.
☹   a, b and d. Risk events almost always have an affect on costs and may be positive or negative depending on the event.

30.   c.   *Earned Value Management*, Fleming and Koppelaman
☺   c. EAC=BAC/CPI. Therefore BAC=EAC*CPI= $100,000*1.2= $120,000.
☹   a, b and d. These are distracter answers.

31.   a   *PMBOK® Guide* Figure 7-3 and Figure 6-4
☺   a. Funding limit reconciliation is a cost budgeting tool not a cost estimate tool.
☹   b, c and d. Analogous estimating, bottom-up estimating and parametric estimating are all tools of cost estimating. Notice this question has the word *not* in it.

32.   a.   *Earned Value Management*, Fleming and Koppelaman
☺   a. EAC=BAC/CPI. Therefore CPI =BAC/EAC= $100,000/$120,000= .83 CPI= .83
☹   b, c and d. These are distracter answers.

33.   c.   *PMBOK® Guide* 7.3.3.4
☺   c. Trend analysis examines project performance over time to determine if performance is improving or deteriorating is called.
☹   a. Variance analysis compares actual project performance to planned performance.
☹   b. Earned value analysis compares actual cost and schedule performance to planned performance.
☹   d. Cost benefit analysis compares the cost of a project to the benefits of the project. In general we only work on projects whose benefits out weigh costs.

34.   a.   any accounting book

☺   a. Your working capital is your current assets minus your current liabilities. Working capital is a measure of how much liquid assets a company has to build the business.

☹   b. Net present value is the present value of inflows minus the present value of outflows. NPV is used in capital budgeting to analyze the profitability of an investment or project.

☹   c. Profit is equal to price-cost. This is a procurement idea. The profit the seller receives is equal to the price they charge minus their costs.

☹   d. Cost is equal to price –profit. This is a procurement idea. A seller's cost is equal to the price they charge minus the profit they make.

35.   a.   Earned Value Management, Fleming and Koppelaman

☺   a. The cumulative CPI has been proved to stabilize once the project is approximately 20% complete.

☹   b, c and d. The cumulative CPI would stabilize before this.

36.   b.   *PMBOK® Guide* 12.1.2.3

☺   b. Indirect costs such as such as overhead and general and administrative are hard for the project manager to influence.

☹   a. Direct costs are incurred for the exclusive benefit of the project. The project manager should be controlling direct costs.

☹   c and d. Variable costs change based on the size of certain elements of the project. Fixed costs do not change based on the size of certain elements of a project. Project managers control direct costs, regardless of whether they are variable or fixed.

37.   c.   Any Accounting Textbook or Web Search

☺   c. Sunk costs are unrecoverable costs should not be taken into consideration. Sunk time is a similar idea.

☹   a, b and d. Cost performance, schedule performance, and risk trends should all be analyzed as management reviews whether to continue or kill a project.

38.   d.   *PMBOK® Guide* 7.3.2.2

☺   d. The BAC for your project is your total project budget. The question says you have a budget of $200/month for six months. Your total project budget is $1,200.

☺   a, b and c. This is a distracter answer.

39.   c. *PMBOK® Guide* 7.3.2.2

☺   c. The planned value (PV) is the budgeted cost of work scheduled. You have $200/month budget and you are at the end of month four. Therefore your PV= $ 800.

☹   a, b and d. These are distracter answers.

40.   c.   Any Accounting Textbook

☺   c. The present value will be lower than $100. $PV = (\text{Future value})/(1 + k)^n$. k= interest rate and n= number of years.

$PV = (\$100)/(1+.15)^2$. PV = $75.61. Another way to think of this is $1 today is worth more than $1 in the future.

☹ a. The present value will be less than the future value but will not go to $0.

☹ b. Since the interest rate is not zero, the present value will always be less than the future value; therefore, the answer must be less than $100.

☹ d. This statement is just the opposite of the right answer. Present value is always smaller than future value when there is a positive rate.

41. a. *PMBOK® Guide* 7.3.2.2

☺ a. The CPI is the cost-efficiency indicator. An index of 1.11 means that for every dollar we spend we get 1.11 dollars of value.

☹ b. This statement is reversed.

☹ c. This is a description of an SPI of 1.11.

42. a. *PMBOK® Guide* Chapter 7— Cost Introduction

☺ a. Lifecycle costing is associated with the life cycle of the product and includes the cost operations and maintenance.

☹ b. Project cost estimating is approximating the cost of the project.

☹ c. Project cost budgeting is aggregating the estimated costs of individual schedule activities or work packages to establish a total cost baseline.

☹ d. Opportunity costs are the costs of lost opportunities.

43. c. *PMBOK® Guide* 7.3.2.2

☹ c. The SPI is the schedule performance indicator. An SPI of 1.11 means that for every day we work we get 1.11 days of work complete.

☹ a. This is a description of an CPI of 1.11.

☹ b. This statement is reversed description of a CPI of 1.11.

☹ d. This statement is the reversed.

44. a. *PMBOK® Guide* 7.1

☺ a. As we know more about the project, the accuracy of the cost estimates should increase.

☹ b, c and d. These statements do not represent the accuracy of cost estimates. The more we know as we progress through the project life cycle, the more accurate the cost estimates.

45. b. *PMBOK® Guide* 7.1.1.1

☺ b. Marketplace conditions and commercial databases are considered as enterprise environmental factors during cost estimating.

☹ a. Cost estimating policies, templates, historical information, and project files are examples of organizational process assets.

☺ c and d. Analogous estimating and parametric estimating are tools not inputs to cost estimating.

46. d. *PMBOK® Guide* 7.1.2.1

☺ d. Analogous estimating is often used when little information is available about the project. In this method we use past similar projects as the basis for our estimate. This method is often quicker, less costly and less accurate.

☹ a. Vendor bid analysis involves using vendor bids as the basis of our estimates.

☹   b. Parametric estimating involves using statistical relationships between variables to create cost estimates.

☹   c. Bottom-up estimating involves estimating the cost of work packages and rolling these estimates up to create a cost estimate for the project.

47.   c.   *PMBOK® Guide* 7.1.2.7

☺   c. Contingency reserves are for known unknowns. Management reserves are for unknown unknowns.

☹   a. Contingency reserves are set up for expected but not certain events (known unknowns).

☹   b. Contingency reserve is included in your baselines.

☹   d. Contingency reserves can be used at the discretion of the project manager.

48.   a.   *PMBOK® Guide* 7.2.2.2 and Figure 7-5

☺   a. If you look at Figure 7-5 you can see that management reserve is the difference between maximum funding and the top of the cost baseline, meaning that management reserve is not part of the cost baseline but are included in the budget for the project.

☹   b. Contingency reserve is for known unknowns whereas management reserve is for unknown unknowns.

☹   c. Management reserve is not part of the cost baseline, contingency reserve is.

☹   d. Management reserve can only be used after the project manager has obtained approval.

49.   c.   *PMBOK® Guide* chapter 7— Cost Introduction

☺   c. Each control account has a code that links it directly to the organization's accounting system.

☹   a. The work package level is the lowest level of the WBS and is where the work is scheduled, cost estimated, monitored and controlled (*PMBOK® Guide* 5.3).

☹   b. There is no such thing as an activity level in the WBS.

☹   d. The planning package level is the level below the control account and above the work package (*PMBOK® Guide* 6.1.2.5).

50.   c.   *PMBOK® Guide* 7.1

☺   c. Management reserve is for unknown unknowns and therefore is not part of the cost estimates.

☹   a, b and d. Typical items in the cost estimates are labor, materials, equipment, services and facilities. They may also include items such as an inflation reserve and contingency costs.

PROJECT QUALITY MANAGEMENT

Sample Questions

Big Picture Things to Know

Read Chapter Eight of the *PMBOK® Guide* before answering the questions in this section.

Quality management has three steps. Know how these steps ensure that the project will satisfy the needs for which it was undertaken.
- Quality Planning—identifying which quality standards are relevant to the project and determining how to satisfy them
- Perform Quality Assurance—applying the planned, systematic quality activities to ensure that the project employs all processes needed to meet requirements
- Perform Quality Control—monitoring specific project results to determine whether they comply with relevant quality standards and identifying ways to eliminate causes of unsatisfactory performance

Also of importance:
- Quality assurance versus quality control
- Which quality tools and techniques belong to quality planning versus perform quality assurance versus perform quality control
- The appropriate time to use each quality tool
- Deming, Crosby, Juran

1. Perform quality assurance includes:

a. applying the planned, systematic quality activities to ensure that the project employs all processes needed to meet requirements
b. identifying which quality standards are relevant determining how to satisfy them
c. monitoring specific project results to determine if they comply with relevant quality standards and identifying ways to eliminate causes of unsatisfactory performance
d. all the activities of the performing organization that determine quality policies, objectives, and responsibilities so that the project will satisfy the needs for which it were undertaken.

2. Which one of the following statements is true about quality and grade?

a. low quality may not always be a problem
b. we should always deliver high grade
c. quality and grade are basically the same thing
d. low grade may not always be a problem

3. Which statement represents the relationship between precision and accuracy?

a. precise measurements are accurate
b. accurate measurements are precise
c. precision and accuracy are not equivalent
d. a high level of precision and accuracy are always required

4. In your lumber company, three standard deviations has been your standard for decades. Your new quality manager wants to adopt a six sigma approach. Which of the following statement is true?

a. six sigma is twice as stringent as three sigma
b. six sigma is the more traditional approach to quality management
c. with three sigma, defects occur only about 3 times in a thousand and with six sigma defects occur only about 3.3 times in a million.
d. six sigma approach means plus or minus three standard deviations on each side of the mean

5. The statistical method that helps identify which factors may influence specific variables of a product or process is:

a. Pareto chart
b. control chart
c. design of experiment
d. inspection

6. A tool that shows how many defects were generated by type of category is:

a. Pareto chart
b. cause and effect diagram
c. flow chart
d. scatter diagram

7. The project team should know the difference between all the following *except*:

a. tolerances and control limits
b. random causes and common causes
c. attribute sampling and variable sampling
d. prevention and inspection

8. Your medical component business is growing at an exponential rate. As far as product testing you are moving to testing samples instead of entire populations. In general, the main reasons to test samples instead of populations include all of the following except:

a. the testing may be destructive
b. the testing is expensive
c. the testing takes a long time
d. the testing is variable related not attribute related

9. Quality control is related to scope verification in that:

a. quality control is about acceptance, whereas scope verification is about meeting requirements
b. quality control is normally performed after scope verification
c. quality control is about meeting requirements, whereas scope verification is about acceptance
d. quality control and scope verification are always performed in parallel

10. Common causes of variation are also called:

a. special causes
b. unusual events
c. control limits
d. random causes

11. The upper and lower control limits are usually set at:

a. +/- 1 sigma
b. +/- 2 sigma
c. +/- 3 sigma
d. +/- 6 sigma

12. If the results fall inside the customer tolerances:

a. the process is in control
b. the results are acceptable to the customer
c. the process should not be adjusted
d. the data is within +/- 3 sigma

13. The pessimistic time to complete Activity A is 22 days. The optimistic time is 10 days. The standard deviation for Activity A is:

a. 1 day
b. 2 days
c. 6 days
d. 12 days

14. Rank ordering of defects is done through:

a. control charts
b. process flowcharts
c. cause and effect diagrams
d. Pareto chart

15. You want to be able to systematically change all of the important factors for a product or process to provide the optimal conditions. Based on this need you are most likely to use:

a. benchmarking
b. control chart
c. design of experiment (DOE)
d. run chart

16. On your factory floor much space is occupied by work in progress. Management has decided to try a pull system. Therefore workers do not automatically receive work in progress from a previous station but need to pull when they need inventory. Another name for this system is:

a. Kanban
b. Kaizen
c. Utility Theory
d. Marginal Analysis

17. Your quality manager comes to you with a list of tools typically used in quality planning. This list is likely to include all the following *except*:

a. brainstorming
b. affinity diagrams
c. force field analysis
d. defect repair review

18. Your quality manager and operations manager are arguing about how much money should be spent on quality. The real question is how to define optimal quality. Marginal analysis states that optimal quality is reached when:

a. the incremental revenue from improvement equals the incremental cost to obtain it
b. quality has the same priority as cost and schedule
c. more money is spent proactively on quality than reactively on quality
d. nothing more can be done to improve quality

19. Your quality control group has recommended statistical sampling, which is often conducted for all the following reasons *except*:

a. sampling often can reduce costs
b. sampling is often a quicker process
c. testing may be destructive so we need to sample
d. attribute sampling measures the degree of conformance

20. You are preparing for the PMI® exam. You decide to test yourself on 40 sample questions in each of the six domains and set priorities based on your results. To do this you are most likely to use a:

a. cause and effect diagram
b. flow chart
c. run chart
d. Pareto diagram

21. Fishbone diagrams are also known as:

a. Ishikawa diagrams
b. control charts
c. Pareto charts
d. network diagrams

22. Your customer is complaining about the reliability and maintainability of your products. You are likely to put more focus on:

a. the project life cycle
b. product design
c. project scope
d. the product life cycle

23. Conformance to requirements means:

a. the product or service satisfies real needs
b. the customer accepts the deliverable
c. the project must produce what is said it would produce
d. doing exactly what the customer wants

24.   The cost of quality is often broken up into two categories:

a. cost of conformance and cost of non-conformance
b. prevention costs and appraisal costs
c. internal failure costs and external failure costs
d. cost of quality assurance and cost of quality control

25. Perform quality control is:

a. applying the planned, systematic quality activities to ensure that the project employs all processes needed to meet requirements
b. identifying which quality standards are relevant to the project and determining how to satisfy them
c. monitoring specific project results to determine if they comply with relevant quality standards and identifying ways to eliminate causes of unsatisfactory performance
d. all the activities of the performing organization that determine quality policies, objectives, and responsibilities so that the project will satisfy the needs for which it was undertaken

26. You are the project manager for a logging company. This month you are charted to deliver 10,000 units that are 60 centimeters each. Your upper control limit on your process is 63 centimeters. Your lower control limits on your process is 57 centimeters. Your mean is 60 centimeters. What percentage of your units will fall between 58 and 62 centimeters?

a. 68.3%
b. 75.5 %
c. 95.5%
d. 99.7%

27. Your customer has asked you to do a "little extra" work. You should:

a. always do what the customer requests
b. evaluate the change request
c. ask your management for direction
d. ask your sponsor for direction

28. "Kaizen" is another name for:

a. just in time
b. continuous improvement
c. quality baseline
d. quality metrics

29. Changes should be:

a. formally documented in writing
b. documented in writing when we have time
c. made first, and documented after the fact
d. processed and implemented regardless of the level of documentation

30. Your project is to paint a very large conference room for your customer. As you are painting, the customer facilities manager asks you to touch up a small scuff mark in an outer hallway. You should:

a. evaluate the change request
b. do as asked because you know that gold plating is always a good idea
c. ignore the request since it is not part of your statement of work
d. wait to see if you have extra paint and if yes, take care of the scuff mark

31. Zero inventory is most associated with:

a. scatter diagrams
b. benchmarking
c. cost-benefit analysis
d. just in time

32. Your organization is spending a tremendous amount of money to ensure you are known for quality products. Scrap and rework are considered what type of costs:

a. internal failure costs
b. external failure costs
c. appraisal costs
d. prevention costs

33. Interrogatory checklists are phrased as:

a. Do this now!
b. Follow the plan.
c. Focus on success.
d. Have you done this?

34. A process improvement plan identifies:

a. the steps for analyzing processes that will facilitate the identification of waste and non-value added activities
b. the quality objectives of the project
c. the operational definitions that describe in very specific terms what something is and how the quality control process measures it
d. how the project management team will implement the performing organization's quality policy

35. Quality audits are a tool and technique of:

a. quality planning
b. perform quality assurance
c. perform quality control
d. quality planning, perform quality assurance, and perform quality control

36. You own an outdoor food stand where your main product is hamburgers. You want to collect data so you can understand the inherent limits of your process. To do this you are most likely to use a:

a. Pareto chart
b. control chart
c. cause and effect diagram
d. trend analysis

37. The basis for quality improvement is:

a. Monte Carlo analysis
b. plan-do-check-act
c. configuration management
d. change control system

38. You are the project manager for a logging company. This month you are charted to deliver 10,000 units that are 60 centimeters each. Your upper control limit on your process is 63 centimeters. Your lower control limit on your process is 57 centimeters. Approximately what percentage of your units will be above 61 centimeters?

a. 68.3%
b. 31.7%
c. 95.5%
d. 15.9%

39. What quality guru is famous for "conformance to requirements"?

a. Deming
b. Juran
c. Taguchi
d. Crosby

40. In the past few years our projects have experienced multiple cost overruns and schedule delays. We have decided early in quality planning that we need to generate some ideas for improvement. Our project management team recommends:

a. design of experiment
b. benchmarking
c. control charts
d. quality audit

41. It has been recommended that your projects should use more statistical techniques especially in quality. One example was a tool used to compute a loss function. This loss function determines the cost of producing products that fail to achieve a target value. This tool is known as:

a. Utility theory
b. Taguchi method
c. Pareto Diagram
d. Failure Mode Effect Analysis (FMEA)

42. Quality is suffering on your project as well as all projects in the organization. People are blaming the quality control department. The owner of quality at the organizational level is:

a. the quality control department
b. the quality assurance department
c. the project managers
d. senior management

43. "Fitness for use" means:

a. the product or service satisfies real needs
b. the customer accepts the deliverable
c. the project must produce what is said it would produce
d. doing exactly what the customer wants

44. Statistical sampling is used over testing the entire population for all the following reasons *except*:

a. lower cost
b. speed
c. testing may be destructive
d. provides more accurate results

45. The 80/20 principle states that 80 percent of problems are due to 20 percent of the causes. This principle is associated with:

a. cause and effect diagrams
b. flowcharts
c. Pareto charts
d. scatter diagrams

46. You are a project manager overseeing relief efforts in disaster areas. You realize that quality is so important on these as well as all projects. One of the fundamental ideas of quality management is:

a. more inspectors will ensure quality products
b. it usually costs more to prevent mistakes than to correct them
c. quality is the responsibility of the members of the quality department
d. quality should be planned and designed into the product, not inspected in

47. You are a project manager who manages the equipment installations and overhauls in an automobile manufacturing facility. Early in the planning process of one of your large projects you are asked to generate ideas for improvement and to provide a basis by which to measure performance. In this example you are most likely to use:

a. control charts
b. Pareto charts
c. scatter diagrams
d. benchmarking

48. As a member of the quality management team it is important to have a strong knowledge of quality control. It is important to know the difference between all of the following pairs of terms *except*:

a. prevention and inspection
b. attribute sampling and variable sampling
c. tolerances and control limits
d. sampling and probability

49. As a member of the quality control department it is your responsibility to teach entry-level courses to all technical personnel. In this course, one of the ideas that must be addressed is tolerances versus control limits. Which statement below is *true*?

a. tolerances should be tighter than control limits
b. a data point may be outside of the control limits but still inside of the tolerances
c. your customer usually sets the control limits
d. your process or equipment usually sets the tolerances

50. Because of your great success on your last project you have been assigned to a new project with a very difficult customer. Based on lessons learned from others, you know it is critical that your project has clear acceptance criteria. Which of the following statements is *false* in regards to acceptance criteria?

a. the criteria includes performance requirements that must be achieved before the project deliverables are accepted
b. the criteria is defined in the project scope statement
c. the deliverables meeting the acceptance criteria signify that customer needs have been satisfied
d. quality control validates that the customers acceptance criteria has been met

PROJECT QUALITY MANAGEMENT

Learning Solutions

1.   a.   *PMBOK® Guide* Chapter 8—Quality Introduction

☺   a. This is the definition of perform quality assurance.

☹   b. This is the definition of quality planning.

☹   c. This is the definition of perform quality control.

☹   d. This is the definition of quality management.

2.   d.   *PMBOK® Guide* Chapter 8—Quality Introduction

☺   d. Low grade may not always be a problem. Low grade is acceptable if the customer only needs low grade.

☹   a. Quality products should always be delivered. Quality is the degree to which a set of inherent characteristics fulfills requirements.

☹   b. We should deliver the grade the customer needs—no more, no less.

☹   c. Quality and grade are very different. Quality is the degree to which a set of inherent characteristics fulfill requirements. Grade is a category assigned to a product or service having the same functional use but different technical characteristics.

3.   c.   *PMBOK® Guide* Chapter 8—Quality Introduction

☺   c. Precision is consistency that the value of repeated measurements are clustered and have little scatter. Accuracy is correctness that the measured value is very close to the true value. They are not equivalent.

☹   a. Precise measurements are consistent.

☹   b. Accurate measurements are correct.

☹   d. The project management team must determine the level of precision and accuracy required. Be careful of answers that contain the word *always*.

4.   c.   Any Text Book on Quality or Six Sigma

☺   c. With three sigma defects occur only about 3 times in a thousand and with six sigma defects occur only about 3.3 times in a million. Six sigma for many organizations is a measure of quality that strives for near perfection.

☹   a. Six sigma is much more than trice as stringent as three sigma. With three sigma defects occur only about 3 times in a thousand and with six sigma defects occur only about 3.3 times in a million

☹   b. Three sigma not six sigma is the more traditional approach to quality management. (PMBOK Guide 8.3.2.2)

☹   d. When people say three sigma they really mean plus or minus three standard deviations on each side of the mean.

5.   c.   *PMBOK® Guide* 8.1.2.3

☺   c. Design of experiments is a statistical method that helps identify which factors may influence specific variables of a product or process under development or in production.

☹   a. Pareto charts help rank order to guide corrective action.

☹   b. Control charts help determine whether or not a process is stable or has predictable performance.

☹   d. An inspection is the examination of a work product to determine whether it conforms to standards.

6.   a.   *PMBOK® Guide* 8.3.2.3

☺   a. Pareto charts show how many defects were generated by type or category of identified cause and help rank order to guide corrective action.

☹   b. Cause and effect diagrams help us understand how various factors may be linked to potential problems.

☹   c. Flow charts show how items in a system relate.

☹   d. Scatter diagrams are used to show the possible relationship between two variables.

7.   b.   *PMBOK® Guide* 8.3

☺   b. Common causes and also called random causes, therefore, there is no difference between them. These causes represent normal process variation.

☹   a. Tolerance limits show what is acceptable, control limits show what is in control The project team should know the difference.

☹   c. Attribute sampling looks at whether the work conforms or does not conform. Variable sampling looks at the degree of conformance. The project team should know the difference.

☹   d. Prevention keeps errors out of the process and inspection keeps errors out of the hands of the customer. The project team should know the difference.

8.   d.   Any Text Book on Statistics

☺   d. We may decide to test samples instead of populations for either attribute sampling or for variable sampling. This is not the reason to test samples.

☹   a, b and c. The three main reasons that organizations test samples instead of populations are; the testing may be destructive, the testing is expensive and the testing takes a long time.

9.   c   *PMBOK® Guide* 5.4

☺   c. Quality control is about meeting requirements, whereas scope verification is about acceptance.

☹   a. This statement is reversed.

☹   b and d. Quality control is normally performed before scope verification, but these processes can be performed in parallel.

10.   d.   *PMBOK® Guide* 8.3

☺   d. Common causes are also called random causes and they represent normal process variation.

☹   a and b. Special causes are also known as unusual events.

☹   c. Control limits represent the level of control we have over our processes.

11.   c.   *PMBOK® Guide* 8.3.2.2

☺   c. Control limits are normally set at +/-3 sigma (standard deviation).

☹   a, b and d. Control limits are normally set at +/-3 sigma (standard deviation).

12.   b.   *PMBOK® Guide* 8.3.2.2

☺   b. Results are acceptable to the customer if they fall within the tolerances.

☹   a. The process is in control if the results are inside the control limits.

☹   c and d. These statements all apply to control limits, not tolerance limits.

13.   b.   Statistical Process Control textbook or Web Search

☺   b. One standard deviation is equal to the absolute value of ((p-o)/6). Therefore, one standard deviation = (22-10)/6= 12/6= 2 days.

☹   a, c and d. One standard deviation is equal to the absolute value of ((p-o)/6).

14.   d.   *PMBOK® Guide* 8.3.2.5

☺   d. Pareto charts show how many defects were generated by type or category of identified cause and help rank order in order to guide corrective action.

☹   a. Control charts help us understand the limits of our process.

☹   b. Process flowcharts help show how various elements of a system interrelate.

☹   c. Cause and effect diagrams illustrate how various factors might be linked to potential problems.

15.   c   *PMBOK® Guide* 8.1.2.3

☺   c. Design of experiments plays a role in optimization of products and processes.

☹   a. Benchmarking involves comparing actual or planned project performance practices to those of other projects to generate ideas for improvement and to provide a basis to measure performance.

☹   b. Control charts help us understand the limits of our process.

☹   d. Run charts show history and the pattern of variation.

16.   a.   Web Search on Kanban

☺   a. Kanban is a signaling system through which just in time (JIT) is managed.

☹   b. Kaizen is another name for continuous improvements.

☹   c. Utility theory is a measure of someone's willingness to take a risk based on their satisfaction meter.

☹   d. Marginal analysis states that optimal quality is reached at the point where the incremental revenue equals the incremental cost to achieve the improvement.

17.   d.   *PMBOK® Guide* 8.3.2.10

☺   d. Defect repair review is an action taken to ensure that product defects are repaired and brought into compliance with requirements and specifications. This is a tool of perform quality assurance and perform quality control.

☹   a, b and c. These tools are all examples of quality planning tools.

18.   a.   web search on Marginal Analysis

☺   a. Marginal analysis states that optimal quality is reached at the point where the incremental revenue equals the incremental cost to achieve the improvement.

☹   b. In theory, quality should have the same priority as cost and schedule.

☹   c. The cost of quality looks at the money spent proactively (cost of conformance) and reactively (cost of non-conformance).

☹   d. There is almost always more than can be done to improve quality, but this improvement comes at a cost.

19.   d.   *PMBOK® Guide* 8.3 and 8.3.2.8
☺   d. This statement is a definition of attribute sampling but not a reason to do sampling.
☹   a, b and c. All of the statements are reasons to do sampling over testing the entire population. Notice the question is asking for the *exception*.

20.   d.   *PMBOK® Guide* 8.3.2.5
☺   d. Pareto charts help rank order to guide corrective action.
☹   a. Cause and effect diagrams illustrate how various factors might be linked to potential problems.
☹   b. Flowcharts show how items of a process interrelate.
☹   c. A run chart may use trend analysis to use history to predict the future.

21.   a.   *PMBOK® Guide* 8.3.2.1
☺   a. Fishbone diagrams are also known as Ishikawa diagrams and cause and effect diagrams.
☹   b, c and d. Fishbone diagrams show how various factors might be linked to potential problems. The diagrams listed all have different purposes.

22.   Quality Management- Ireland
☺   b. The assessment of products is often evaluated an compared to nine 'ilities' including reliability and maintainability. Reliability is the degree to which a product performs its intended function under specified conditions for a specified period of time. Product design will play a large role in determining how a product stands up to this 'ilities".
☹   a. The project life cycle is used to divide projects into phases to provide better management control. Look for an answer that will have more an effect on reliability and maintainability. (PMBOK Guide 2.1)
☹   c. The project scope is the work that needs to be accomplished so as to meet the product scope. Look for an answer that will have more an effect on reliability and maintainability. (PMBOK Guide 5 Introduction)
☹   d. The product life cycle includes the entire life of the product. Operations and divestment are part of this life cycle. Look for an answer that will have more an effect on reliability and maintainability. (PMBOK Guide 2.1.3)

23.   c.   *PMBOK® Guide* Chapter 8—Quality Introduction
☺   c. Conformance to requirements means that the project must produce what it said it would produce.
☹   a. The product must satisfy real needs is the definition of fitness for use.
☹   b. The customer accepting the deliverables is the definition of scope verification.
☹   d. We may never do exactly what the customer wants. The focus should be on meeting requirements.

24.   Quality Management- Ireland
☺   a. The two categories of the cost of quality are cost of conformance and cost of non-conformance.
☹   b. Prevention and appraisal costs are two categories under the cost of conformance.
☹   c. Internal failure and external failure costs are two categories under the cost of non-conformance.

☹   d. This is an interesting answer but not complete. Don't forget about the costs of quality planning. Look for an answer that looks at quality from a different perspective.

Cost of Conformance	Prevention Costs Appraisal Costs
Cost of Non-Conformance	Internal Failure Costs External Failure Costs Measurement and Test Equipment

25.   c.   *PMBOK® Guide* Chapter 8—Quality Introduction
☺   c. This is the definition of perform quality control.
☹   a. This is the definition of perform quality assurance.
☹   b. This is the definition of quality planning.
☹   d. This is the definition of quality management.

26.   c.   Statistical Process Control textbooks or Web Search
☺   c. One standard deviation is equal to the absolute value of ((p-o)/6). Therefore, one standard deviation = (63-57)/6= 6/6= 1 centimeter. The mean is 60 centimeters. 58 centimeters is – 2 standard deviations from the mean, and 62 centimeters is + 2 standard deviations from the mean. We are looking for the answer that represents +/- 2 standard deviations from the mean. 95.5 % of the data will fall within +/- 2 standard deviations.
☹   a. 68.3% of the data represents +/- 1 standard deviation. That range would be the mean of 60 centimeters plus 1 centimeter and the mean minus 1 centimeter (59 -61 centimeters).
☹   b. This is a made-up number.
☹   d. 99.7 % of the data will fall in the range of +/- 3 standard deviations, which is 57-63 centimeters.

27.   b.   *PMBOK® Guide* 4.6
☺   b. If the customer wants to change the scope of the project, the first step is to evaluate the change request.
☹   a. Be careful of the word *always*. We don't always do what the customer requests, and we certainly don't do it blindly.
☹   c. We are the manager on the project. We should not go to management without evaluating the change request first and looking at options.
☹   d. Our sponsor gives us money. We need to evaluate the change request first to know if we are going to need more money.

28.   b.   Web search on "Kaizen"
☺   b. "Kaizen" is the Japanese term for continuous improvement.
☹   a, c and d. These are distracter answers.

29.   a.   *PMBOK® Guide* 8.2.1.5

☺   a. Changes should be formally documented in writing.

☹   b, c and d. Changes should be documented in writing before processed and implemented.

30.   a.

☺   a. This customer has asked for a change. The customer may believe this "change" is so small it is insignificant. But it is a change request and we should evaluate.

☹   b. Gold plating is never a good idea.

☹   c. We should never ignore the customer.

☹   d. This answer is not being proactive. If we have extra paint and do the work we are gold plating. Not good. If we don't have extra paint we are ignoring the customer. Not good.

31.   d.   Web search on "Just in Time"

☺   d. "Just in time" leads to zero inventory.

☹   a. Scatter diagrams show the possible relationship between two variables.

☹   b. Benchmarking a tool to generate ideas for improvement and to provide a basis by which to measure performance.

☹   c. Cost-benefit analysis looks at the cost benefit trade off of meeting quality requirements.

32.   a.   Quality Management- Ireland

☺   a. Scrap and rework are considered internal failure costs.

☹   b. Future business losses would be an example of an external failure cost.

☹   c. Inspection and testing of the product would be an example of an appraisal cost.

☹   d. Training would be an example of a prevention cost.

33.   d.   *PMBOK® Guide* 8.1.3.3

☺   d. Interrogatories are used to ask a question. Answer d is the only question.

☹   a, b and c. Imperatives are used for giving direction. These statements are all examples of imperatives.

34.   a.   *PMBOK® Guide* 8.1.3

☺   a. The process improvement plan details the steps for analyzing processes that will facilitate the identification of waste and non-value added activities.

☹   b. The quality baseline records the quality objectives of the project.

☹   c. This is the definition of the quality metrics.

☹   d. This is the definition of the quality management plan.

35.   b.   *PMBOK® Guide* Figure 8-1

☺   b. A quality audit is a tool and technique of perform quality assurance only.

☹   a and c. Quality audits are not tools and techniques of quality planning or perform quality control.

☹   d. This answer is only partially correct.

36.	b.	*PMBOK® Guide* 8.3.2.2
☺	b. Control charts help us understand the limits of our process.
☹	a. Pareto charts help rank order to guide corrective action.
☹	c. Cause and effect diagrams illustrate how various factors might be linked to potential problems.
☹	d. Trend analysis uses history to forecast future results.

37.	b.	*PMBOK® Guide* Chapter 8—Quality Introduction
☺	b. The plan-do-check-act cycle, as defined by Shewhart and popularized by Deming, is the basis for quality improvement.
☹	a. Monte Carlo analysis is a risk quantification and a schedule development tool and technique.
☹	c and d. Configuration management and change control system are tools and techniques for integrated change control.

38.	d. Statistical Process Control textbook or Web Search
☺	d. 15.9 % of the data will be above 61 centimeters. One standard deviation is equal to the absolute value of $((p-o)/6)$. Therefore, one standard deviation = $(63-57)/6 = 6/6 = 1$ centimeter. The mean is 60 centimeters. 61 centimeters is +1 standard deviation from the mean. and 59 centimeters is -1 standard deviation from the mean. Therefore, 68.3 % of the data will be between 59 and 61 centimeters. 100-68.3= 31.7 will be outside of 59 and 61. 31.7/2= 15.9 will be above 61 centimeters.
☹	a. 68.3 % of the data will be between 59 and 61 centimeters because this range represents +/- 1 standard deviations.
☹	b. 31.7% of the data will be outside the range of 59 and 61 centimeters because 100%-68.3% =31.7%.
☹	c. 95.5 % of the data will be between 58 and 62 centimeters because this range represents +/- 2 standard deviations.

39.	d.	Web Search on names
☺	d. Crosby is famous for "conformance to requirements."
☹	a. Deming is famous for "reduction of variance."
☹	b. Juran is famous for "fitness for use."
☹	c. Taguchi is famous for the "loss function."

40.	b.	*PMBOK® Guide* 8.1.2.2
☺	b. Benchmarking involves comparing actual or planned project performance practices to those of other projects to generate ideas for improvement and to provide a basis to measure performance.
☹	a. Design of experiments is a statistical method that helps identify which factors may influence specific variables of a product or process under development or in production.
☹	c. Control charts help understand the limits of our process.
☹	d. A quality audit is a tool of quality assurance, not quality planning. They are structured reviews to determine whether project activities comply with organizational policies, processes, and procedures.

41. b.   web search on Taguchi Method
☺ b. The Taguchi method computes a loss function used to determine the cost of producing products that fail to achieve a target value.
☹ a. Utility theory is a measure of a person's willingness to take a risk.
☹ c. Pareto Diagrams are based on the Pareto principle or the 80/20 rule which holds that a relatively small number of causes will typically product a large majority of the problems or defects. Pareto Diagrams help us set priorities.
☹ d. FMEA is used to identify potential failure modes, determine their effect on the operation of the product, and identify actions to mitigate the failures.

42. d. Most quality theories wills state that the person doing the work owns the work
☺ d. Senior management owns quality at the organizational level.
☹ a. The quality control department does not own quality at the organizational level. The own the quality of the work they do.
☹ b. The quality assurance department does not own quality at the organizational level. The own the quality of the work they do.
☹ c. A project manager is responsible for the quality of his project.

43. a.   *PMBOK® Guide* Chapter 8—Quality Introduction
☺ a. The product or service satisfies real needs is the definition of fitness for use.
☹ b. The customer accepts the deliverable is the definition of scope verification.
☹ c. The project producing what is said it would produce is the definition of conformance to requirements.
☹ d. Fitness for use is meeting real needs, not doing whatever the customer wants.

44. d.   *PMBOK® Guide* Chapter 8—Quality Introduction
☺ d. Statistical sampling will *not* provide more accurate results than testing the entire population.
☹ a and b. Statistical sampling is less expensive and quicker than testing the entire population.
☹ c. Testing may be destructive. If you test the entire population you will have nothing to use or sell.

45. c.   *PMBOK® Guide* 8.3.2.5
☺ c. Pareto charts are based off of the Pareto principle, which states that a relatively small number of causes will typically produce a large majority of the problems or defects. These charts rank order causes so as to guide corrective action.
☹ a. Cause and effect diagrams illustrate how various factors might be linked to potential problems or effects. These diagrams do not rank order causes.
☹ b. Flowcharts show how elements in a system relate but do not rank order.
☹ d. Scatter diagrams show the pattern of relationship between two variables. These diagrams do not rank order.

46. d.   *PMBOK® Guide* 8.1.1.3
☺ d. Quality should be planned and designed into the product, not inspected into the product as one of the major tenants of quality management.
☹ a. Quality should be designed, not inspected into the product.
☹ b. This statement is reversed. It usually costs less to prevent than to correct errors.
☹ c. Quality is the responsibility of everyone, not just the quality department.

47.   d.   *PMBOK® Guide* Figure 8-1
☺   d. Benchmarking is a quality planning and quality assurance tool associated with finding best practices and providing a basis for measuring performance.
☹   a, b and c. Control charts, Pareto charts and scatter diagrams are all tools of quality control, not quality planning. The question tells us we are in planning. Therefore, these answers cannot be correct.

48.   d.   *PMBOK® Guide* 8.3
☺   d. The question is referencing knowing the difference in pairs. Sampling and probability is not a pair. The project management team, though, should understand sampling and probability.
☹   a. Prevention and inspection create a pair of ideas often contrasted. Prevention is proactive, inspection is reactive.
☹   b. Attribute sampling and variable sampling make up a pair often contrasted. With attribute sampling, the data either passes or fails. With variable sampling, we look at the degree of conformance.
☹   c. Tolerances and control limits create a pair of ideas often contrasted. Tolerance limits helps us understand if the result is acceptable. A control limit helps us understand if the result is in control.

49.   b. Any Statistical Quality Control Text
☺   b. A data point may fall outside the control limits but still be inside the tolerances.
☹   a. In general, tolerances should be wider than control limits. We want our control to be tighter than the customer or market requires.
☹   c. The customer or market usually sets the tolerances—what is acceptable.
☹   d. Our process or equipment usually sets the control limits. The control limits show how well we can control the process.

50.   d.   *PMBOK® Guide* 8.1.1.3
☺   d. Formal acceptance, not quality control, validates the customer's acceptance criteria has been met. Quality control is about correctness, not acceptance.
☹   a, b and c. These statements are all true. The question is looking for the *false* statement.

PROJECT HUMAN RESOURCES MANAGEMENT

Sample Questions

PROJECT HUMAN RESOURCES MANAGEMENT
– *PMBOK® Guide* Chapter 9
Big Picture Things to Know

Read Chapter Nine of the *PMBOK® Guide* before answering the questions in this section.

Human resource management has four steps. Know how these steps help organize and manage the project team.

- Human Resource Planning—identifying and documenting project roles, responsibilities, and reporting relationships, as well as creating the staffing management plan
- Acquire Project Team—obtaining the human resources needed to complete the project
- Develop Project Team—improving the competencies and interaction of team members to enhance project performance
- Manage Project Team—tracking team member performance, providing feedback, resolving issues, and coordinating changes to enhance project performance

Also of importance:
- Motivational theories by Maslow, McGregor, Vroom, Herzberg
- Conflict resolution techniques
- Power bases for the project manager
- Leadership styles

1. All of the following are steps of project human resource management *except*:

a. human resource planning
b. manage stakeholders
c. manage project team
d. acquire project team

2. Virtual teams support all the following *except*:

a. people on different shifts
b. people who need to co-locate
c. people with mobility handicaps
d. people who must live in widespread areas

3. All of the following are outputs of human resource planning *except*:

a. project staff assignments
b. roles and responsibilities
c. project organization charts
d. staffing management plan

4. Pre-assignment, negotiation, acquisition, and virtual teams are tools and techniques of:

a. human resource planning
b. develop project team
c. acquire project team
d. manage project team

5. When differences of opinions initially become a negative factor between project team members:

a. the project manager should take responsibility to resolve
b. the senior managers of the organization should take responsibility to resolve
c. the project manager should work with the functional managers to resolve
d. the team members should take responsibility to resolve

6. One tool and technique to help manage the project team is:

a. recommended corrective actions
b. recommended preventative actions
c. issue log
d. team building

7. Zero sum rewards are rewards that:

a. cost no money
b. only a limited number of project team members can receive
c. everyone can receive
d. everyone or no one must receive

8 Maslow's lowest level, physiological needs, can be met in the workplace through:

a. rest periods, adequate compensation
b. safe working conditions
c. creative work
d. friendly co-workers

9. Examples of Herzberg's hygiene factors include all the following except:

a. compensation
b. working conditions
c. opportunity for achievement
d. relationships with peers

10. The technique used to manage conflict when a project situation is too important to be compromised and involves incorporating multiple ideas and viewpoints from people with different perspectives is:

a. smoothing
b. collaborating
c. withdrawing
d. forcing

11. Constraints that limit flexibility in the human resource planning process include all the following *except*:

a. organizational structure
b. economic conditions
c. collective bargaining agreements
d. incompatible communication software

12. The lead engineer on your team, who has authored 25 papers and holds 12 patents, seems to have more influence over the direction of the team than you do. This is an example of :

a. referent power
b. expert power
c. reward power
d. formal power

13. Under McGregor's Theory Y, management view is that most people:

a. dislike their work and will try to avoid it
b. lack ambition
c. are self-centered
d. are creative, imaginative, and ambitious

14. The type of power anyone can earn, regardless of their position is:

a. formal power
b. reward power
c. penalty power
d. expert power

15. The technique to manage conflict that involves emphasizing areas of agreement while avoiding points of disagreement is:

a. smoothing
b. collaborating
c. withdrawing
d. forcing

16. The leadership style that has the most risk of "perceived lip service" is:

a. consultative in a group
b. consensus
c. autocratic
d. directing

17. Maslow's highest level, self-actualization needs, can be met in the workplace through:

a. rest periods, adequate compensation
b. safe working conditions
c. creative work
d. friendly co-workers

18. Your manager seems to seek no input and make decisions on her own. This leadership style is known as:

a. directing
b. autocratic
c. consensus
d. consultative

19. You have been put in charge of a team, comprised of very experienced members, that has been very successful in the past. Your least likely leadership style in this situation is:

a. consensus
b. consultative
c. autocratic
d. facilitating

20. The stages of team development in order are:

a. storming, forming, performing, norming
b. forming, storming, performing, norming
c. forming, storming, norming, performing
d. storming, norming, forming, performing

21. Herzberg's hygiene theory stresses:

a. some job factors lead to satisfaction whereas others can only prevent dissatisfaction
b . some job factors lead to satisfaction and to dissatisfaction
c. some job factors lead to satisfaction in some people and dissatisfaction in other people
d. job satisfaction and dissatisfaction exist on the same continuum

22. The theory that people choose behaviors that they believe will lead to desired rewards or outcomes is:

a. Maslow's Hierarchy
b. McGregor's Theory Y
c. Vroom's Expectancy Theory
d. Ouchi's Theory Z

23. The theory that high levels of trust, confidence, and commitment to workers on the part of management leads to high level of motivation and productivity on the part of workers is:

a. Vroom's Expectancy theory
b. Ouchi's Theory Z
c. McGregor's Theory X
d. Herzberg's Hygiene Theory

24. The conflict resolution technique that definitely resolves the conflict quickly but should only be used as a last resort is:

a. compromising
b. forcing
c. confronting
d. withdrawing

25. The new technician working on your team is constantly name dropping and mentioning what the sponsor would like the team to do. This is an example of:

a. expert power
b. referent power
c. penalty power
d. formal power

26 You are walking through the construction site for your project when a fire breaks out and chaos will likely ensue. The site safety manager is most likely to use which conflict resolution technique in this situation?

a. problem solving
b. compromising
c. withdrawal
d. forcing

27. You are struggling to get your team members focused on your project. It seems that there are unclear priorities across the projects in your organization. Setting priority across projects is most often handled by:

a. the project managers
b. the project stakeholders
c. senior management
d. the functional managers

28. You and your team members are developing the project plan. To do this well, we should analyze the requirements and expectations of the:

a. the project team
b. the project management team
c. the project stakeholders
d. the functional managers

29. At this point in project planning, the plan needs to be integrated. This integration should be accomplished by:

a. the project team
b. the project manager
c. senior management
d. the project stakeholders

30. Which of the following statements about conflict is true?

a. conflict should be avoided
b. conflict is always bad
c. conflict is best resolved by separating the parties
d. conflict can be positive

31. The primary source of conflict on projects is:

a. personality
b. cost
c. technical
d. schedule

32. Which of the following is not a part of problem solving?

a. problem definition
b. alternative identification
c. risk management
d. decision making

33. When comparing fringe benefits and perquisites. we determine that:

a. they are basically the same thing
b. fringe benefits are standard; perquisites are special awards
c. fringe benefits are special awards; perquisites are standard
d. a corner office is an example of a fringe; insurance is an example of a perquisite

34. Policies and procedures that protect team members from safety hazards are often included in the risk register as well as in the:

a. project management plan
b. staffing management plan
c. communications plan
d. project organizational chart

35. The tool and technique often used when the performing organization lacks the in-house staff needed to complete the project is:

a. pre-assignment
b. negotiation
c. acquisition
d. virtual teams

36. Co-location is a tool used in:

a. human resource planning
b. acquire project team
c. develop project team
d. manage project team

37. Your project team members seem to be experiencing internal conflict. Initially you try to let them work things out themselves but the conflict has only escalated. At this point, who should facilitate resolution?

a. the team members
b. senior management
c. functional managers
d. the project manager

38. The objectives of develop project team include the following *except*:

a. enhance project performance
b. increase productivity
c. improve skills of team members to increase their ability to complete project activities
d. obtain the appropriate people to staff the project

39. The project team is:

a. the same as the project management team
b. a subset of the project management team
c. all the project stakeholders
d. bigger than the project management team

40. You are having an early team meeting and trying to define the project stakeholders. You remind your team that stakeholders:

a. always support your project
b. provide funding for your project
c. may be positive or negative
d. help set priorities among projects

41. Dealing with other cultures can be new to many team members. Conflict arises for many reasons, often because of a lack of understanding and communication. In general, the least productive way to deal with conflict is by:

a. confrontation
b. problem solving
c. withdrawal
d. collaborating

42. The adage that the more you put into something, the less you get out of it proportionately is known as:

a. law of diminishing returns
b. learning curve theory
c. opportunity costs
d. sunk costs

43. Training materials are often considered a:

a. variable cost
b. fixed cost
c. opportunity cost
d. sunk cost

44. The wages of the project manager are usually considered a:

a. direct cost
b. indirect cost
c. sunk cost
d. opportunity cost

45. Travel costs on a project are usually considered to be:

a. indirect
b. fixed
c. direct
d. sunk

46. Your latest project is to implement a new document management system to support all formal documents in your company. The project is deep into implementation and it seems there are many unidentified informal alliances present. Also certain groups have informal power that is driving your project in an unexpected direction. To prevent these surprises, what type of environmental factors should have been identified earlier?

a. organizational
b. interpersonal
c. logistical
d. political

47. Several of your team members hope to move into project management positions. They will all be taking the CAPM® exam shortly and are busy studying the *PMBOK® Guide*. They come to you and ask for help understanding the difference between human resource planning and activity resource estimating. You explain that:

a. these are two different names for the same process step
b. human resource planning is related to defining roles, responsibilities and relationships whereas activity resource estimating is related to determining the type, quantity and timing of needed resources
c. human resource planning leads to cost estimating, whereas activity resource estimating leads to acquire project team
d. an output of human resource planning is the resource breakdown structure; an output of activity resource estimating is the project organization chart

48. Your organization is having trouble managing human resources across multiple projects. Management asks for a visual to show how many resources are needed by category over time on each project. You meet with the other project managers to develop standards to produce:

a. project organizational charts
b. resource histograms
c. project team directories
d. performance reports

49. You are managing a team that is struggling with feelings of trust and cohesiveness. When you suggest some team building activities, most of the team members seem to sigh heavily. One way to deal with this is to:

a. accept that the team does not want team building and do nothing
b. force team building activities and mandate attendance
c. use the activities of the project, such as building a WBS, to obtain team building as a secondary effect
d. do team building with only the team members who want to participate

50. Your organization is using more and more teams to improve project performance. One of your projects is to develop a list of indicators of effective team performance. Typical indicators include all the following *except*:

a. improvement in an individual's skills that help him perform better
b. improvement in competencies that help the team perform better
c. decreases in staff turnover
d. increases in zero sum rewards for team members

PROJECT HUMAN RESOURCES MANAGEMENT

Learning Solutions

PROJECT HUMAN RESOURCES MANAGEMENT
– PMBOK® Guide Chapter 9

1. b.   *PMBOK® Guide* Figure 9-1
    ☺ b. Manage stakeholders is the fourth step of project communications management.
    ☹ a. Human resource planning is step one of project human resource management.
    ☹ c. Manage project team is step four of project human resource management.
    ☹ d. Acquire project team is step two of project human resource management.

2. b.   *PMBOK® Guide* 9.2.2.4 and 9.3.2.5
    ☺ b. Co-location involves placing all of the most active team members in the same physical location. Virtual team members spend little or no time face to face.
    ☹ a, c and d. All of these ideas can be supported by the virtual team format.

3. a.   *PMBOK® Guide* Figure 9-1
    ☺ a. Project staff assignments are an output of acquire project team not human resource planning.
    ☹ b. c and d. Roles and responsibilities, project organizational charts, and the staffing management plan are all outputs of human resource planning.

4. c.   *PMBOK® Guide* Figure 9-1
    ☺ c. The list represents all the tools and techniques of acquire project team.
    ☹ a. examples of tools and techniques of human resource planning are organizational charts and position description.
    ☹ b. An example of a tool and technique of develop project team is team-building.
    ☹ d. An example of a tool and technique of manage project team is observation and conversation.

5. d.   *PMBOK® Guide* 9.4.2.3
    ☺ d. The team members should be initially responsible for resolving their own conflicts.
    ☹ a. Once the conflict escalates the project manager needs to facilitate.
    ☹ b. Senior management should set priorities across projects but not be responsible for conflict inside of a project.
    ☹ c. Functional managers are responsible for assisting with problems related to team member performance.

6. c.   *PMBOK® Guide* Figure 9-1
    ☺ c. An issue log is a written log that documents the persons responsible for resolving specific issues by a target date. It is a tool and technique for manage project team.
    ☹ a and b. The recommended corrective actions and recommended preventive actions are outputs not tools of manage project team.
    ☹ d. Team building is a tool and technique of develop project team.

7. b.   *PMBOK® Guide* 9.3.2.6
    ☺ b. Zero sum rewards are win-lose rewards that only a limited number of project team members can achieve such as team member of the month.
    ☹ a. Zero sum rewards may or may not cost money.
    ☹ c. Not everyone, at least not at the same time, can win a zero sum reward. They are for a limited number of team members.
    ☹ d. This statement is just the opposite of a zero sum reward.

8.   a.   Verma, *Human Resource Skills for the Project Manager*, page 61

☺   a. Rest periods and adequate compensation are examples of ways to address physiological needs at the lowest level of Maslow's hierarchy.

☹   b. safe working conditions represent the level above physiological needs.

☹   c. creative work represents a way to meet the top level of self actualization.

☹   d. friendly coworkers represents the middle level, which addresses social needs.

9.   c.   Verma, *Human Resource Skills for the Project Manager*, page 65

☺   c. Opportunity for achievement is a motivating agent, not a hygiene factor.

☹   a, b and d. These items are all hygiene factors according to Herzberg. Hygiene factors alone are not enough to motivate people.

10.   b.   Verma, *Human Resource Skills for the Project Manager* Table 4-1

☺   b. Collaborating is the technique we use to manage conflict when we incorporate multiple ideas and viewpoints into the solution.

☹   a. Smoothing involves emphasis on areas of agreement and de-emphasis on areas of disagreement.

☹   c. Withdrawing involves pulling away from a conflict.

☹   d. Forcing involves making the other party do it your way.

11.   d.   *PMBOK® Guide* 9.1.1.1 and 10.1.1.4

☺   d. Incompatible communication software is a constraint of communication planning not human resource planning.

☹   a. b and c. Organizational structure, economic conditions, and collective bargaining agreements are all constraints that may affect human recourse planning.

12.   b.   Verma, *Human Resource Skills for the Project Manager* Table 4-1

☺   b. Expert power is derived from some one's knowledge and experience in a particular field.

☹   a. Referent power is derived from one's ability to refer to another party.

☹   c. Reward power is derived from one's ability to give rewards. Rewards may or may not be financial.

☹   d. Formal power is derived from one's position in an organization.

13.   d.   Verma, *Human Resource Skills for the Project Manager*, page 70

☺   d. Theory Y is a positive view management has of workers.

☹   a, b and c. These statements are all a negative view of workers from management. Therefore, these statements represent the McGregor's Theory X not Theory Y.

14.   d.   Verma, *Human Resource Skills for the Project Manager,* Figure 7-9

☺   d. Expert power is derived from one's knowledge, not one's position.

☹   a, b and c. Formal, reward, and penalty power may all be associate or derived from one's position in the organization.

15.   a.   Verma, *Human Resource Skills for the Project Manager*, Table 4-1
☺   a. Smoothing involves emphasizing areas of agreement and avoiding points of disagreement.
☹   b. Collaborating is the technique we use to manage conflict when we incorporate multiple ideas and viewpoints into the solution.
☹   c. Withdrawing involves pulling away from a conflict.
☹   d. Forcing involves making the other party do it your way.

16.   a.   Verma, *Human Resource Skills for the Project Manager*, page 218
☺   a. Consultative in a group refers to group decision making where the project manager invites ideas and suggestions of team members in a meeting. If the project manager does not take these ideas into account when making the decisions, though, the PM runs the risk of being perceived as doing "lip service" and not really using the team members input.
☹   b. Consensus refers to sharing problems with team members in a group and then reaching a decision by consensus.
☹   c. Autocratic style refers to the project manager making a decision without input from others.
☹   d. Directing style refers to the project manager telling others what to do.

17.   c.   Verma, *Human Resource Skills for the Project Manager*, page 61
☺   c. Creative work is how the workplace can help meet the Maslow's needs for self-actualization.
☹   a. Rest periods and adequate compensation can help meet Maslow's physiological needs.
☹   b. Safe working conditions can help meet Maslow's safety/security needs.
☹   d. Friendly co-workers can help meet Maslow's social needs

18.   b   Verma, *Human Resource Skills for the Project Manager*, page 218
☺   b. Autocratic style refers to the project manager making a decision without input from others.
☹   a. Directing style refers to the project manager telling others what to do.
☹   c. Consensus refers to sharing problems with team members in a group and then reaching a decision by consensus.
☹   d. Consultative in a group refers to group decision making where the project manager invites ideas and suggestions of team members in a meeting and the project manager makes the final decision.

19.   c.   Verma, *Human Resource Skills for the Project Manager*, page 218
☺   c. Autocratic style refers to the project manager making a decision without input from others. You are less likely to use this style with a very senior group of people.
☹   a. Consensus refers to sharing problems with team members in a group and then reaching a decision by consensus.
☹   b. Consultative in a group refers to group decision making where the project manager invites ideas and suggestions of team members in a meeting and the project manager makes the final decision.
☹   d. Facilitating refers to coordinating the work of the team.

20.   c.   Verma, *Human Resource Skills for the Project Manager*,   page 227
☺   c. Forming, storming, norming, performing is the correct order.

☹   a, b and d. see solution c. during forming, team members are polite. During storming, team members confront each other. During norming. people confront issues, not people. During performing, the team members settle down to open and productive effort.

21.   a.   Verma, *Human Resource Skills for the Project Manager,* page 64

☺   a. Some job factors called motivational factors lead to satisfaction, whereas others, called hygiene factors, can only prevent dissatisfaction.

☹   b, c and d. If provided appropriately, hygiene factors can prevent dissatisfaction but cannot lead to satisfaction. Motivational factors related to the work itself can lead to job satisfaction, but cannot prevent dissatisfaction. They are not on the same continuum.

22.   c.   Verma, *Human Resource Skills for the Project Mana*ger, page 65-73

☺   c. Vroom's Expectancy Theory states that people choose behaviors that they believe will lead to desired results and that they will be rewarded attractively for those results.

☹   a. Maslow's Hierarchy is a model of motivation that suggests that each of us has a hierarchy of five types of needs. The bottom level is physiological needs. Level two is safety, level three is social, level four is esteem, and the top level is self-actualization.

☹   b. McGregor's Theory Y describes management's view that most workers are self-disciplined, can direct and control themselves, desire responsibility, and accept them willingly.

☹   d. Ouchi's Theory Z is based on Japanese styles and philosophies and states that high levels of trust, confidence, and commitment to workers on the part of management leads to high level of motivation and productivity on the part of workers.

23.   b.   Verma, *Human Resource Skills for the Project Manager,* page 65-73

☺   b. Ouchi's Theory Z is based on Japanese styles and philosophies and states that high levels of trust, confidence, and commitment to workers on the part of management leads to high level of motivation and productivity on the part of workers.

☹   a. Vroom's Expectancy Theory states that people choose behaviors that they believe will lead to desired results and that they will be rewarded attractively for those results

☹   c. McGregor's Theory X describes management's view that most workers dislike their work and try to avoid it.

☹   d. Herzburg's Hygiene Theory states that some job factors lead to satisfaction, whereas others can only prevent dissatisfaction and are not sources of satisfaction. Hygiene factors related to the work itself, if provided appropriately, prevent dissatisfaction. Motivational factors related to the work itself can increase job satisfaction.

24.   b.   Verma, *Human Resource Skills for Project Managers* Table 4-1

☺   b. Forcing involves pushing one viewpoint at the expense of another. This is the technique often used in an emergency situation. Hard feelings may come back in other forms after forcing.

☹   a. Compromising is giving something to receive something. Both parties get some degree of satisfaction.

☹   c. Confronting, also called problem solving, treats conflict as a problem to be solved. This technique provides ultimate resolution.

☹   d. Withdrawal involves giving up, pulling out or retreating. This technique does not solve the problem.

25. b. Verma, *Human Resource Skills for Project Manager,* page 233

☺ b. Referent power refers to the potential influence one has due to the strength of the relationship between the leader and the followers.

☹ a. Expert power is derived from one's knowledge.

☹ c. Penalty power refers to the negative things a project manager might do.

☹ d. Formal power, often called legitimate power, is derived from one's position in an organization.

26. d. Verma, *Human Resource Skills for the Project Manager*, Table 4-1

☺ d. Forcing involves pushing one viewpoint at the expense of another. This is the technique often used in an emergency situation. Hard feelings may come back in other forms after forcing.

☹ a. Problem solving treats conflict as a problem to be solved. This technique provides ultimate resolution but takes time.

☹ b. Compromising is giving something to receive something. Both parties get some degree of satisfaction.

☹ c. Withdrawal involves giving up, pulling out, or retreating. This technique does not solve the problem.

27. c. *PMBOK® Guide* 1.6.2

☺ c. Senior management should set priorities across projects.

☹ a. A project manager sets the priorities to manage inside the project.

☹ b. The project stakeholders are everyone and anyone who can impact or be impacted by the project. Stakeholders are too big and diverse a group to be setting priorities.

☹ d. Functional managers negotiate with project managers and assign resources to projects.

28. c. *PMBOK® Guide* 2.2

☺ c. We need to analyze the requirements and expectations of the stakeholders when developing the project plan.

☹ a, b and d. These groups are all subsets of stakeholders. In this instance, we want the bigger answer.

29. b. *PMBOK® Guide* Chapter 4-Integration Introduction

☺ b. The project manager holds primary for responsible for integration.

☹ a. The project team does a lot of the work of the project but does not own the integration.

☹ c. Senior management owns the integration of projects into portfolios but not the integration inside of a project.

☹ d. Project stakeholders is too large and diverse a group to own the integration of a project.

30. d. Verma, *Human Resource Skills for the Project Manager*, page 94

☺ d. Conflict can be positive is a true statement.

☹ a. Positive conflict should be stimulated and negative conflict should be resolved effectively.

☹ b. Conflict can be positive or negative.

☹ c. People must work together to resolve conflict.

31.   d.   Verma, *Human Resource Skills for the Project Manager,* page 102

☺   d. Schedules are ranking number one.

☹   a. Personality is ranked number seven.

☹   b. Cost is ranked number six.

☹   c. Technical is ranked number four.

32.   c.   *PMBOK® Guide* 1.5.5

☺   c. Risk management is the process of risk management planning, identification, analysis responses, and monitoring and control on a project.

☹   a, b and d.   Problem solving is the combination of problem definition, alternative identification and analysis, and decision-making.

33.   b.   General Knowledge: check your human resource policies

☺   b. Fringe benefits are standard like health insurance; perquisites are special awards like a corner office.

☹   a. Fringe and perquisites are not the same thing.

☹   c and d. Both of these statements are reversed.

34.   b.   *PMBOK® Guide* 9.1.3.3

☺   b. The staffing management plan may describe how we are going to protect team members from safety hazards.

☹   a. The project management plan is a true answer, but look for one that is more specific.

☹   c. The communication plan describes who gets what information when, etc.

☹   d. The project organizational chart is a graphical display of project team members and their reporting relationships.

35.   c.   *PMBOK® Guide* 9.2.2

☺   c. When the performing organization lacks the in-house staff needed to complete the project, the required services may be acquired for outside sources

☹   a. Pre-assignment means the project team members are assigned in advance.

☹   b. Negotiation is a tool used to fill staff assignments. For example, the project manager may need to negotiate with functional managers or other project managers for resources.

☹   d. Virtual teams is a tool used when the organization has team members locating in different locations, on different shifts, telecommuting, etc.

36.   c.   *PMBOK® Guide* Figure 9-1

☺   c. Co-location means that many or all of the project team members sit in the same physical location. Co-location aids in the step develop project team.

☹   a. Human resource planning determines roles, responsibilities, and reporting relationships. This happens before we develop the project team and before co-location.

☹   b. Acquire project team is the process of obtaining the human resources needed for the project, which happens before develop project team and before co-location.

☹   d. Manage project team involves tracking team member performance, providing feedback, resolving issues, and coordinating changes to enhance project performance. Co-location should be done before this step if co-location is going to occur.

37.   d.   *PMBOK® Guide* 9.4.2.3

☺   d. Once the conflict escalates, the project manager needs to get involved.

☹   a. The team members should be initially responsible for resolving their own conflicts, but if the conflict escalates, the project manager needs to facilitate.

☹   b. Senior management should set priorities across projects but not be responsible for conflict inside of a project.

☹   c. Functional managers are responsible for assisting with problems related to team member performance.

38.   d.   *PMBOK® Guide* 9.3

☺   d. Obtain the appropriate people to staff the project is done during acquire project team not develop project team.

☹   a, b and c. These items are all objectives of develop project team.

39.   d.   *PMBOK® Guide* Figure 2-5

☺   d. The project management team is the subset of the project team directly involved in project management activities.

☹   a and b. See explanation of answer d.

☹   c. The project team is a subset of all project stakeholders. Stakeholders are everyone involved or affected by the project.

40.   c.   *PMBOK® Guide* 2.2

☺   c. Stakeholders may have a positive or negative influence on a project.

☹   a. Stakeholders may or may nor support your project.

☹   b. The sponsor provides funding for your project.

☹   d. Senior management set priorities among projects.

41.   c.   Verma, *Human Resource Skills for the Project Manager*

☺   c. Withdrawal means we pull away from the conflict. The conflict will not get resolved this way.

☹   a and b. Confronting and problem solving are two names for the same technique. With this technique we treat the conflict as a problem to be resolved. This usually leads to a long-term solution.

☹   d. Collaborating is a technique we use when the views of the parties are too important to compromise. This also leads to a long-term solution.

42.   a.   Any Accounting Textbook or Web Search

☺   a. The law of diminishing returns states that the more you put into something the less you get out of it, from a proportional standpoint.

☹   b. Learning curve theory states that the more workers do something the greater the increase in productivity.

☹   c. Opportunity cost is the value of the opportunity lost if another option is chosen.

☹   d. A sunk cost is money spent that cannot be recovered by future actions.

43.   a.   Any Accounting Textbook or Web Search
☺   a. A variable cost is a cost that varies directly in relation to output.
☹   b. Fixed costs do not change, regardless of the change in variable (number of students).
☹   c. Opportunity costs are the costs associated with an opportunity not realized.
☹   d. Sunk costs are funds that have been spent on a project that cannot be recovered.

44.   a.   *PMBOK® Guide* 12.1.2.4
☺   a. Direct costs are costs billed directly to a project.
☹   b. Indirect costs are billed across multiple projects and operations.
☹   c. Sunk costs are funds that have been spent on a project that cannot be recovered.
☹   d. Opportunity costs are the costs associated with a opportunity not realized.

45.   c.   *PMBOK® Guide* 12.1.2.4
☺   c. Travel costs are usually billed directly to a project.
☹   a. Indirect costs are allocated across multiple projects and operations. Travel is usually billed to the associated project only.
☹   b. Fixed costs do not change as the variable changes. As the amount of travel changes, the cost for total travel will change.
☹   d. Sunk costs are funds that have been spent on a project that cannot be recovered.

46.   d.   *PMBOK® Guide* 9.1.1.1
☺   d. Political factors include informal power, informal alliances and individual goals and agendas.
☹   a. An example of an organizational factor is which departments will be involved in the project.
☹   b. An example of an interpersonal factor is the type of formal and informal relationships exist.
☹   c. Examples of logistical factors are physical distance, time zones and different countries.

47.   b.   *PMBOK® Guide* 6.3 and 9.1
☺   b. This statement describes human resource planning and activity resource estimating very well.
☹   a. Human resource planning and activity resource estimating are very different steps. Human resource planning is related to people; activity resource estimating is related to all resources such as people, equipment, and materials.
☹   c. This statement is reversed. Human resource planning leads to acquire project team and activity resource estimating leads to cost estimating.
☹   d. This statement is reversed. The project organization chart is an output of human resource planning and the resource breakdown structure is an output of activity resource estimating.

48.   b.   *PMBOK® Guide* Figure 9-6
☺   b. Resource histograms are visuals that show how many resources by category are needed over time.
☹   a. A project organizational chart is a graphical display of project team members and their reporting relationships.
☹   c. Project team directories list project team members, etc.
☹   d. Performance reports document performance information.

49.   c.   *PMBOK*® *Guide* 9.3.2.3

☺   c. Doing the work of the project, such as building the WBS, and building the network diagram can be great ways to build the team without using the phrase, "team building activity."

☹   a. Team development is critical to team and project success. We must develop this team even more importantly because the team is struggling with trust and cohesiveness.

☹   b. Usually we do not *force* or *mandate*. Answers with these words are often wrong unless the question is asking what *not* to do.

☹   d. Doing team building with only part of the team will not achieve the desired results.

50.   d.   *PMBOK*® *Guide* 9.3.3.1 and 9.3.2.6

☺   d. Zero sum rewards, often called win-lose rewards, are rewards that only a limited number of team members can achieve. These rewards can actually hurt team performance.

☹   a. Improvement in an individual's skills can have a positive effect on team performance.

☹   b. Improvements in competencies can have a positive effect on team performance.

☹   c. A decrease in staff turnover is a positive indicator.

PROJECT COMMUNICATION MANAGEMENT

Sample Questions

Big Picture Things to Know

Read Chapter Ten of the *PMBOK® Guide* before answering the questions in this section.

Communications has four Steps. Know how these steps help ensure timely and appropriate generation, collection, distribution, storage, retrieval, and ultimate disposition of project information.

- Communications Planning—determining the information and communication needs of the project stakeholders
- Information Distribution—making needed information available to project stakeholders in a timely manner
- Performance Reporting—collecting and distributing performance information, including status reporting, progress measurement, and forecasting
- Manage Stakeholders—managing communications to satisfy the requirements of and resolve issues with project stakeholders

Also of importance:
- Communications model
- Verbal, non-verbals, para linguals
- Formal and informal, written and verbal communication
- Leadership styles
- Number of the communication channels

PROJECT COMMUNICATIONS MANAGEMENT
– *PMBOK® Guide* Chapter 10

1. The most effective means for communicating and resolving issues with stakeholders is:

a. electronic mail
b. a face-to-face meeting
c. a telephone call
d. a video conference

2. Stakeholder management is usually the responsibility of:

a. the project sponsor
b. the performing organization
c. the project team
d. the project manager

3. One of your team members asks you who should get a copy of the performance report just completed. You respond:

a. all stakeholders
b. all key stakeholders
c. follow the project plan
d. follow the communications management plan

4. Lessons learned sessions, especially on projects that yielded less than desirable results, should be conducted with:

a. key internal stakeholders
b. team members
c. key internal and key external stakeholders
d. key internal stakeholders and team members

5. In the communications model, distance is an example of:

a. encoding
b. the message
c. the medium
d. noise

6. You realize that as you increase the number of stakeholders, you increase the number of communication channels. Your current project has 10 stakeholders total. How many communications channels are there on this project?

a. 10
b. 45
c. 50
d. 100

7. A project report is an example of what type of communication?

a. formal written
b. informal written
c. formal verbal
d. informal verbal

8. Ad hoc conversations with our peers are examples of what type of communication?

a. vertical
b. horizontal
c. formal verbal
d. informal written

9. Examples of information gathering and retrieval systems include:

a. electronic data bases
b. email
c. voicemail
d. video conferencing

10. The performance measurement baseline typically integrates all of the following *except*:

a. quality
b. cost
c. scope
d. schedule

11. Estimate at completion (EAC) and estimate to complete (ETC) are examples of:

a. forecasts
b. requested changes
c. recommended corrective actions
d. performance reports

12. Communications planning is often tightly linked with:

a. enterprise environmental factors
b. organizational influences
c. both enterprise environmental factors and organizational influences
d. neither enterprise environmental factors nor organizational influences

13. In the communication model, who is responsible to encode the initial message?

a. the sender
b. the sender and the receiver
c. the receiver
d. the sender or the receiver

14. On an international project, what type of communication is often not practical?

a. electronic mail
b. electronic tools
c. telephone calls
d. a face-to-face meeting

15. All of the following statements are true about communication blockers *except*:

a. the phrase "this will never work" is an example
b. they can get in the way of communication
c. they should be addressed proactively by the project manager
d. they should be ignored at all costs

16. The primary role of a communications expeditor is to:

a. ensure communication happens quickly
b. set a good example for communication
c. bring parties together that need to communicate
d. escalate communication issues

17. The primary reasons for unproductive meetings include all of the following *except:*

a. not following an agenda
b. inept leadership
c. undisciplined participants
d. too much work

18. Management has asked for a report that summarizes what has been accomplished on the project to date. To satisfy this request you should:

a. provide a status report
b. provide a forecast
c. hold a status review meeting
d. provide a progress report

19. Your CPI= .8 and your SPI=1.1. How is your project doing?

a. ahead of schedule, under budget
b. ahead of schedule, over budget
c. behind schedule, under budget
d. behind schedule, over budget

20. An example of horizontal communication is:

a. with your peers
b. with your team
c. with your management
d. with your suppliers

21. If the earned value is higher than the planned value:

a. the project is ahead of schedule
b. the project is behind schedule
c. the project is over budget
d. the project is under budget

22. If the actual cost is higher than the earned value:

a. the project is ahead of schedule
b. the project is behind schedule
c. the project is over budget
d. the project is under budget

23. If your project is running on budget, your CPI will be:

a. 0
b. 1
c. greater than 1
d. less than 1

24. EAC= (BAC/CPI) is the equation used for estimate at completion when:

a. past performance shows that the original estimating assumptions were fundamentally flawed
b. current variances are seen as atypical
c. conditions have changed
d. current variances are seen as typical of future variances

25. The forecasted estimate at completion is also called the:

a. EV
b. EAC
c. BAC
d. PV

26. If your project is over budget your CV will be:

a. negative
b. positive
c. 0
d. 1

27. A measure of how much work is done is:

a. PV
b. EV
c. AC
d. BAC

28. A measure of how much work should be done is:

a. PV
b. EV
c. AC
d. VAC

29. A measure of how much more money you need to spend is:

a. PV
b. ETC
c. EAC
d. BAC

30. If you assume that you will continue to spend at the same rate, you will use which of the following terms to help calculate your estimate at completion?

a. CPI
b. CV
c. SV
d. EAC

31. Cost estimates based on project team members' recollection are generally:

a. useless
b. less reliable than documented performance
c. more reliable than documented performance
d. the most reliable form of estimating

32. Earned value rules include all the following *except*:

a. variance thresholds for costs
b. computation formulas for determining estimate to complete
c. earned value credit criteria
d. definition of the WBS level at which earned value technique analysis will be performed

33. In face-to-face meetings most of the communication is:

a. verbal
b. non-verbal
c. para lingual
d. through words

34. Which of the following is not a step of project communications management?

a. communications planning
b. manage stakeholders
c. manage project team
d. information distribution

35. Which of the following is not one of the four dimensions of communicating?

a. written and oral, listening and speaking
b. internal and external
c. positive and negative
d. formal and informal

36. Lessons learned are:

a. a good idea
b. a professional obligation of the project manager
c. usually worth the effort on troubled projects
d. performed once at the end of every project

37. The collection of all baseline data is part of:

a. communications planning
b. information distribution
c. performance reporting
d. cost estimating

38. Lessons learned are documented so that they become part of the historical database for:

a. the project
b. the project and the performing organization
c. the stakeholders
d. the project and the stakeholders

39. You have been working as an engineer for years and your manager recommends you start considering a career path in project management. She informs you that you are a great communicator and communication is key for success as a project manager. In general, how much time does a project manager spend communicating?

a. 30%
b. 50%
c. 70%
d. 90%

40. You have been told that your project is a make-or-break project for the company. As such, everyone on the project team will officially report to you and not to the functional manager. In addition, all of the key team members will be co-located. Co-location is also known as:

a. weak matrix
b. tight matrix
c. balanced matrix
d. strong matrix

41. Your management has asked you to turn over information about where the project stands today. In reality your management wants a:

a. status report
b. forecast
c. progress report
d. lessons learned

42. Which of the following is not one of the key parts of the communications model?

a. noise
b. message
c. medium
d. words

43. The five major conflict resolution techniques are:

a. confronting, problem solving, compromising, smoothing, and withdrawal
b. confronting, problems solving, smoothing, withdrawal, and forcing
c. confronting, problem solving, smoothing, compromising, and forcing
d. confronting, smoothing, compromising, withdrawal, and forcing

44. Your customer is external to your company. As your customer accepts the project deliverables, you are most likely to want to receive:

a. formal verbal communication
b. informal verbal communication
c. formal written communication
d. informal written communication

45. Status review meetings should be held:

a. at the same frequency throughout the life of the project
b. at the same level for all stakeholders to be fair
c. at various frequencies and levels based on the needs of the project and stakeholders
d. for the customer once a month, regardless of the project status

46. Hausmann Associates is working on a large design/build project for a semiconductor factory. You realize as the project manager that it is important to have a process to collect baseline data and distribute performance information. The process that is most likely to do this is:

a. information distribution
b. performance reporting
c. manage stakeholders
d. scope planning

47. Hausmann Associates is working on a large design/build project for a new customer. This customer has requested that all communication occurs through email. Issues seem to be occurring and you remind your customer that issue resolution can be accomplished most effectively through:

a. conference calls
b. electronic mail
c. face-to-face meetings
d. instant messaging

48. Your manager, Rob Roberts, has been very supportive on your design/build contract for American Semiconductor Corporation (ASC). In fact, your manager likes to be involved in day-to-day activities on your project as well as projects being managed by other project managers. As the project manager on this contract you remind Rob that as a project manager you have responsibility for:

a. stakeholder management
b. managing priorities across projects
c. making decisions on changing project objectives
d. providing financing for the project

49. The contract with American Semiconductor Corporation is over and did not go as well as expected. You suggest to your manager that a lesson learned review be conducted with both key internal and external personal. Your manager reminds you that the project did not go as well as planned and it is best not to broadcast this information. You remind him that lessons learned are:

a. usually a good idea
b. always a good idea
c. a professional obligation
d. a time to only talk about positive lessons

50. You are working on your first global project. It seems you spend more time on communication than anything else. Many of your team members are having a hard time understanding you. It seems that distance is a major obstacle. Distance is an example of:

a. the medium
b. the noise
c. the message
d. the encoding

PROJECT COMMUNICATION MANAGEMENT

Learning Solutions

1. b. *PMBOK® Guide* 10.4.2
☺ b. Face-to-face meetings are the most effective means for communicating and resolving issues with stakeholders. During a face-to-face meeting, verbals, non-verbals, and para linguals can all be transmitted.
☹ a, c and d. Notice the question uses the work *effective*, not the word *practical*. If a face-to-face meeting is not warranted or practical, telephone calls, electronic mail, and other electronic tools are useful for exchanging information and dialoguing.

2. d. *PMBOK® Guide* 10.4 and 2.2
☺ d. The project manager is usually responsible for stakeholder management.
☹ a. The project sponsor provides the financial resources, in cash or kind, for the project.
☹ b. The performing organization provides the employees who are most directly involved in doing the work of the project.
☹ c. The project team performs the work of the project.

3. d. *PMBOK® Guide* 10.3.3.1 and 10.1.3.1
☺ d. The communications management plan describes many things, including the person or group who will receive information.
☹ a. Be careful with any answer that contains the word *all*. It is unlikely that any report would go to *all* stakeholders. Remember that stakeholders can include many groups of people, both internal and external. It is highly unlikely that all of these groups would be getting a performance report.
☹ b. "Key stakeholders" is certainly a better answer than *all stakeholders*, but still, we distribute information based on the communications plan.
☹ c. The project plan may be a true statement but it is too vague. The communications plan is a subset of the project plan and the better answer.

4. c. *PMBOK® Guide* 10.2.2.4
☺ c. Project managers have a professional obligation to conduct lessons learned for all projects with key internal and external stakeholders, particularly if the project yielded less than desirable results.
☹ a. "Internal stakeholders" is a true statement, but we must also share lessons learned with external stakeholders.
☹ b and d. Team members are a subset of internal stakeholders and not the complete audience for lessons learned.

5. d. *PMBOK® Guide* Chapter 10 Communications—Introduction
☺ d. Noise is anything that interferes with the transmission. Distance is an example.
☹ a. Encode is to translate thoughts or ideas into a language that is understood by others.
☹ b. The message is what is actually being sent; it is the output of encoding.
☹ c. The medium is the method used to convey the message.

6.   b.   *PMBOK® Guide* 10.1.2.1

☺   b. The number of channels= ((n*n)-n)/2 where n is the number of people. In this example n=10 and, therefore, we have 45 channels.

☹   a, c and d. These numbers are not the answer you get when using the formula; the number of channels= ((n*n)-n)/2.

7.   a.   *PMBOK® Guide* 10.2.2.1

☺   a. Formal written communication examples include project reports, project plans, etc.

☹   b. An informal written example would be a memo.

☹   c. A formal verbal example would be a project presentation.

☹   d. An informal verbal example would be an ad hoc conversation.

8.   b.   *PMBOK® Guide* 10.2.2.1

☺   b. Horizontal communication is communication with your peers.

☹   a. Vertical communication is either up or down in the organization. An example of vertical up would be communication with your management.

☹   c. A formal verbal example would be a project presentation. The example in the question is verbal, but not formal.

☹   d. An informal written would be a memo. The example in the question is informal, but not written.

9.   a.   *PMBOK® Guide* 10.2.2.2

☺   a. Electronic data bases are examples of information gathering and retrieval systems.

☹   b, c and d. Email, voicemail, and video conferencing are examples of information distribution methods.

10.   a.   *PMBOK® Guide* 10.3.1.5

☺   a. Quality parameters may be included in the performance measurement baseline, but are not typically included.

☹   b, c and d. Cost, scope, and schedule are the three parameters that typically make up the performance measurement baseline.

11.   a.   *PMBOK® Guide* 10.3.3.2

☺   a. EAC is a forecast of how much we think the project will cost. ETC is a forecast of how much more money we expect to spend.

☹   b. Requested changes are formal requests to expand or reduce the project scope, etc. EAC and ETC are not requested changes, but forecasts of what to expect.

☹   c. Recommended corrective actions are actions to bring expected future performance back on plan. EAC and ETC are not recommended correct actions; they are forecasts of the future.

☹   d. Performance reports are documents and presentations that provide organized work performance information including earned value management parameters and calculations.

12. c. *PMBOK® Guide* 10.1
☺ c. Communications planning is closely linked to both enterprise environmental factors and organizational influences because the project's organizational structure will have a major effect on the project's communications requirements.
☹ a and b. These answers are both true, but look for a more complete answer.
☹ d. This answer is just the opposite of the right answer.

13. a. *PMBOK® Guide* Chapter 10 Communications—Introduction
☺ a. Encode means to translate the thoughts or ideas into a language that is understood by others. The sender does this.
☹ b, c and d. The sender encodes the initial message and the receiver decodes the initial message.

14. d. *PMBOK® Guide* 10.4.2
☺ d. Face-to-face meetings are often not practical on international projects due to money and time constraints.
☹ a, b and c. Electronic mail, electronic tools, and telephone calls may be more practical on international projects due to money and time constraints.

15. d. Verma, *Human Resource Skills for the Project Manager,* pages 24-25
☺ d. Communication blockers must be dealt with so that they do not interrupt the project.
☹ a, b and c. These statements are all true. The question is asking for the *exception*.

16. c. Verma, *Organizing Projects for Success*, page 148
☺ c. A communications expeditor is one who brings parties together to communicate.
☹ a, b and d. The expeditor may do all these things, but these are not the primary role of the expeditor.

17. d. Verma, *Human Resource Skills for the Project Manager*, pages 29-31
☺ d. Too much work is not a reason for unproductive meetings; it may be an outcome of unproductive meetings.
☹ a, b and c. All of the reasons came out of a study conducting on unproductive meetings.

18. d. *PMBOK Guide* 4.5.3.3 and 10.3.3
☺ d. A progress report describes what has been accomplished to date.
☹ a. A status report tells where we are today, not what we have accomplished.
☹ b. A forecast predicts the future.
☹ c. A status review meeting describes where we are today, not what we have accomplished to date. Also a meeting is a tool and technique, not an output that we can give to someone.

19. b. *PMBOK® Guide* 7.3.2
☺ b. An index less than one is not good. An index greater than one is good. A CPI of .8 means that we are over budget. An SPI of 1.1 means that we are ahead of schedule.

☹   a. The project is ahead of schedule. For it to be under budget, the CPI would need to be less than one.

☹   c. If we were behind schedule, our SPI would be less than one. If we were under budget, our CPI would be greater than one.

☹   d. If we were behind schedule, our SPI would be less than one. We are over budget.

20.   a.   *PMBOK® Guide* 10.2.2

☺   a. Horizontal communication is with your peers.

☹   b, c and d. These are all examples of vertical communication.

21.   a.   *PMBOK® Guide* 7.3.2.2

☺   a. $SV = EV - PV$. If this answer is a positive number, meaning if $EV > PV$, then your project is running ahead of schedule.

☹   b. The EV would be less than PV if the project was behind schedule.

☹   c and d. AC is required information to determine cost variances since $CV = EV - AC$.

22.   c.   *PMBOK® Guide* 7.3.2.2

☺   c. $CV = EV - AC$. If the answer is a negative number, meaning if your AC is higher than your EV, then your project is running over budget.

☹   a and b. PV is required information to determine schedule variance since $SV = EV - PV$.

☹   d. The AC would be less than the EV if your project was under budget.

23.   b.   *PMBOK® Guide* 7.3.2.2

☺   b. $CPI = EV/AC$. If you are running on budget your $EV = AC$ which means your $CPI = 1$.

☹   a. CPI= 0 would only occur if you have accomplished no work and spent no money.

☹   c. CPI>1 when the project is running under budget.

☹   d. CPI <1 when the project is running over budget.

24.   d.   *PMBOK® Guide* 7.3.2.2

☺   d. $EAC = (BAC/CPI)$ is the formula when current variances are seen as typical of future variances and we should use the present CPI to predict the future.

☹   a and c. In these situations, use the formula $EAC = AC + ETC$.

☹   b. In this situation, use the formula $EAC = AC + (BAC - EV)$.

25.   b.   *PMBOK® Guide* 7.3.2.2

☺   b. EAC is the forecast of the most likely total cost of the work based on project performance and risk quantification.

☹   a. EV is the earned value; it is a measure of work actually completed.

☹   c. BAC is the budget at completion and is equal to the total cumulative PV at completion.

☹   d. PV is the planned value; it is the budgeted cost for the work scheduled to be completed at a given time.

26.　a.　*PMBOK® Guide* 7.3.2.2
☺　a. CV= EV-AC. If your project is running over budget, your AC will be greater than your EV and your CV will be negative.
☹　b. Your CV will be positive if your project is running under budget.
☹　c. Your CV will be 0 if your project is running right on budget.
☹　d. Your CV will be 1 if your project is running $1 under budget.

27.　b.　*PMBOK® Guide* 7.3.2.2
☺　b. EV is the earned value; it is the budgeted cost of work performed.
☹　a. PV is the planned value; it is the budgeted cost of work scheduled to be completed.
☹　c. AC is the actual cost; it is the total cost incurred for the work completed.
☹　d. BAC is the budget at completion; it is equal to the total cumulative PV at completion.

28.　a.　*PMBOK® Guide* 7.3.2.2
☺　a. PV is the planned value; it is the budgeted cost for the work scheduled to be completed at a given time.
☹　b. EV is the earned value; it is the budgeted cost of work performed.
☹　c. AC is the actual cost; it is the total cost incurred for the work completed.
☹　d. VAC is variance at completion; it is a measure of the total variance expected at the end of the project.

29.　b.　*PMBOK® Guide* 7.3.2.2
☺　b. ETC is estimate at completion; it is an estimate for completing the remaining work.
☹　a. PV is the planned value; it is the budgeted cost for the work scheduled to be completed at a given time.
☹　c. EAC is the forecast of the most likely total cost of the work, based on project performance and risk quantification.
☹　d. BAC is the budget at completion; it is equal to the total cumulative PV at completion.

30.　a.　*PMBOK® Guide* 7.3.2.2
☺　a. If we assume that we will continue to spend at the same rate then EAC=BAC/CPI.
☹　b and c. CV and SV are not part of the EAC formula.
☹　d. EAC is what we are calculating; it will not help in the calculation.

31.　b.　*PMBOK® Guide* 7.1.1.2
☺　b. Team member knowledge is useful but generally less reliable than documented performance
☹　a and d. The information is useful, but not the most reliable.
☹　c. This statement is reversed.

32.　a.　*PMBOK® Guide* Chapter 7 Cost—Introduction
☺　a. Variance thresholds for costs will be defined and used, but are not part of the earned value rules.
☹　b, c and d. These are all examples of earned value rules. The question is looking for the *exception*.

33.   b.   Web search on "communications models"

ex. Mehrabian, Albert. "Communication without words," *Psychology Today* (September 1968)

☺   b. One model (Mehrabian) states that 55% of communication is nonverbal, 38% of communication is through para linguals, and 7% of communication is through words.

☹   a and d. Only a small amount of communication occurs through the words we use.

☹   c. Para linguals include tone of voice, pitch, and cadence, and accounts for less than half the communication.

34.   c.   *PMBOK® Guide* Figure 10-1

☺   c. manage project team is a step in human resource management not communications management.

☹   a, b and d. These are all steps of communications management. The question is asking for the one that is *not* a step in communications management.

35.   c.   *PMBOK® Guide* 10.2.2.1

☺   c. "Positive and negative" is not one of the four dimensions of communicating.

☹   a, b and d. These items represent three of the four dimensions of communicating.

36.   b.   *PMBOK® Guide* 10.2.2.4

☺   b. As a project manager, it is our professional responsibility to conduct lessons learned.

☹   a. Yes, lessons learned are a good idea, but look for a stronger answer.

☹   c. This statement is true, but look for a stronger answer.

☹   d. The lessons learned should be performed throughout the life of the project, not just at the end.

37.   c.   *PMBOK® Guide* 10.3

☺   c. Performance reporting involves collection of all baseline data and the distribution of performance information to stakeholders.

☹   a. Communication planning determines the information and communication needs of the stakeholders.

☹   b. Information distribution is making the information available to the stakeholders..

☹   d. Cost estimating is developing an approximate cost to complete each scheduled activity for the project.

38.   b.   *PMBOK® Guide* 10.2.3.1

☺   b. Both the project and the performing organization will use the lessons learned.

☹   a. Good answer, but look for an answer that is more complete.

☹   c and d. "Stakeholders" is too broad an answer for this question.

39.   d.   Merdedith et al. *Project Management, A Managerial Approach*, page 126

☺   d. As project managers, we spend most of our time communicating.

☹   a, b and c. All of these numbers are too low.

40.   b.   *PMBOK® Guide* 9.3.2.5
☺   b. This is a definitional question. Another name for co-location is "tight matrix".
☹   a, c and d. These answers are organizational structures not co-location.

41.   a.   *PMBOK Guide* 4.5.3.3 and 10.3.3
☺   a. Status reports state where the project is today.
☹   b. Forecasts predict the future.
☹   c. Progress reports state what has been accomplished to date.
☹   d. Lessons learned are project records that describe the learning gained from a project.

42.   d.   *PMBOK® Guide* Chapter 10—Introduction
☺   d. Words are not one of the key components of the communication model.
☹   a, b and c. The parts of the model include encode, message, medium, noise, and decode.
        Notice the question says *not*.

43.   d.   Verma, *Human Resource Skills for the Project Manager*, page 117
☺   d. This is the correct list, according to Verma.
☹   a. Forcing is missing from this list.
☹   b. Compromising is missing from this list.
☹   c. Smoothing is missing from this list.

44.   c.   *PMBOK® Guide* 10.2.2.1
☺   c. Because your customer is external and the question is about acceptance, we want the
        communication to be formal and written.
☹   a. Verbal makes this wrong.
☹   b. Informal and verbal make this wrong.
☹   d. Informal makes this wrong.

45   c.   *PMBOK® Guide* 10.3.2.3
☺   c. The needs of the project and stakeholders should determine the frequency and level of these
        meetings.
☹   a and b. The word "same" makes both these answers wrong.
☹   d. The project status should determine the frequency and level of the meetings.

46.   b.   *PMBOK® Guide* 10.3
☺   b. Performance reporting includes the collecting and distribution of performance information,
        including baseline data.
☹   a. Information distribution is the process of making needed information available to
        stakeholders in a timely manor.
☹   c. Manage stakeholders is the process of managing communications to satisfy the requirements
        of, and resolve issues with, project stakeholders.
☹   d. Scope planning is the process of creating a project scope plan.

47.   c.   *PMBOK® Guide* 10.4.2

☺   c. Face-to-face meetings are the best way to resolve issues if they are practical.

☹   a, b and d. Non-verbals are lost in conference calls, electronic mail, and instant messaging. Non-verbals provide a significant portion of the received message.

48.   a.   *PMBOK® Guide* 10.4

☺   a. Stakeholder management is usually the responsibility of the project manager.

☹   b. Senior management has the responsibility to manage priorities across projects.

☹   c. The person who issues the project charter, such as the project initiator or sponsor, should be responsible for making decisions on changing project objectives. The project objectives are defined in the project charter.

☹   d. The project sponsor provides the financial resources for the project.

49.   c.   *PMBOK® Guide* 10.2.2.4

☺   c. Lessons learned, especially on projects that did not go well, are a professional obligation.

☹   a. The word *usually* makes this answer wrong.

☹   b. This is a good answer but look for a stronger answer.

☹   d. Lessons learned should be for both positive and negative lessons.

50.   b.   *PMBOK® Guide* Chapter 10—Communications Introduction

☺   b. Noise is anything that gets in the way of the transmission and understanding of the message. Distance is an example of noise.

☹   a. The medium is the method we use to send the message. An example would be email.

☹   c. The message is what we are sending.

☹   d. Encoding is translating ideas into a form that others will understand.

PROJECT RISK MANAGEMENT
Sample Questions

Big Picture Things to Know

Read Chapter Eleven of the *PMBOK® Guide* before answering the questions in this section.

Risk management has six steps. Know how these steps help increase the probability and impact of positive events and decrease the probability and impact of negative events.

- Risk Management Planning—deciding how to approach, plan, and execute the risk management activities for a project
- Risk Identification—determining which risks might affect the project and documenting their characteristics
- Qualitative Risk Analysis—prioritizing risks for subsequent further analysis or action by assessing and combining their probability or occurrence and impact
- Quantitative Risk Analysis—numerically analyzing the effect on overall project objectives of identified risks
- Risk Response Planning—developing options and actions to enhance opportunities, and to reduce threats to project objectives
- Risk Monitoring and Control—tracking identified risks, monitoring residual risks, identifying new risks, executing risk response plans, and evaluating their effectiveness throughout the project life cycle

Also of importance:
- Qualitative versus Quantitative risk analysis tools
- Different risk responses
- Risks may be positive (opportunities) or negatives (threats)

1. Risk identification diagramming techniques include the following *except*:

a. Delphi
b. cause and effect
c. system or process
d. influence

2. As a project manager on an information technology project, you realize that there are risks related to new technology, schedule, cost, etc. Your manager suggests that you contract some of the work out as a proactive way to deal with risk. All of the following are true when contracting to a seller except:

a. the risk is eliminated
b. the buyer's risk exposure is minimized
c. the buyer may be exposed to new risks
d. this response is often called transfer

3. The tornado diagram is most often associated with:

a. sensitivity analysis
b. expected monetary value
c. decision tree analysis
d. simulations

4. Your manager on the construction project seems to avoid risk at all costs. In fact the cost of your project is going up significantly because of your manager's view of risk. Your manager might be classified as being:

a. risk prone
b. risk –neutral
c. risk adverse
d. risk tolerance

5. The triangular distribution gathers information from all of the following scenarios *except*:

a. most likely
b. mean
c. optimistic
d. pessimistic

6. History shows that your construction firm ignores lessons learned when it comes to risk. Management believes that if we don't talk about risk it will not happen. In this situation we are likely to see more:

a. contingency plans
b. backup plans
c. fallback plans
d. workaround plans

7. Which of the following is used as a model for a schedule risk analysis?

a. work breakdown schedule
b. PDM schedule
c. duration estimates
d. schedule management plan

8. Your project has 30% probability of having to pay $20,000 in damages and a 40% probability of receiving $30,000 in damages. What is the expected monetary value of this situation?

a. - $ 6,000
b. + $ 6,000
c. - $ 12,000
d. + $ 12,000

9. All of the following are strategies to deal with risks with potentially positive impacts on project objectives *except*:

a. mitigation
b. exploit
c. share
d. enhance

10. You have been working all week in Baltimore and plan to fly home late tonight to New York. There is a surprise snow storm in New York and a risk the airport may close. You cancel your flight and rent a car to get home. As you are driving you hear on the radio that the highway is closing 50 miles north of you. The closing of the highway is an example of a:

a. residual risk
b. risk impact
c. secondary risk
d. workaround

11. Examples of mitigation include all of the following *except*:

a. establishing a contingency reserve
b. adopting a less complex processes
c. conducting more tests
d. choosing a more stable supplier

12. In your product development group, risk management has always been a low priority. Management does not want to talk about risk until the risk event has occurred. You are trying to explain the importance of timing to them. One idea you share is:

a. as we move further into a project the amount at stake goes up
b. as we move further into a project the level of uncertainty increases
c. as we move further into a project, the amount at stake goes down
d. as we move further into a project, the risk of failing increases

13. Project risks are:

a. always negative
b. always positive
c. may be positive or negative
d. may begin positive but always turn negative

14. While working on a construction project, it is brought to your attention that you need an environmental permit. You are concerned that the permitting agency may take longer than planned to issue the permit. If this occurs, the project will be three weeks late, and may run over budget by $20,000. Quality may also suffer, but you do not know how to quantify the quality degradation. The risk event in the above scenario is:

a. the project will finish three weeks late
b. the uncertainty that the project may run over budget
c. the degradation in quality
d. the permitting agency possibly taking longer than planned to issue the permit

15. The risks placed on a watch list for continued monitoring usually include:

a. risks requiring a near-term response
b. risks assessed as important, based on qualitative risk analysis
c. risks assessed as not important, based on qualitative risk analysis
d. risks requiring additional analysis and response

16. Your organization is in the process of identifying risks for your project. You explain that there are really two types of risks called:

a. pure and insurable
b. pure and business
c. legal liability and personnel-related
d. direct property damage and indirect consequential loss

17. The risk register should include all the following *except*:

a. SWOT analysis
b. list of identified risks
c. list of potential responses
d. root causes of a risk

18. We are presently trying to identify potential risks on our project. In our organization, the senior people often dominate a meeting and everyone else goes along with their ideas. One risk identification technique that keeps one person from having an undue influence on the outcome is:

a. brainstorming
b. SWOT analysis
c. root cause analysis
d. Delphi technique

19. You are the project manager for a large construction company. Risk management is a large part of what you manage. Your management tells you to focus on the business risks and they will focus on the pure risks. How is your organization most likely to deal with pure risks?

a. hire more staff
b. build contingency into the schedule
c. build contingency into the budget
d. buy insurance

20. As the new business manager for a large construction company, it is important for you to be able to quantify new opportunities. You are looking at a new venture now and have determined that there is a 20% probability of income in year one of $40,000. There is a 30% probability of income in year one of $10,000 and there is a 50% probability of a loss of $20,000 in the first year. What is the expected monetary value of this venture for year one?

a. $30,000
b. $10,000
c. $ 1,000
d. $ 0

21. Reserve analysis looks at:

a. plan versus actual on cost performance
b. plan versus actual on schedule performance
c. the amount of contingency reserve remaining versus the amount of risk remaining
d. the amount of money remaining versus the amount of work remaining

22. As the manager of a new business group you are constantly evaluating opportunities. Opportunity A has a probability of 40%. Opportunity B has a probability of 70%. Also, Opportunity A has a high risk score that is a much higher risk score than Opportunity B. This tells you to:

a. put more focus on opportunity A
b. put more focus on opportunity B
c. share your focus equally between both opportunities
d. put both opportunities on a watch list since they both have a high risk score

23. Deviations from the project plan may indicate:

a. the project team has apathy for the project
b. poor teamwork
c. potential impacts of threats and opportunities
d. the need for more quality inspectors

24. Your risk manager likes to use expected monetary value to quantify risk. It seems that some of your stakeholders though ignore expected monetary value and base risk decisions on the satisfaction they will obtain from each option. This theory is called:

a. hierarchy of needs
b. hygiene theory
c. utility theory
d. expectancy theory

25. Workaround plans are:

a. unplanned before the risk event occurs
b. developed to aid in risk avoidance
c. associated with risk mitigation
d. the same as contingency plans

26. Several of your key engineers are constantly showing up late for work. When they do arrive they are dressed very well, much better than is standard practice in your firm. You are wondering if what you are noticing is really a warning sign that they have been interviewing at other companies. Another name for a warning sign is:

a. risk event
b. risk impact
c. risk score
d. risk trigger

27.   Examples of risk mitigation include:

a. insurance
b. performance bonds
c. warrantees
d. building a prototype

28. Your firm is discussing the best way to estimate project durations. Your schedule expert finally steps up and says we need to use a technique that take into account probability and path convergence. In reality she is suggesting:

a. PERT analysis
b. CPM analysis
c. three point estimating
d. Monte Carlo analysis

29. Risk response planning focuses on:

a. positive risks
b. negative risks
c. both positive and negative risks
d. emerging risks

30. Your organization has agreed to utilize a contingent response strategy. For some risks, it is appropriate for the project team to make a response that will only be used under certain predefined conditions such as:

a. a risk trigger occurs
b. a customer request
c. a workaround occurs
d. a contingency occurs

31. Opportunities in the high risk (dark zone) of the probability and impact matrix:

a. can be obtained the most easily and offer the lowest benefit
b. can be obtained the most easily and offer the highest benefit
c. may be the most difficult to obtain and should be monitored
d. may be the most difficult to obtain and thus do not need to be monitored

32. You manage a small training company. An incredible opportunity arises but you believe your organization is not big enough to win alone. Your risk response strategy is most likely:

a. share
b. transfer
c. accept
d. mitigate

33. Data typically developed during the project risk analysis leads to what type of probability distributions?

a. s-curves
b. uniform distributions
c. asymmetrical distributions
d. Pareto diagrams

34. Your map making company has been managing risk for years by trial and error. You have just hired a risk manager who says that contingency plans and workaround plans are not the same thing. Your present manager states that they are the same thing. In reality:

a. contingency plans are associated with active acceptance whereas workarounds are planned after the risk event occurs
b. workarounds are associated with active acceptance and contingency plans with mitigation
c. contingency plans and workarounds are different names for the same idea
d. contingency plans are associated with mitigation and workarounds are associated with passive acceptance

35. Monte Carlo Analysis is a tool and technique of:

a. schedule development and quantitative risk analysis
b. qualitative risk analysis, quantitative risk analysis, and schedule development
c. quantitative risk analysis and cost estimating
d. cost estimating and qualitative risk analysis

36. You are trying to group your risks in order to develop effective risk responses. One effective way to do this is to categorize your risks by:

a. the people affected
b. the deliverables affected
c. the area of the WBS affected
d. the root causes

37. The cost management plan and schedule management plan are used in:

a. risk identification
b. qualitative risk analysis
c. risk monitoring and control
d. risk response planning

38. Risks requiring a near-term response may be considered more urgent to address. Indicators of priority may include the following *except*:

a. time to affect a risk response
b. symptoms and warning signs
c. risk rating
d. risk brainstorming

39. You have just taken over a project that has been running smoothly for seven months. As part of the risk register you see a watch list, which typically includes risks that:

a. have a high risk rating
b. may require a very near term response
c. warrant more analysis
d. are not accessed as important

40. Quantitative risk analysis includes:

a. modeling and simulation
b. risk probability and impact assessment
c. probability and impact matrix
d. risk categorization

41. Risk monitoring and control includes all the following *except*:

a. variance and trend analysis
b. technical performance measurement
c. modeling and simulation
d. reserve analysis

42. Threats that are in the high-risk zone of the probability and impact matrix:

a. should be placed on a watch list
b. should be addressed through a contingency plan
c. may not require any proactive management
d. may require an aggressive response strategy

43. You have moved into the project management role on a project with more than 80 percent of the work done. There seems to have been little work done as far as risk. You should start with:

a. risk identification
b. risk monitoring and control
c. risk qualification
d. risk quantification

44. Expected monetary value results are:

a. always positive
b. always negative
c. generally positive for opportunities and generally negative for threats
d. generally zero for opportunities and generally negative for threats

45. Performance reports and work performance information are useful in:

a. qualitative risk analysis
b. quantitative risk analysis
c. risk response planning
d. risk monitoring and control

46. Your company, Hausmann Associates, is in the final stages of the design/build of a semiconductor factory for a major customer. At the last customer meeting, the company finance manager mentioned the possibility of building another factory in the near future. This is an opportunity your company wants. The most likely strategy you are to use is:

a. exploit
b. mitigate
c. transfer
d. avoid

47. Hausmann Associates is early in the planning stage for the design/build of a factory. As you are doing early risk management planning you realize that you need a systematic way to identify risk. To do this you are most likely to use:

a. sensitivity analysis
b. expected monetary value
c. decision tree analysis
d. a risk breakdown structure

48. During the planning for a large design/build construction project you find through qualitative analysis that you have multiple risks that are both high probability and high impact. The decision is made to conduct quantitative analysis on these risks so as to describe the situations under consideration and the implications of each of the available choices and possible scenarios. To do this you are most likely to use:

a. decision tree analysis
b. sensitivity analysis
c. risk probability and impact assessment
d. risk urgency assessment

49. You are deeply involved in the monitoring and control of your design/build project. Several risk events have occurred unexpectedly and you do not have risk response plans in place. Therefore, you are most likely to go to a:

a. contingency plan
b. fallback plan
c. backup plan
d. workaround plan

50. Hausmann Associates has been awarded the design/build contract for a major semiconductor factory. During planning, you realize that this is a risky project and you want to do a great job early on with risk identification. Who are you most likely to include in this process?

a. the project manager should complete risk identification alone to make sure it is done correctly
b. the project manager and the team should complete risk identification
c. the project manager, the team, and other key stakeholders should be involved in risk identification
d. the project manager and the sponsor should complete risk identification

PROJECT RISK MANAGEMENT

Learning Solutions

1.   a.   *PMBOK® Guide* 11.2.2

☺   a. This question tells us that we are in the risk identification step. The question is asking about risk identification tools and techniques. Be careful of the word *except*. All answers listed are tools and techniques of risk identification. The Delphi method is an information-gathering technique of risk identification, not a diagramming technique, and thus is the item on the list that does *not* belong (the right answer). The Delphi technique is a way to reach a consensus of experts. Multiple rounds are used and this technique helps to reduce bias in the data.

☹   b, c and d. Cause and effect, system or process, and influence are all diagramming techniques of the risk identification step. The question is asking for the *exception*.

2.   a.   PMBOK Guide 11.5.2

☺   a. Transferring the risk does not eliminate the risk. It gives another party ownership for the management of the risk.

☹   b. As a buyer moves the risk to the seller, the buyer's exposure is minimized, though often not eliminated completely.

☹   c. New risks often emerge as risk response plans are put in place. The buyer may now be exposed to litigation, etc.

☹   d. Shifting the risk to a seller is often called transfer or deflection.

3.   a.   *PMBOK® Guide* 11.4.2.2

☺   a. The tornado diagram is the typical display of sensitivity analysis.

☹   b, c and d. The tornado diagram has no association with these tools.

4.   c.   Web Search

☺   c. A person or organization who avoids risk is called risk adverse.

☹   a. A person or organization who seeks out risk is called risk prone.

☹   b. A person or organization that is neither risk adverse or risk prone is called risk neutral..

☹   d. Risk tolerance is the amount of risk a person or organization is willing to accept.

5.   b.   *PMBOK® Guide* 11.4.2.1

☺   b. The mean is not gathered when interviewing someone using a triangular distribution method; the mean is a calculated value.

☹   a, c and d. The most likely, the optimistic, and the pessimistic are all collected values when gathering information through a triangular distribution.

6.   d.   PMBOK Guide 11.6.3.3

☺   d. Workaround plans are unplanned responses to risks. If our organization does not proactively address risk, we are likely to need more workarounds.

☹   a. Contingency plans are the most common method to actively accept a risk. In this question the organization is not developing contingency plans. The organization is doing nothing in regards to risk.

☹   b and c. Backup plans and fallback plans are examples of contingency plans. Often these terms are used for our second contingency in the case the first one does not work completely. If our organization does not have contingency plans they will not have backup or fallback plans.

7.   b.   *PMBOK® Guide* 11.4.2.2

☺   b. The precedence diagramming method (PDM) schedule is the model used for schedule risk analysis. One reason for this is that the PDM schedule will show path convergence.

☹   a. The work breakdown structure (WBS) is one model used for cost risk analysis, not schedule risk analysis.

☹   c. Duration estimates alone are not enough for schedule risk analysis. We need a diagram that shows the entire schedule including path convergence.

☹   d. The schedule management plan is a plan that describes how we will manage changes to the project schedule. It is a plan, not a model.

8.   b.   PMBOK Guide 11.4.2.2 (theory)

Amount at Stake	Risk Probability	Expected Monetary Value
-$20,000	30%	-$20,000*30%= -$6,000
$30,000	40%	$30,000*40%=$12,000
		EMV of Venture= +$6,000

9.   a   *PMBOK® Guide* 11.5.2.2

☺   a. Mitigation is a tool to lower the probability and/or lower the negative impact on project objectives, not positive impact. Be careful of the word *except*.

☹   b. Exploit is a tool for risks with a potentially positive impact. Be careful of the word *except*.

☹   c. Share is a tool for risks with a potentially positive impact. Be careful of the word *except*.

☹   d. Enhance is a tool for risks with a potentially positive impact. Be careful of the word *except*.

10.   c.   *PMBOK® Guide* 2000 11.5.3.3

☺   c. A secondary risk is a risk that emerges as the direct result of implementing a risk response.

☹   a. A residual risk is a risk that remains after risk responses have been taken.

☹   b. Impact is the amount at stake for a risk. In this example, the impact might be that you will not get home this evening.

☹   d. A workaround is an unplanned response to a risk event.

11.   a   *PMBOK® Guide* 11.5.2.1

☺   a. A contingency reserve is not a change to how we are going to do the work of the project and thus is associated with acceptance, not mitigation. Be careful of the word *except*.

☹   b, c and d. Mitigation is the lowering of the probability or impact of an adverse risk event. The examples listed are all examples of mitigation. Be careful of the word *except*.

12.   a.   PMBOK Guide 2.1.1 and Risk Management- Wideman

☺   a. Early in the project, we have not invested a lot and thus the amount at stake is low. The further we get into a project, the more has been invested, and thus the more is at stake.

☹   b. The level of uncertainty is highest at the beginning of the project. The certainty of completion generally gets higher as the project continues and thus the level of uncertainty decreases.

☹   c. Early in the project, we have not invested a lot and thus the amount at stake is low. The further we get into a project, the more has been invested, and thus the more is at stake.

☹   d. The risk of failing to achieve the objectives is highest at the start and gets lower as the project continues.

13. c. *PMBOK® Guide* Chapter 11— Risk Introduction

☺ c. Risks are uncertain events that may have either a positive or negative effect on at least one project objective.

☹ a, b and d. Risks can have either a positive or negative effect.

14. d. *PMBOK® Guide* Chapter—11 Introduction

☺ d. The risk event is what might occur, not the impact of it.

☹ a. The project will finish three weeks late is the impact, not the event.

☹ b. The uncertainty that the project may run over budget is the impact, not the event.

☹ c. The degradation in quality is the impact, not the risk event.

15 c. *PMBOK® Guide* 11.3.3.1

☺ c. A watch list is used for risks assessed as not important based on qualitative risk analysis.

☹ a. Risks requiring a near-term response are usually viewed as important and thus would not be placed on a watch list.

☹ b. Risks assessed as important will often be run through quantitative analysis, not placed on a watch list.

☹ d. Risks requiring additional analysis will often be run through quantitative analysis, not placed on a watch list.

16. b. Project Risk- Wideman

☺ b. Pure risks carry only the chance for a loss. Business risks carry a chance for either gain or loss.

☹ a. Pure and insurable as they relate to risk mean the same thing. A pure (insurable) risk carries only the chance for a loss. An example would be property damage.

☹ c. Legal liability and personnel are both types of insurable risk. Most organizations would by insurance to deal with these risks.

☹ d. Direct property damage and indirect consequential loss are examples of insurable risks. Most organizations would buy insurance to deal with these risks.

17. a. *PMBOK® Guide* 11.2.2.2

☺ a. SWOT analysis is a tool and technique of risk identification, not a part of an output. Be careful of the work *except*.

☹ b, c and d. The risk register details identified risks, including description, category, cause, probability of curing, impact on objects, etc.

18. d. *PMBOK® Guide* 11.2.2.2

☺ d. The Delphi technique is an information-gathering technique used as a way to reach experts on a subject. The Delphi technique helps reduce bias in data and prevents anyone from having an undue influence on the outcome.

☹ a. During brainstorming some people may have an undue influence. Sometimes the loudest person in the room influences the outcome.

☹ b. SWOT analysis ensures a look at a project from it's strengths, weaknesses, opportunities, and threats perspective.

☹ c. Root cause analysis is an analytical technique. It is not related to preventing people from dominating meetings and having an undue influence.

19.   d. Project Risk-Wideman

☺   d. A pure risk is another name for an insurable risk. Most organizations buy insurance to shift the risk to another party.

☹   a, b and c. A pure risk is another name for an insurable risk. Most organizations buy insurance to shift the risk to another party.

20.   c. formula EMV= amount at stake* risk probability

Amount at Stake	Risk Probability	Expected Monetary Value
$ 40,000	20%	$40,000*20%= $8,000
$ 10,000	30%	$10,000*30%= $3,000
($20,000)	50%	-$20,000*50%= -$10,000
		EMV of Venture Total= $1,000

21.   c.   *PMBOK® Guide* 11.6.2.5

☺   c. Reserve analysis compares the amount of contingency reserve remaining versus the amount of risk remaining.

☹   a. Earned value analysis compares plan versus actual on cost performance through the CPI.

☹   b. Earned value analysis compares plan versus actual on schedule performance through the SPI.

☹   d. Earned value analysis compares the amount of money remaining versus the amount of work remaining through the TCPI (to complete performance index).

22.   a.   PMBOK Guide 11.3.2.2

☺   a. The risk score is the probability multiplied by the impact. We should put our focus on Opportunity A since it has the highest risk score.

☹   b and c. The risk score is the probability multiplied by the impact. We should put our focus Opportunity A since it has the highest risk score.

☹   d. Watch lists are for low priority risks. Since Opportunity A has a high risk score we should actively manage it, not put it on a watch list.

23.   c.   *PMBOK® Guide* 11.6.2.3

☺   c. Deviations from the baseline plan may indicate the potential impact of threats or opportunities. If the deviations are positive, it may be the result of opportunities. If the deviations are negative, it may be the result of threats.

☹   a. Apathy is often demonstrated through a total lack of conflict.

☹   b. Unproductive meetings are a sign of poor teamwork.

☹   d. In general. the people doing the work should inspect the quality of the work.

24.   c. Project Risk-Wideman
☺   c. Utility theory assumes that any decision is made on the basis of the utility maximization principle, according to which the best choice is the one that provides the highest utility (satisfaction) to the decision maker.
☹   a. Maslow's Hierarchy of needs is related to motivation, not a person's view of risk.
☹   b. Herzberg's Hygiene theory is related to motivation, not a person's view of risk.
☹   d. Vroom's expectancy theory is related to motivation, not a person's view of risk.

25.   a.   *PMBOK® Guide* 11.6.3.3
☺   a. Workarounds are unplanned responses to emerging risks.
☹   b. Clarifying requirements, obtaining information, improving communication, and acquiring expertise are examples of changing the project management plan to aid in risk avoidance (*PMBOK® Guide* 11.5.2.1).
☹   c. Designing redundancy is associated with risk mitigation (*PMBOK® Guide* 11.5.2.1).
☹   d. Contingency plans are planned responses associated with active acceptance (*PMBOK® Guide* 11.5.2.2).

26.   d   *PMBOK® Guide* 11.2.3.2
☺   d. A risk trigger is a warning sign that a risk event is about to occur or has just occurred.
☹   a. A risk event is what might happen.
☹   b. The risk impact is the severity of the consequences.
☹   c. The risk score is the risk probability multiplied by the risk impact. The higher the risk score, the higher the priority.

27.   d.   *PMBOK® Guide* 11.5.2.1
☺   d. Building a prototype is an example of risk mitigation.
☹   a, b and c. Insurance, performance bonds, and warrantees are examples of transference, not mitigation.

28.   d.   *PMBOK® Guide* 6.5.2.4
☺   d. Monte Carlo analysis is a schedule analysis technique that takes into account that paths often converge into one activity.
☹   a. PERT analysis uses a weighted average to calculate activity durations. It does not take into account path convergence.
☹   b. CPM analysis calculates a single deterministic early and late start and finish date for each activity. CPM does not take into account probability.
☹   c. Three point estimating calculates the mean for activities based on three data points. It does not take into account probability or path convergence.

29.   c.   *PMBOK® Guide* 11.5
☺   c. Risk response planning is the process of developing options, and determining actions to enhance opportunities and reduce threats to the project's objectives.
☹   a and b. Risk response planning looks at both positive and negative risks.
☹   d. Emerging risks are risks that were previously unidentified or accepted passively (*PMBOK® Guide* 11.6.3.3).

30.   a.   *PMBOK® Guide* 11.5.2.4

☺   a. A risk trigger is a warning sign that a risk event is about to occur or has just occurred. This can trigger the contingency response.

☹   b. A customer request in general does not trigger a contingency response. A customer request often triggers an evaluation of the request.

☹   c. A workaround is an unplanned response to a risk event. It does not trigger a contingency. A workaround is triggered after a risk event occurs if the contingency does not work or if there is not a contingency.

☹   d. If the risk trigger occurs than the response (the contingency) will be used.

31.   b.   *PMBOK® Guide* 11.3.2

☺   b. Opportunities are positive risk events. Those in the high risk are those that have the highest probability (can be obtained the most easily) and offer the highest impact (highest benefit).

☹   a. Opportunities in the high-risk zone have the highest benefit, not the lowest benefit.

☹   c. Opportunities in the high-risk zone have the highest probability and thus can be obtained the most easily.

☹   d. Opportunities in the high-risk zone have the highest probability and thus can be obtained the most easily.

32.   a.   *PMBOK® Guide* 11.5.2.2

☺   a. Sharing an opportunity involves allocating ownership for the benefit of the project. A typical example would be forming a joint venture to go after an opportunity.

☹   b. Transfer is a strategy for threats not opportunities.

☹   c. Accept is not likely to win you this opportunity. Active acceptance would be to develop a contingency and passive acceptance would be to do nothing. Look for a more proactive strategy.

☹   d. Mitigate is a strategy for threats not opportunities

33.   c.   *PMBOK® Guide* 11.4.2.1

☺   c. Asymmetrical distributions depict shapes that are compatible with the data typically developed during the project risk analysis.

☹   a. S-curves are usually associated with the cost baseline.

☹   b. Uniform distributions can be used if there is no obvious value that is more likely than any other between specified high and low bounds, such as the early concept stage of design.

☹   d. Pareto diagrams are associated more with quality control not risk analysis.

34.   a.   *PMBOK® Guide* 11.5.2.3 and 11.6.3.3

☺   a. Contingency plans are the most common active acceptance strategy. Workarounds are reactive after the risk event has occurred.

☹   b. Workarounds are reactive after the risk event has occurred. They are not associated with active acceptance. Contingency plans are associated with active acceptance, not mitigation.

☹   c. Contingency plans are the most common active acceptance strategy. Workarounds are reactive after the risk event has occurred.

☹   d. Contingency plans are associated with active acceptance, not mitigation. Workarounds are reactive after the risk event has occurred. They could be associated with passive acceptance.

35.   a.   *PMBOK*® *Guide* 11.4.2.2 and 6.5.2.4

☺   a. Monte Carlo analysis is a simulation tool used in schedule development and quantitative risk analysis.

☹   b. Monte Carlo analysis is a simulation tool that is not part of qualitative risk analysis.

☹   c. Monte Carlo analysis is a simulation tool that is not part of cost estimating.

☹   d. Monte Carlo analysis is a simulation tool that is not part of either cost estimating or qualitative risk analysis.

36.   d.   *PMBOK*® *Guide* 11.3.2.4

☺   d. The root causes are an effective way to developing effective risk responses.

☹   a, b and c. These are not causes of risks, but effects of risk. It is more useful to group by cause then by effect if we want to develop effective risk responses.

37.   a.   *PMBOK*® *Guide* 11.2.1.4

☺   a. Risk identification has the project management plan as an input. The cost management plan and schedule management plan are subsets of the project management plan.

☹   b, c and d. These steps have the risk management plan, not the cost and schedule management plan, as an input.

38.   d.   *PMBOK*® *Guide* 11.3.2.5

☺   d. Risk brainstorming is a tool and technique of risk identification. The output of brainstorming provides a list of risks. Brainstorming itself is not an indicator of priority, it is a tool and technique.

☹   a. The time to effect a risk response can be one indicator of priority. The longer it takes to affect a response, the higher the priority the risk.

☹   b. If there are no symptoms or warning signs, the priority of the risk may be higher.

☹   c. The risk rating is the impact multiplied by the probability. The higher the rating, the higher the priority may be.

39.   d.   *PMBOK*® *Guide* 11.3.3.1

☺   d. Risks on the watch list are accessed as not important and need to be watched only.

☹   a. Watch list risks are of low importance and, therefore, probably do not have a high-risk rating.

☹   b. Watch list risks are of low importance and, therefore, probably do not require a very near term response.

☹   c. Watch list risks are of low importance and, therefore, probably do not require more analysis.

40.   a.   *PMBOK*® *Guide* 11.4.2.2

☺   a. Modeling and simulation are tools and techniques for quantitative risk analysis.

☹   b. Risk probability and impact assessment is a tool and technique of qualitative risk analysis (*PMBOK*® *Guide* 11.3.2.1).

☹   c. Probability and impact matrix is a tool and technique of qualitative risk analysis (*PMBOK*® *Guide* 11.3.2.2).

☹   d. Risk categorization is a tool and technique of qualitative risk analysis (*PMBOK*® *Guide* 11.3.2.4).

41.   c.   *PMBOK® Guide* 11.4.2.2

☺   c. Modeling and simulation are tools and techniques of quantitative risk analysis, not risk monitoring and control.

☹   a. Variance and trend analysis is a tool and technique of risk monitoring and control (*PMBOK® Guide* 11.6.2.3).

☹   b. Technical performance measurement is a tool and technique of risk monitoring and control (*PMBOK® Guide* 11.6.2.4).

☹   d. Reserve analysis is a tool and technique of risk monitoring and control (*PMBOK® Guide* 11.6.2.5).

42.   d.   *PMBOK® Guide* 11.3.2

☺   d. High-risk zone threats are the highest risks with a potential negative impact and, therefore, may require an aggressive response plan.

☹   a and b. Threats in the low-risk zone should be addressed through a contingency or placed on a watch list.

☹   c. Threats in the high-risk zone will require proactive management.

43.   a.   *PMBOK® Guide* Figure 11-1

☺   a. From the list, risk identification is the first step.

☹   b. Risk monitoring and control is the last step of risk management. The other steps on the list need to be done first.

☹   c. Risk qualification happens after risk identification.

☹   d. Risk quantification happens after risk qualification, which happens after risk identification.

44.   c.   *PMBOK® Guide* 11.4.2.2

☺.   c. EMV for opportunities is positive, but negative for threats.

☹   a. EMV is usually negative for threats.

☹   b. EMV is usually positive for opportunities.

☹   d. EMV is usually positive, not zero, for opportunities.

45.   d.   *PMBOK® Guide* 11.6.1

☺   d. Risk monitoring and control have performance reports and work performance as inputs.

☹   a, b and c. Performance reports and work performance information are not used as inputs in these steps.

46.   a.   *PMBOK® Guide* 11.5.2.2

☺   a. Exploit is the strategy used to make sure that opportunities are realized.

☹   b, c and d. Mitigate, transfer and avoid are all strategies to deal with threats, not opportunities.

47.   d.   *PMBOK® Guide* 11.1.3

☺   d. A risk breakdown structure provides a structure to systematically identify risk.

☹   a, b and c. Sensitivity analysis, expected monetary value analysis and decision tree analysis are all tools for quantitative risk analysis, not for risk identification.

48.   a.   *PMBOK® Guide* 11.4.2.2

☺   a. Decision tree analysis often using a decision tree to show the situation and implications of each available choices.

☹   b. Sensitivity analysis helps determine which risks have the most potential impact on the project.

☹   c and d. Risk probability and impact assessment along with risk urgency assessment are both qualitative risk analysis tools, not quantitative risk analysis tools.

49.   d.   *PMBOK® Guide* 11.6.3.3

☺   d. A workaround plan is an unplanned response to emerging risks. This is the correct answer since the question says you have no risk response plans in place.

☹   a, b and d. Contingency plans, fallback plans and backup plans are all examples of risk response plans. The question says you have no risk response plans in place.

50.   c.   *PMBOK® Guide* 11.2

☺   c. The project manager, the team and other key stakeholders should be involved in risk identification. Key stakeholders outside the project team may provide additional objective information.

☹   a. It is not likely that the project manager would be able to complete risk identification alone.

☹   b. The project manager and the team is a good answer, but look for an even better answer.

☹   d. The sponsor may or may not be involved in risk identification. Usually we think of the sponsor as the person or organization providing the financing for the project.

PROJECT PROCUREMENT MANAGEMENT

Sample Questions

Big Picture Things to Know

Read Chapter Twelve of the *PMBOK® Guide* before answering the questions in this section.

Procurement management has six steps. Know how these steps help the project team acquire the products, services, or results from the outside.

- Plan Purchase and Acquisitions—determining what to purchase or acquire and determining when and how
- Plan Contracting—documenting products, services, and result requirements and identifying potential sellers
- Request Seller Responses—obtaining information, quotations, bids, offers, or proposals as appropriate
- Select Sellers—reviewing offers, choosing among potential sellers, and negotiating a written contract with each seller
- Contract Administration—managing the contract and the relationship between the buyer and the seller
- Contract Closure—completing and settling each contract

Also of importance:
- Contract types
- Centralized and decentralized contracting

1. All the following statements about time and materials contracts are true *except*:

a. they are a hybrid type of arrangement that contains aspects of both cost-reimbursable and fixed-price arrangements
b. the seller receives a profit in addition to being reimbursed for allowable costs
c. the full value of the agreement is not defined at contract award
d. the exact quantity of items to be delivered is not defined at contract award

2. You are managing the equipment installation side of a brand new factory. To meet the schedule end date provided by management, you need your supplier, Kirkpatrick and Associates to start work, and incur costs, before you can award them a contract. In this situation you are most likely to give Kirkpatrick and Associates a:

a. purchase order
b. request for proposal
c. purchase agreement
d. letter of intent

3. We are in the process of creating our procurement documents. All of the following are names used when the seller selection decision is based on price *except*:

a. bid
b. tender
c. quote
d. proposal

4. As the project manager of the equipment installation side of a new factory, you expect to deal repeatedly with Lewis and Associates, a plumbing firm. You don't know the exact quantity or exact products you will buy from this firm, but you expect to be buying from them often over the next 18 months. You are most likely to want to sign a:

a. purchase order
b. request for proposal
c. purchase agreement
d. letter of intent

5. A bidder conference is typically held during what step?

a. plan contracting
b. plan purchase and acquisitions
c. select sellers
d. request seller responses

6. You are the manager of the design/build of a large manufacturing facility. With your customer, you have signed a Fixed Price Incentive Contract. You know that is this type of contract the risk is shared between the buyer and the seller. The time at which you organization picks up all of the financial risk is called:

a. contract award
b. contract breach
c. contract termination
d. point of total assumption

7. A contract change control system is normally part of what process step?

a. plan contracting
b. contract administration
c. request seller responses
d. select sellers

8. You are managing the design/build of a small office building. With your customer, you have signed a Cost Plus Incentive Contract. The pricing for the contract is:

target cost:	$100,000
target fee:	$ 8,000
max fee $	$ 12,000
min fee $	$ 4,000
share ratio	60/40 (buyer/seller)

You complete the work for $105,000. What is the fee you will receive?

a. $8, 000
b. $10,000
c. $4,000
d. $6, 000

9. During the make-or-buy analysis your team considered the immediate need for specialized hardware as well as the long-term expressed by the organization. If the organization anticipates a long-term need for the item then:

a. the cost charged to the project may be more than actual costs
b. the cost charged to the project will be the actual costs
c. the cost charged to the project may be less than actual costs
d. the cost charged to the project may include the organization's investment for the future

10. You are managing the design/build of a small office building. With your customer, you have signed a Cost Plus Incentive Contract. The pricing for the contract is:

target cost: $100,000
target fee: $ 8,000
max fee $ 12,000
min fee $ 4,000
share ratio   60/40

You complete the work for $105,000. What is the total price the buyer will pay?

a. $105,000
b. $109,000
c. $111,000
d. $113, 000

11. "The proposed project manager needs to be a certified Project Management Professional" is an example of using a:

a. screening system
b. weighting system
c. independent estimate
d. seller rating system

12. As you are managing the multiple projects for your customer, the British Government. Each contract seems to have a different type such as Time and Materials, to Cost Reimbursable and even some fixed price contracts. The corporate accountant calls you to state you are about to hit your PTA (point of total assumption) on one of the contracts. The accountant must be talking about which type of contract?

a.   Time and Materials
b.   cost plus fixed fee
c.   cost plus incentive
d.   fixed price incentive

13. Termination of a contract may occur for all of the following reasons *except*:

a. completion
b. cause
c. mutual agreement
d. convenience

14. You are heavily involved in the sale of construction services to a large manufacturing firm. During the negotiation, your organization's contracts manager takes over and pushes for the contract type to be cost plus percentage cost instead of the originally planned cost plus fixed fee. You realize that your contracts manager may be assuming:

a. the contract will run over the estimated costs
b. the contract will run under the estimated costs
c. the buyer is taking too much risk
d. the buyer needs the seller to take more risk before they will sign the contract

15. Multiple sources for critical products may be used to:

a. mitigate risks
b. lower costs
c. obtain quantity discounts
d. reward the lowest bidder

16. As a house builder you often take on more work than you can handle. For years you have delivered homes late, but you continue to be profitable. Your current project is running 90 days late and the home buyer states that she is going after punitive damages. Punitive damages represent:

a. the exact amount due to the injured party for his loss
b. the amount agreed to in advance
c. the specific performance stated in the contract
d. the amount above what would barely compensate the injured party for his loss

17. The Oral presentations of the potential sellers are often given:

a. during the bidder conference
b. after proposal submission
c. during the procurement audit
d. after contract award

18. As a project manager in the pharmaceutical industry your contractors at times question your authority. When this issue arises, you point them to the contract where your authority is documented. This type of authority is called:

a. apparent authority
b. expressed actual authority
c. implied actual authority
d. non-apparent authority

19. The cost of proposal preparation is normally at:

a. no direct cost to the buyer
b. a direct cost to the buyer only if the buyer does not buy from the seller
c. a direct cost to the buyer only if the buyer does buy from the seller
d. a direct cost to the buyer regardless of whether the buyer buys from the seller

20. Right now all of the procurement professionals in your organization work in a centralized organization. A consultant has come in and recommended that you move to decentralized contracting. All of the following are positives of decentralized contacting except:

a. more loyalty to the project
b. easier access to contracting expertise
c. more in depth understanding of the needs of the project
d. clearly defined career paths for contracting professionals

21. An emergency has occurred and you need a safety contractor fast to do some consulting work for you. In this circumstance you are most likely to use a:

a. fixed price
b. fixed price incentive
c. cost plus incentive
d. time and materials

22. As part of plan purchase and acquisitions you are trying to decide if you should rent or buy a piece of equipment. To rent the equipment will cost $100/week. To purchase the equipment will be $900 plus a usage cost of $10/week. On what day will the cost to rent equal the cost to buy?

a. 8 weeks
b. 10 weeks
c. 15 weeks
d. 20 weeks

23. A procurement audit:

a. identifies any weaknesses in the seller's work processes or deliverables
b. determines whether project activities comply with organizational and project policies, processes and procedures
c. documents the effectiveness or risk responses in dealing with identified risks and their root causes, as well as the effectiveness of the risk management processes
d. reviews processes from plan purchases and acquisitions through contract administration

24. During plan purchase and acquisitions you need to write a contract statement of work for your supplier. Based on the work to be done, you need to specify to the seller exactly how to do the work. This type of statement of work is often known as:

a. design
b. functional
c. performance
d. statement of objective

25. During contract administration, the project team should be focusing on:

a. the bidder conference
b. the oral presentation
c. the make-or-buy analysis
d. the buyer-conducted performance review

26. You have decided to end your contract with your newest supplier, even though this supplier wants to continue. You no longer need or want the work done. You check your contract to see if you are allowed to terminate for:

a. cause
b. default
c. convenience
d. mutual consent

27. Joint ventures are an example of what positive risk strategy?

a. transfer
b. exploit
c. share
d. enhance

28. As a computer manufacturer you often purchase components from suppliers. One of your contracts has an interpretation issue. It states that fifty (15) units need to be delivered. In general this would be interpreted to mean that the seller must:

a. deliver fifty units
b. deliver fifteen units
c. deliver nothing since there is a contradiction in the contract
d. deliver thirty three units

29. Direct costs are:

a. costs of doing business
b. a percentage of indirect costs
c. costs such as overhead and general and administrative
d. costs incurred for the exclusive benefit of the project

30. You have sent out your request for proposals.   The suppliers all have questions. You decide to hold a meeting to make sure everyone understands the contract statement of work. You are most likely in:

a. plan contracting
b. request seller responses
c. select sellers
d. plan purchase and acquisitions

31. Standard forms help us:

a. plan contracting
b. request seller responses
c. plan purchases and acquisitions
d. select sellers

32. After negotiation, your procurement manager types up a memo documenting the discussions. Several of the ideas in this memo do not make it into the final contract. In general what will hold up in court is:

a. the official contract
b. the negotiation memo
c. a combination of the official contract and the negotiation memo
d. neither the official contract or the negotiation memo

33. Your organization has decided to subcontract out some of your technology development versus doing it in house. Your team is in the process of documenting products, services, and results requirements for your potential suppliers. This is done in:

a. scope planning
b. scope definition
c. create WBS
d. plan purchase and acquisitions

34. The government of your country is sending out a request for proposal for a very large long term research and development project. What contract type are they most likely to use?

a. fixed price
b. cost reimbursable
c. time and materials
d. unit price

35. Your management states that the organization is thinking about pulling the procurement people out of the project teams and into a centralized group. The advantage of this is:

a. you have more control over the procurement resources
b. the procurement people will gain a better understanding of the needs of the project
c. the procurement people will really be part of your project team
d. the organization will have stronger buying power

36. Several meetings are held during the contract life cycle. The meeting where sellers try to "sell" themselves and their proposals is called:

a. contract kick-off meeting
b. bidder conference
c procurement audit
d. oral presentation

37. Your external customer has requested a copy of your work breakdown structure. You give them a:

a. bill of materials
b. contract work breakdown structure
c. organizational breakdown structure
d. work breakdown structure

38. As a project manager you are attending your first negotiation with a very large potential client. Two of your company's best sales people, Bill and Russ, are with you and really leading the negotiation effort. The customer is finding Bill very difficult to deal with and keep looking to Russ to support their case. After the negotiation effort is over and the contract signed Russ and Bill congratulate each other. Bill and Russ were most likely using what negotiation tactic?

a. lying
b. missing man
c. Fait Accompli
d. good guy/bad guy

39. The project manager is part of a team making a critical source selection decision. Seven potential suppliers have all submitted bids. The selection criteria states that price will be a critical element in the selection process. Six of the bids are all in the same price range. One of the bids is significantly lower than the others. This bid is from an unknown supplier. The corporate procurement manager suggests that this low bid be eliminated. What is the likely concern of the procurement manager?

a. the other six potential suppliers will question why the low bidder won the contract
b. selecting the low bidder goes against the published selection criteria
c. the higher six bidders did not understand the request for bid
d. the low bidder may be buying in to the contract

40. All of the following are typical examples of a Force Majeure *except*:

a. earthquake
b. major fire
c. your organization mismanaging its cash flow
d. epidemic

41. Typical reasons for using a non-competitive form of procurement include all the following *except*:

a. you have a long-term friendship with the seller
b. the project is under extreme schedule pressure
c. the seller has a unique qualification
d. other mechanisms exist to make sure you get a fair price

42. As a buyer, the lowest risk contract type for you from a financial view is:

a. time and materials
b. cost-plus-incentive fee
c. cost-plus-fee
d. lump sum

43. You are the PM for an organization buying training services. You hire Seller A to provide the services. Seller A subcontracts out some of the work to Subcontractor B. Subcontractor B is not performing up to your standards. In this case, privity tells us to:

a. deal directly with Subcontractor B since you have privity with them
b. deal directly with Seller A since you have privity with them
c. deal with both Seller A and Subcontractor B since you have privity with both of them
d. do nothing since you have no direct contract with Subcontractor B

44. Contract closeout and contract termination are:

a. different names for the same idea
b. contract closeout comes first, than termination
c. closeout is ending the contract after the work is done; termination is ending the contract while there are still open items
d. contract termination comes first, then contract closeout

45. The major difference between a contract and a project is that:

a. there are no major differences
b. a contract is usually bigger than a project
c. a project is usually bigger than a contract
d. a contract is a legal relationship; a project is not

46. The Colorado State Government has announced it will be awarding a contract for several road construction projects in the Denver area. Hausmann Associates wants to go after this work but is greatly concerned about unforeseen conditions related to traffic and weather issues in the area. Based on this situation, to get into a low risk contract, Hausmann Associates is most liked to try to negotiate:

a. firm-fixed price contract
b. fixed-price- incentive contract
c. cost-plus-incentive contract
d. fixed cost contract

47. Based on falling revenues and profits, Hausmann Associates is in strong need of a project management methodology. At this point your team is working on a make-or-buy analysis. You are most likely in what step?

a. plan contracting
b. request seller responses
c. plan purchase and acquisitions
d. select sellers

48. Hausmann Associates has subcontracted out many of the design aspects of a highway construction project to Person's Corporation. Hausmann decides to review Person's progress to deliver scope and quality. This review is often called:

a. bidder conference
b. oral presentation
c. procurement audit
d. buyer-conducted performance review

49. Hausmann Associates is in the process of a make-or-buy decision related to a project management methodology tool. If Hausmann decides to make a purchase, its ideas will be documented in the:

a. procurement management plan
b. contract management plan
c. project management plan
d. scope management plan

50. You are an independent contractor working to support a large customer headquartered in London with a large manufacturing facility in Stockholm. You rotate your time, traveling back and forth from London to Stockholm every other week. Due to a major blizzard, you are unable to get to the manufacturing facility for several days. Your failure to be in Stockholm is allowed as the storm is considered a temporary excuse for non-performance. Another name for this clause in the contract is:

a. privity
b. force majeure
c. consideration
d. enterprise environmental factor

51. You are working under a large Fixed Price Incentive Contract. The pricing for the contract is:

target cost: $100,000
target profit: $ 10,000
target price $110,000
share ratio   80/20
Price ceiling $125, 000.
You complete the work for a cost of $120,000. What is the profit you will receive?

a. $ 4,000
b. $ 5,000
c. $ 6, 000
d. $10,000

52. You are working under a large Fixed Price Incentive Contract. The pricing for the contract is:

target cost: $100,000
target profit: $ 10,000
target price $110,000
share ratio   70/30
Price ceiling $125, 000.
You complete the work for a cost of $120,000. What is the price the buyer will pay?

a. $ 120,000
b. $ 124,000
c. $ 125, 000
d. $ 126,000

53. You are working under a large Fixed Price Incentive Contract. The pricing for the contract is:

target cost: $100,000
target profit: $ 10,000
target price $110,000
share ratio   80/20
Price ceiling $125, 000.

The Point of total assumption for this contract is?

a. $ 110,000
b. $ 118,750
c. $ 120,000
d. $ 125,000

PROJECT PROCUREMENT MANAGEMENT

Learning Solutions

1. b.   *PMBOK® Guide* 12.1.2.3
☺   b. This question has the word *except* in it; therefore, we are looking for the answer that does not belong or is not true. This statement is the definition of a cost-reimbursable contract, not a time and materials contract.
☹   a, c and d. These are all true statements and thus not the correct answer. T&M contracts resemble cost reimbursable type arrangements in that they are open-ended. They resemble fixed price from the standpoint that the price per hour or per day is fixed. Neither the full value of the agreement nor the exact quantity of items to be delivered are defined.

2. d.   Garrett World Class Contracting page 128
☺   d. A letter of intent is a pre-contract agreement that often unofficially encourage sellers to start work.
☹   a. A purchase order is the simplest form of a firm fixed contract. The statement is asking about what you would use before you can award a contract.
☹   b. A request for proposal is a document used to request proposals from sellers. This document will not get the seller to start work.
☹   c. A purchase agreement sets the terms and conditions that apply to transactions between parties. The seller in general though will not start work until there is a contract.

3. d.   *PMBOK® Guide* 12.2.3.1
☺   d. Proposals are used when the buyer wants to make the decision based on best value, not low price. The question states that we are creating our procurement documents. We most likely are in the plan contracting process step since procurement documents are one of this process's outputs.
☹   a, b and c. Bid, tender, and quotation are terms that are generally used when the seller selection decision will be based on price (as when buying commercial or standard items), while a term such as proposal is generally used when other considerations, such as technical approach, are paramount.

4. c.   Garrett World Class Contracting, page 123
☺   c. A purchase agreement sets the terms and conditions that apply to transactions between parties. It is often used when the parties do not know the exact quantity or exact products that will be exchanged. This agreement reduces the time to form a contract since the terms and conditions are already in place each time.
☹   a. A purchase order is the simplest for of a firm fixed price contract. You will not want to use a firm fixed price contract since you do not know the exact quantity or exact products you are buying.
☹   b. A request for proposal is a document used to request proposals from sellers.
☹   d. A letter of intent is a pre-contract agreement that often unofficially encourage sellers to start work.

5. d.   *PMBOK® Guide* Figure 12-1
☺   d. Request seller response is the process when we receive responses from prospective sellers. A tool and technique of this step is to hold a bidder conference. This meeting is held with potential sellers before the sellers complete and submit their proposals.

☹   a. Plan contracting is the process in which the buyers prepare their documents. This is too early to hold the bidder conference.

☹   b. Plan purchase and acquisitions is the process in which the buyer does their make-or-buy analysis. This is too early to hold the bidder conference.

☹   c. Select sellers is the process in which the buyer reviews the submitted proposals and selects one or more sellers. This is too late for the bidder conference.

6.   d. Garrett World Class Contracting, page 114

☺   d. The point of total assumption is the point where the sharing relationship changes to a share ratio to 0/100. At this point the seller picks up 100 % of the cost risk.

☹   a. Contract award is the point when the buyer and the seller sign the contract.

☹   b. Contract breach is the failure without legal excuse to perform a promise of the contract.

☹   c. Contract termination is the end of the contract while at least one party still has open obligations.

7.   b.   *PMBOK® Guide* 12.5.2

☺   b. Contract administration is the process where each party ensures that both parties meet their contractual obligations. The contract change control system is a tool and technique of this step.

☹   a. Plan contracting is the process in which the buyer prepares the documents needed to support the successor steps. This is too early for the contract change control system.

☹   c. Request seller responses is the process in which the buyer obtains responses from the potential sellers. This is too early for the contract change control system.

☹   d. Select sellers is the process in which the buyer reviews the submitted proposals and selects one or more sellers. This is too early for the contract change control system.

8.   d.   Garrett World Class Planning page 113

☺   d. The seller completed the work for $105,000. This is an overrun of $5,000. Since the seller overran, their fee is going to be decreased by their share (40%) of the share ratio.

Fee adjustment= 40%*$5,000= $2,000

Seller fee = target fee-fee adjustment

Seller fee = $8,000-$2,000= $6,000

At this point you must confirm that the seller fee is above the minimum fee, if not the minimum fee will be paid to the seller.

☹   a, b and c. These are distracter answers.

Contract type	Cost Plus Incentive
Do we have an overrun or under run? How much?	Overrun of $5, 000
Will the seller's fee be increased or decreased for an overrun?	Decreased by the seller's % of the overrun. (go to share ratio, take 2nd %)
Decreased by how much? (Seller's % *overrun)	40% of $5,000= $2,000
Seller fee=target fee-adjustment	Seller fee= $8,000-$2,000 Seller fee= $6,000
Is fee between max and min fee?	Yes so Seller fee=$6,000

9.	c.	*PMBOK® Guide* 12.1.2.1
☺	c. The cost charged to the project may be less than actual costs with the difference representing the organization's investment for the future.
☹	a, b and d. If the organization anticipates a long-term need for the product, the organization may pick up part of the cost of the product, and thus the cost charged to the project will be less than actual costs.

10.	c.	Garrett World Class Planning page 113
☺	c. The seller completed the work for $105,000. This is an overrun of $5,000. Since the seller overran their fee is going to be decreased by their share (40%) of the share ratio.
Fee adjustment= 40%*$5,000= $2,000
Seller fee = target fee-fee adjustment
Seller fee = $8,000-$2,000= $6,000
At this point you must confirm that the seller fee is above the minimum fee, if not the minimum fee will be paid to the seller
Total price= actual cost + seller fee.
Total price= $105,000+$6,000
Total price= $111,000
☹	a, b and d. These are distracter answers.

Contract type	Cost Plus Incentive
Overrun or under run? How much?	Overrun $5, 000
Will the seller's fee be increased or decreased for an overrun?	Decreased by the seller's % of the overrun. (go to share ratio-take 2nd %)
Decreased by how much?	40% of $5,000= $2,000
Seller fee=target fee-adjustment	Seller fee= $8,000-$2,000 Seller fee= $6,000
Is fee between max and min fee?	Yes so Seller fee=$6,000
Actual price= actual cost+ actual fee	Actual price= $105,000+6,000 =$111,000

11.	a.	*PMBOK® Guide* 12.4.2.3
☺	a. A screening system involves establishing minimum requirements of performance.
☹	b. A weighting system is a method for quantifying qualitative data. The seller's PM being or not being a PMP is not qualitative. It is absolute. Either the PM is or is not a PMP®.
☹	c. An independent estimate is a should cost estimate. The seller's PM being a PMP® is an example of a minimum requirement.
☹	d. A seller rating system looks at criteria such as past performance. This information is used in addition to the screening system to select a seller.

12.	d.	Garrett, World Class Contracting, page 114
☺	d. The point of total assumption is the point where the sharing relationships changes for the share ratio to 0/100. At this point the seller picks up 100 % of the cost risk. In a fixed price incentive the buyer and seller share the risk according to the share ratio. If the seller continues to overrun eventually the seller hits the PTA. The PTA is caused by the price ceiling.

☹   a. Time and materials contracts do not have a point of total assumption. There is no share ratio in the Time and materials contract. The seller is reimbursed a fixed price per hour or day (the time portion of the contract) and at cost for materials.

☹   b. The cost plus fixed fee has no point of total assumption. There is no share ratio in a cost plus fixed fee. The seller is reimbursed 100 % for overruns as long as the overruns are allowable. The buyer has 100% of the cost risk.

☹   c. The cost plus percentage cost has no point of total assumption. There is no share ratio in a cost plus percentage cost. The seller is reimbursed 100 % for overruns as long as the overruns are allowable. The buyer has 100% of cost risk.

13.   a   *PMBOK® Guide* 12.6

☺   a. Completion is the normal end of a contract after all the work is completed. Termination is the early end of the contract before some aspect of the contract is complete.

☹   b. Termination for cause means the contract terminates because one of the parties is not meeting at least one of its obligations.

☹   c. Termination by mutual agreement means the contract ends because both parties feel it is in their best interests to end the contact even though there are still open obligations.

☹   d. Termination for convenience means that one of the parties, usually the buyer, has the right granted to them in the contract to end the contract because it is convenient for them.

14.   a.   Garrett, World Class Contracting, page 110

☺   a. On a cost plus fixed fee contract the seller's profit remains the same when the contract runs over the estimated costs. On a cost plus percentage cost contract the seller's profit goes up if the contract overruns the estimated costs. Your contracts manager is probably assuming the contract will overrun the estimated costs and is pushing for the cost plus percentage cost so as to obtain the extra profit.

☹   b. On a cost plus percentage cost contract the sellers profit goes down if the contract runs under the estimated costs. If your contracts manager is assuming the contract will under run the estimated cost, he would not push for a cost plus percentage cost contract because this will provide for a lower profit. On a cost plus fixed fee, the seller's profit does not go down if the contract runs under its estimated costs.

☹   c. The cost plus percentage cost has more buyer risk than the cost plus fixed fee.

☹   d. The cost plus percentage cost provides the seller with less risk, not more risk, than the cost plus fixed fee.

15.   a.   *PMBOK® Guide* 12.4

☺   a. Mitigation of risks is often a driving reason to use multiple sources for the same product.

☹   b and c. Multiple sources often result in higher costs. One reason for this is the loss of possible quantity discounts.

☹   d. The lowest bidder is not rewarded when multiple sources are used since the work is spread out instead of all going to the lowest bidder.

16.   d. Garrett World Class Contracting, page 59

☺   d. Punitive damages are often set to punish the other party and represent the amount above what would barely compensate the injured party for his loss.

☹   a. Compensatory damages the exact amount due to the injured party for his loss.

☹   b. Liquidated damages represent the amount agreed to in advance.

☹   c. In most cases, the injured party is awarded damages (money). At times though a party is forced to perform the specifics of the contract.

17.   b.   *PMBOK® Guide* 12.2.3.3

☺   b. After proposal submission the seller is often asked to supplement its proposal with an oral presentation. The oral presentation is meant to provide additional information.

☹   a. During the bidder conference is too early for the oral presentation. The seller has not submitted a proposal at this point.

☹   c. During the procurement audit is too late for the oral presentation. The procurement audit is held during contract closeout.

☹   d. After the contract award is too late for the oral presentation. The seller has been selected by the time of contract award, so the oral presentation would serve no purpose.

18.   b.   Garrett World Class Contracting, page 37

☺   b. Expressed actual authority is intended authority that is put in writing such as in a contract.

☹   a. Apparent authority is not actually granted (like in a contract) but may rest with the agent if the agent is allowed to exercise such authority and the other party has a reasonable basis to believe the agent has such authority.

☹   c. Implied actual authority is intended authority that is often implied based on a persons position in the organization.

☹   d. Non-apparent authority is a made up term.

19.   a.   *PMBOK® Guide* 12.3

☺   a. The cost of the proposal is normally at no direct cost to the buyer.

☹   b, c and d. The cost of the proposal is normally at no direct cost to the buyer, regardless of whether the buyer buys for the seller.

20.   d.

☺   d. Clearly defined career paths for contracting professionals is an positive of centralized, not decentralized contracting.

☹   a. More loyalty to the project is an positive decentralized contracting.

☹   b. Easier access to contracting expertise is a positive of decentralized contracting.

☹   c. If procurement people are part of the project team, they are likely to have a more in depth understanding of the needs of the project.

21.   d.   *PMBOK® Guide* 12.1.2.3

☺   d. Time and materials contracts are often used when the buyer is purchasing services. When the buyer needs a contractor quickly, time and materials are often used since they can be set up quickly without a definite quantity specified.

☹   a and b. Fixed price contracts are used when the product is well defined. Often in an emergency we do not have time to define the product well before the seller must start working.

☹   c. The cost plus incentive contract is a complex contract to set up and thus often not used in an emergency.

22. b.
☺   b. $100*W= $900+$10*W. ($100-$10)*W= $900. $90* W = $900. W= 10 weeks. At 10 Weeks the cost to rent will equal the cost to purchase.
☹   a. c and d. These are distracter answers.

23. d.   *PMBOK® Guide* 12.6.2
☺   d. A procurement audit is a structured review of the procurement process.
☹   a. The quality process identifies any weaknesses in the seller's work processes or deliverables.
☹   b. A quality audit, not procurement audit, is used to identify inefficient and ineffective policies, processes, and procedures (*PMBOK® Guide* 8.2.2.2).
☹   c. A risk audit, not procurement audit, examines and documents the effectiveness of risk responses (*PMBOK® Guide* 11.6.2.2).

24. a.
☺   a. A design statement of work describes how the buyer wants the seller to accomplish the work.
☹   b. A functional statement of work describes the functional characteristics required in the end product.
☹   c. A performance statement of work defines the performance parameters that the product must be able to meet.
☹   d. A statement of objective describes the output or objectives the buyer is looking for from the seller.

25. d.   *PMBOK® Guide* 12.5.2.2
☺   d. The buyer-conducted performance review is a tool and technique of contract administration.
☹   a. The bidder conference is a tool of request seller responses and not contract administration.
☹   b. The oral presentation is done after the receipt of proposals in request seller responses.
☹   c. The make-or-buy analysis is a tool of plan purchase and acquisitions not contract administration.

26   c.   PMBOK Guide 12.6
☺   c. For one party to terminate for convenience, it must be specified in the contract that they have the right to do so. Terminate for convenience means that one party feels it is in their best interest (convenient for them) to end the contract.
☹   a and b. Termination for cause or default implies that one party terminates with the other because they believe the other party is in breech.
☹   d. Termination for mutual consent means both parties feels it is in their best interest to terminate. In this question the supplier wants to continue so it is not an example of termination by mutual consent.

27. c.   *PMBOK® Guide* 11.5.2.1.2
☺   c. Sharing examples includes actions that form risk-sharing partnerships, teams, special-purpose companies or joint ventures.
☹   a. Transfer involves shifting the negative impact or a threat along with ownership of the response to a third party (*PMBOK® Guide* 11.5.2.1).

☹ b. Exploit helps to eliminate the uncertainty associated with a particular upside risk by making the risk definitely happen (*PMBOK® Guide* 11.5.2.2).

☹ d. Enhance modifies the size of an opportunity by increasing probability and/or positive impacts and by identifying and maximizing key drivers of these positive-impact risks (*PMBOK® Guide* 11.5.2.2).

28. a.

☺ a. The guideline states that words prevail over figures (numbers). Therefore the fifty would prevail over the 15.

☹ b. The guideline states that words prevail over figures (numbers) not figures over words. Therefore the fifty would prevail over the 15.

☹ c. If the seller delivers no components they are in breech of contract.

☹ d. We do not split the difference between fifty and 15. We follow the guideline that words prevail over figures.

29. d. *PMBOK® Guide* 12.1.2.3

☺ d. Costs incurred for the exclusive benefit of the project are called direct costs.

☹ a, b and c. Costs of doing business are billed to the project indirectly. Indirect costs are usually calculated as a percentage of direct costs. They include costs such as overhead and general administrative.

30. b. *PMBOK® Guide* 12.3.2.1

☺ b. Request seller responses is when we hold the bidder conference. The bidder conference is the meeting being described in the question.

☹ a. Plan contracting is the process where the buyer prepares the documents needed to support the successor procurement steps. This is too early for the bidder conference (*PMBOK® Guide* 12.2).

☹ c. Select sellers is the step where we select sellers. To do this we must have the bids or proposals from the sellers. Therefore, this is too late to hold the bidder conference (PMBOK® Guide 12.4).

☹ d. Plan purchase and acquisitions is the process where we decide what products or services we should produce externally versus internally. This is too early for the bidder's conference because we have not sent out the request for proposal yet.

31. a. *PMBOK® Guide* 12.2

☺ a. Plan contracting is the process where the buyer prepares the documents needed to support the successor procurement steps. Standard forms help us create these documents.

☹ b. Request seller responses is the step after we have created the documents and thus the step after we have used the standard forms.

☹ c. Plan purchase and acquisitions is the process where we decide what products or services we should produce externally versus internally. This process occurs before we create our documents to send to the sellers and thus happens before we use the standard documents.

☹ d. Select sellers is the process where we select our sellers. At this point, we have already sent our documents to the sellers, such as the request for proposal, and thus have already used the standard forms.

32.   a.

☺   a. The official contract is what will hold up in court, not items agreed to before the contract that were not put in the contract.

☹   b. The official contract is what will hold up in court, not items agreed to before the contract (the negotiation memo) that were not put in the contract.

☹   c. and d. The official contract is what will hold up in court, not items agreed to before the contract or a combination of both.

33.   d.   *PMBOK® Guide* 12.1.3.2

☺   d. Plan purchase and acquisitions has the contract statement of work as an output. The contract statement of work defines just the portion of the project scope that will be included within the contract.

☹   a. Scope planning is the process where we create the scope management plan. The scope management plan describes how the project scope will be defined, documented, verified, managed, and controlled. It does not describe the scope of the project or the scope of the supplier contracts (*PMBOK® Guide* 5.2.).

☹   b. Scope definition is the process of defining the project scope statement. The project scope statement describes in detail the project's deliverables and the work required to create those deliverables. The scope statement does not differentiate what scope will be done internally and what work will be done externally (*PMBOK® Guide* 5.2).

☹   c. Create WBS is the process of developing the deliverable-oriented hierarchy for the project. The WBS does not differentiate what deliverables will be done internally and what work will be done externally (*PMBOK® Guide* 5.3).

34.   b.   *PMBOK® Guide* 12.1.2.3

☺   b. A cost reimbursable contract is used when the buyer may be able to describe the output they are looking for but the seller is not able to estimate with certainty the cost for the work. Often research and development is done with a cost reimbursable contract.

☹   a. Fixed price contracts are used when the buyer can completely define the statement of work and the seller believes that can come up with a good internal cost estimate for that work. That is usually not the case with research and development.

☹   c and d. Time and materials and unit price are the same contract type and thus neither can be the right answer. Usually time and materials are used for small contracts. The question says the project is a very large long term project and thus we are not likely to use time and materials.

35.   d.   General Management Knowledge

☺   d. The organization will have stronger buying power if it buys as an entire organization versus each area buying independently.

☹   a, b and c. These are all advantages of a decentralized contracts group and disadvantages of a centralized group.

36.   d.   *PMBOK® Guide* 12.3.3.3

☺   d. The oral presentation is held after a proposal is submitted. It is often when the potential contract is won or lost for the seller.

☹   a. The contract kickoff meeting is often held right after a contract is signed and before the work starts.

☹   b. The bidder conference is held prior to the proposal being submitted and is used to make sure all potential sellers understand the requirements (*PMBOK® Guide* 12.3.2).

☹   c. The procurement audit is a meeting held during contract closure to identify lessons learned (*PMBOK® Guide* 12.6.2.1).

37.   b.   *PMBOK® Guide* Glossary and 5.3.3.2

☺   b. The contract work breakdown structure is the part of the WBS maintained by the seller.

☹   a. A bill of materials is the hierarchy for the product.

☹   c. The organizational breakdown structure relates the work packages to the organizational structure.

☹   d. The work breakdown structure is for the whole project, not just the part being done by a specific seller.

38.   d.

☺   d. The good guy/bad guy is a negotiation tactic in which one person acts as if they agree with the other side while their negotiation team mate acts opposed to the other side.

☹   a. Lying is a negotiation tactic in which one party does not tell the truth.

☹   b. Missing man is a negotiation tactic in which one party claims that they cannot agree to what is on the table. They may state that they can agree to only a different form of what is on the table.

☹   c. Fait Accompli is a negotiation tactic in which we claim a topic is over and cannot be reopened.

39.   d.   *PMBOK® Guide* 12.1.3.1 and 12.4.3.3

☺   d. The type of contracts to be used is listed in the procurement management plan. This plan describes how the procurement will be managed.

☹   a. How to administer the contract is described in the contract management plan.

☹   b. One output of select sellers is the contract management plan, not the procurement management plan.

☹   c. A description of the performance requirements that the buyer and seller must meet is found in the contract.

40.   c.   *PMBOK® Guide* 2000 Edition 11.2.1.3

☺   c. Your organization mismanaging its cash flow is not a Force Majeure. Force Majeure clauses excuse a party from liability if some unforeseen event beyond the control of that party that prevents it from performing its obligations under the contract. Organizations should properly manage their cash flow.

☹   a, b and d. Earth quakes, major fires, and epidemics are unforeseen events often designated as Force Majeures.

41.   a.   General Management Knowledge

☺   a. Your have a long-term friendship with the seller is not a typical reason for using a non-competitive environment. Your friend's business should compete along with other potential suppliers.

☹   b, c and d. The project is under extreme schedule pressure, the seller has a unique qualification, or other mechanisms exist to make sure you get a fair price are all valid reasons to procure through a non-competitive environment.

42.   d.   *PMBOK® Guide* 12.1.2.3

☺   d. Lump Sum is another name for the firm fixed price contract. This contract provides the lowest financial risk for the buyer because the buyer knows exactly how much the product will cost when they sign a contract.

☹   a. With time and materials contracts the buyer pays for effort, not completion. Therefore, the buyer does not know how much the product will cost. This is a financial risk for the buyer.

☹   b and c. On cost contracts, the buyer reimburses the seller for the seller's actual cost plus a fee that represents profit. The buyer does not know exactly how much the seller's actual costs will be and thus the buyer does not know the final price for the product when they sign the contract. This is higher risk for the buyer.

43.   b.   Web search on *privity*

☺   b. Deal directly with Seller A since you have privity with them. Privity is the legal relationship between a buyer and seller or seller and subcontractor. In this example you have privity with Seller A only since you have a contract with Seller A only.

☹   a and c. You have no privity with Subcontractor B since you have no direct contract with Subcontractor B.

☹   d. You can do something because you have privity (a legal relationship) with Seller A. Seller A then should then solve the issue with Subcontractor B.

44.   c.   *PMBOK® Guide* 12.6

☺   c. Closeout is ending the contract after the work is done; termination is ending the contract while there are still open items.

☹   a. Contract closeout and termination are not the same idea. With termination there is still at least one open obligation.

☹   b and d. When you end a contract, you either do it through closeout (all the work is done) or through termination (you end but there are still open obligations.) You do not do both closeout and termination.

45.   d.   *PMBOK® Guide* glossary

☺   d. A contract is a legal relationship, a project is not.

☹   a. A contract is a legal relationship between two separate legal entities. A project does not define the legal relationship. A project is a temporary endeavor undertaken to create a unique product, service, or result.

☹   b and c. The definition of a contract or a project is not related to the size.

46.   c.   *PMBOK® Guide* 12.1.2.3

☺   c. The cost-plus-incentive contract is considered lower risk for the seller since the seller is reimbursed for all allowable costs plus receives profit.

☹   a. A firm fixed price contract is part of the fixed price category of contracts. Fixed price contracts are higher risk for the seller and lower risk for the buyer.

☹   b. A fixed price incentive contract is part of the fixed price category of contracts. Fixed price contracts are higher risk for the seller and lower risk for the buyer.

☹   d. There is no such thing as a fixed cost contract.

47.   c.   *PMBOK® Guide* Figure 12-1

☺   c. The make-or-buy analysis is a tool and technique of plan purchase and acquisitions.

☹   a, b and d. Plan contracting, request seller responses and select sellers are all steps that occur after the make-or-buy analysis occurs.

48.   d.   *PMBOK® Guide* Figure 12-1

☺   d. A buyer-conducted performance review is held during the contract administration step and is a meeting where the buyer reviews the seller's progress.

☹   a. A bidder conference is held during the request seller responses and is a meeting in which sellers can receive answers to their questions on the solicitation.

☹   b. An oral presentation is often held after the buyer receives the proposals back from the potential sellers (*PMBOK® Guide* 12.3.3.3).

☹   c. A procurement audit is held during the contract closure step. The purpose of the audit is to collect lessons learned.

49.   a.   *PMBOK® Guide* Figure 12-1

☺   a. A procurement management plan describes how the buyer will manage a purchase.

☹   b. A contract management plan describes how the buyer will administer a contract.

☹   c. A project management plan describes how an organization will manage a project.

☹   d. A scope management plan describes how the project scope will be defined, managed and controlled.

50.   b.   Web Search on terms

☺   b. Force majeure means greater force. These clauses excuse a party from liability if some unforeseen event beyond the control of the party prevents it from performing its obligations under the contract.

☹   a. Privity is the legal relationship between the parties of a contract.

☹   c. Consideration is the reason a party gets into a contract.

☹   d. Enterprise environmental factors are any internal or external environmental factors that influence the project's success (*PMBOK® Guide* Glossary).

51. b.   Garrett World Class Contracting

Contract type	Fixed Price Incentive
Do we have an overrun or under run? How much?	Overrun of $20, 000
Will the seller's profit be increased or decreased for an overrun?	Decreased by the seller's % of the overrun. (go to share ratio, take 2nd %)
Decreased by how much? (Seller's % *overrun)	20% of $20,000= $4,000
Seller profit=target profit-adjustment	Seller profit= $10,000-$4,000 Seller profit= $6,000
Actual price= actual cost + actual profit	Price= $120,000 + $6, 000 Price= $126,000
Is actual price less than the ceiling price?	No, therefore the actual price = the ceiling price = $ 125,000.
Do we need to change the profit?	Yes, since the actual price is $125,000 and the actual cost is $120,000 the actual profit is $5,000.

52.   b.   Garrett World Class Contracting

Contract type	Fixed Price Incentive
Do we have an overrun or under run? How much?	Overrun of $20, 000
Will the seller's profit be increased or decreased for an overrun?	Decreased by the seller's % of the overrun. (go to share ratio, take 2nd %)
Decreased by how much? (Seller's % *overrun)	30% of $20,000= $6,000
Seller profit=target profit-adjustment	Seller profit= $10,000-$6,000 Seller profit= $4,000
Actual price= actual cost + actual profit	Price= $120,000 + $4, 000 Price= $124,000
Is actual price less than the ceiling price?	Yes, Therefore the actual price is $124,000 and profit is $4,000.

53. b.   Garrett World Class Contracting

PTA= ((ceiling price-target price)/buyer share ratio + target cost
PTA= (($125,000-$110,000)/.8) + $100,000
PTA=$118, 750
The PTA (point of total assumption) is the point at which the seller assumes 100% of the cost risk.

Professional and Social Responsibility

Sample Questions

Big Picture Things to Know

Professional responsibility requires you to find answers that are:

- Legal
- Ethical
- Address the issue in the question

Remember: Do the right thing.
These should be the easiest questions on the exam.

Much of the information can be gained through practical experience and confirmed in the following publications:

PMI® Publications:
- *PMI® Code of Ethics and Professional Conduct* (Effective January 2007)

Other Publications related to professional and social responsibility:

- *Doing Business Internationally: The Guide to Cross-Cultural Success* by Walker et al.
- *Global Literacies: Lesson on Business Leadership and National Cultures* by Robert Rosen et al.
- *The Cultural Dimension of International Business* by Gary P. Ferraro

PROFESSIONAL and SOCIAL RESPONSIBLITY

1. You are new to your organization and are having your team put together a cost estimate for senior management. As the numbers come to you, they all seem high. After questioning the team, it seems that it is common practice to estimate 15% higher than expected costs, knowing that senior management often cuts estimates by 15%. Before you pass the estimates to senior management you should:

a. turn the estimates in as they are, knowing that the estimates are probably 15% high
b. add 5% to the estimates so that when senior management cuts them by 15%, you will still come in under budget and look like a real cost-saver
c. work with your team to develop estimates that are realistic and be ready to defend your numbers to management
d. go to your management and ask them what to do

2. One of your team members often uses a loud deep voice to get his message across. The pitch and tone of one's voice is often known as:

a. para linguals
b. non-verbals
c. verbals
d. body language

3. You have noticed that when your engineer Max interacts with others, his colleagues often back up a few inches. It seems that Max invades others' personal space. You decide to talk to Max about spatial relationships, which is also known as:

a. proxemics
b. linguistics
c. sociology
d. psychology

4. It seems that your stakeholders are constantly in conflict. As a PM we know we must balance stakeholders' interests. At times, though, conflict must be resolved in favor of:

a. the project manager
b. senior management
c. the customer
d. the team

5. Your team is made up of members of many different culture groups. In this situation it is best to:

a. ignore the differences across the cultural groups and hope they go away
b. discuss cultural differences at team meetings
c. treat everyone of the team exactly the same, to be fair
d. use the same communication methods for everyone on the project; we need to be fair to all team members

6. Your manager likes to exaggerate the status of your project progress to your customer. You should:

a. provide the information your manager wants, even if it is an exaggeration, and let your manager take responsibility for its accuracy
b. meet with your team to find ways to support your manager's exaggerations
c. provide accurate information to your manager even if it puts your relationship at risk
d. try to switch projects and deal with a different manager

7. As you are studying for the PMI exam, your manager gives you a copy of a set of sample questions. After reviewing the questions you realize that the binding of a book has been broken and the pages copied in violation of the copyright. In this case you should:

a. not use the book, but not tell your manager so as to protect the relationship
b. give the book back to your boss and tell him it makes you uncomfortable
c. make more copies of the book and try to sell them at a high profit
d. report this violation of copyright laws

8. You have just switched companies and your new organization has asked you to develop a project management process. You developed one at your last company and have an "unofficial copy." In this case, you should:

a. use this unofficial copy as the primary basis for the new methodology
b. use your knowledge to develop the requested methodology
c. ask your new manager for advice on using this unofficial copy as a template
d. tell you manager you cannot develop this methodology since you did very similar work in your last position

9. You have been sent to a customer site in a different country at the last minute to deal with a major delay. You had no time to prepare for the visit or learn about the customs or language of the other country. As you enter your hotel room, you struggle to turn on the lights, lock the door, and later work the shower. As you go out to eat, you struggle to find foods you recognize. It is likely you are experiencing:

a. time zone issues
b. linguistics issues
c. culture shock
d. virtual team shock

10. Your management has asked you if you would be interested in a long-term assignment overseas to manage a very strategic project. There are always questions to ask about a new position. Before you accept this offer it is especially important to ask yourself:

a. how adaptable am I?
b. how different will the new culture be from mine?
c. how will my new resources react to me?
d. what is the status of this strategic project?

11. You are managing a construction project. Your environmental engineer lets you know that he/she believes the environmental affects on the local community may be much greater than initially estimated. At this point, you should:

a. keep the information quiet unless someone asks
b. have the environmental findings confirmed
c. inform your customer immediately
d. inform the local community immediately

12. You are closing out your contract with your customer and realize there are contradictions in the acceptance criteria of the contract that do not favor your organization. At this point, you should:

a. work out the contradictions with your customer
b. keep quiet unless someone brings up the contradictions
c. search the contract for other contradictions to support your case
d. make a list of all "extras" you have given your customer to support your case

13. You have started a new job at a new organization and your manager asks you to share information about your last company's proprietary processes. This makes you feel uncomfortable and, based on your employee handbook, this request violates company policy. In this case, you should:

a. share everything you know about your last company to make you look good
b. share only part of what you know about your last organization
c. share nothing
d. share nothing and report the violation of company policy

14. As part of your project, many parts will cross international borders. It seems that at some borders you need to pay a fee. In this case, you should:

a. follow the practices of the other countries as long as they do not violate any laws
b. refuse to pay the fees because this is not the standard practice in your country
c. do whatever it takes to get the parts to their final destination by another method
d. hire a third party to pay this fee for you

15. Your project has an SPI of 1.1 and a CPI of 1.2. At the last project review, your customer seemed frustrated even though all the project indices are good. What is the first thing you should do?

a. meet with your management to update them on the situation
b. meet with your customer to determine their frustration
c. crash or fast track to improve your SPI
d. resource level to improve your CPI

16. You have a team member who seems to believe that his/her culture is superior to other cultures. You can see this in the member's reaction to cultural discussions, different foods, and others' clothes. As a project manager, you decide to coach this member because his/her attitude is affecting the project. You work with this member to help him/her understand:

a. culture shock
b. ethnocentrism
c. transnational
d. empathy

17. You are working on an international project in a developing country. As you drive to work each day, you pass children begging in the streets. You look at their parents and think of your own children. It is important as we work in different environments to demonstrate empathy for others. Empathy is:

a. the ability to understand someone else's feelings
b. the ability to walk in someone else's shoes so as to give them guidance
c. the ability to relate to someone so as to coach them
d. the ability to teach others about your superior culture

18. You are a consultant in the field of project management. While with Customer A, you learn about their proprietary overhead rates. A few months later, you are now under contract with Customer B. Customer B is competing on a large contract with your previous Customer A. What should you do?

a. share the overhead rates of Customer A because Customer B is paying you for your knowledge
b. share the overhead rates of Customer A, but take no money for this information
c. share high-level information about Customer A's cost structure
d. do not share proprietary information

19. You are at a trade meeting where suppliers are giving away gift coupons including all expense weekends at high-end resorts. What should you do?

a. accept the gift and then ask permission of your management to keep it
b. see if other customers are accepting the coupon and if so go ahead and accept
c. accept the coupon for a weekend at a resort but then give it to your manager to use
d. not accept the coupon

20. Your colleague is applying to take the exam to become a PMP. You realize on his/her application that he/she is reporting false information. You should:

a. tell the employees manager
b. tell the human resource manager of your company
c. do nothing
d. report this violation to PMI

Professional and Social Responsibility

Learning Solutions

1. c.   *PMI® Code of Ethics and Professional Conduct*
☺ c. Work with your team to develop estimates that are realistic and be ready to defend your numbers to management. We should always submit truthful and accurate information.
☹ a and b. Both of these responses state that we should submit false information. This is not acceptable.
☹ d. We do not need to check with management. We should always submit truthful information.

2. a.   Web search on communication models
☺ a. Para linguals include pitch, amplitude, rate and voice quality.
☹ b. Non-verbals include body language such as leaning forward or backward, crossing arms, making eye contact etc.
☹ c. Verbals are the words we choose.
☹ d. Body language is an example of non-verbals.

3. a.   Ferraro, 1998 *The Cultural Dimension of International Business*, page 86
☺ a. Proxemics is the study of personal space.
☹ b. Linguistics is the study of language.
☹ c. Sociology is the study of society.
☹ d. Psychology is the study of the human mind.

4. c.   *PMI® Code of Ethics and Professional Conduct*
☺ c. As the project manager, we should strive to balance stakeholders' interests. When this cannot be done, we need to resolve conflict in favor of the customer.
☹ a, b and d. See the comments for answer c.

5. b.   General Management Knowledge
☺ b. Cultural differences should not be ignored but openly discussed and appreciated.
☹ a. Cultural differences will affect the project; we cannot ignore them.
☹ c. Treating everyone the same does not mean we are being fair; we need to show respect for cultural differences.
☹ d. Different team members may have different communication needs; we should use the communication methods that make sense and are in the communication plan.

6. c.   *PMI® Code of Ethics and Professional Conduct*
☺ c. We should always tell the truth in communications.
☹ a. You are responsible for the information you provide. We should tell the truth in all of our communications.
☹ b. We should tell the truth and not ask our team to come up with false information to support exaggerations.
☹ d. This is the easy way out. We must address the issue and not run away from it.

7. d.   *PMI® Code of Ethics and Professional Conduct*
☺ d. We need to report violations of policies, laws, or ethics.
☹ a and b. These responses do not resolve the issue.
☹ c. This answer is illegal.

8.   b.   *PMI® Code of Ethics and Professional Conduct*
☺   b. We have the right to use our knowledge.
☹   a. We do not have the right to use proprietary documents owned by other companies even if we developed those documents.
☹   c. Our new manager giving us permission does not make this acceptable.
☹   d. We have the right to use our knowledge to develop this methodology even if we developed similar methodologies at another company.

9.   c.   Ferraro, 1998 *The Cultural Dimension of International Business*, page 142
☺   c. Culture shock is the feeling of confusion and anxiety experienced by somebody suddenly encountering an unfamiliar cultural environment.
☹   a. Time-zone issues include trying to schedule meetings with people working in different time zones.
☹   b. Linguistic issues are issues surrounding language.
☹   d. Virtual team shock is a made-up phrase. Expect there may be a few fictional phrases on the exam as distracter answers.

10.   a.   Walker et al. 2003 *Doing Business Internationally*, pages 34-35
☺   a. Your adaptability and having an open attitude is the most important thing to think about in this situation.
☹   b, c and d. These are all good questions but you need to select the most important question.

11.   b.   *PMI® Code of Ethics and Professional Conduct*
☺   b. There are two hints in the question: the word *believes* and the word *may*. Based on these words, we need to confirm. We report facts.
☹   a. We do not hide information.
☹   c and d. Both of these responses use the word *immediately*. We need to confirm before we inform others.

12.   a.   *PMI® Code of Ethics and Professional Conduct*
☺   a. We should try to work out issues with our customer.
☹   b. We do not hide information.
☹   c and d. Supporting our case turns this into a negotiation. We want to work things out, not get into our positions.

13.   d.   *PMI® Code of Ethics and Professional Conduct*
☺   d. We not only need to not share proprietary information, but we also need to report this violation of company policy.
☹   a and b. This is unacceptable behavior and violates company policy.
☹   c. This is a good start, but we need to see if there is a more complete answer.

14   a.   General Management Knowledge
☺   a. We should follow the practices of the countries we are dealing with as long as the practices do not violate any laws.

☹ b. Standard practice may vary from country to country. We need to ask if the standard practice of the other country violates any laws.

☹ c. Be careful of any answer that says *do whatever it takes*. It general this is not a positive answer

☹ d. Hiring a third party does not change anything. We need to ask if it is right or wrong to pay the fees.

15. b.   General Management Knowledge

☺ b. Even though the indices are good, we need to investigate with our customer to understand what is behind their frustration.

☹ a. We are management. We do not want to give our management an update until we can tell them the reason behind the frustration.

☹ c. The project SPI is 1.1. The means the project is ahead of schedule. There is no reason at this time to crash or fast track.

☹ d. The project CPI is 1.2. This means the project is under budget. There is no reason to resource level. In fact, resource leveling may or may not improve our CPI.

16. b.   Walker et al. 2003 *Doing Business Internationally*, page vii

☺ b. Ethnocentrism is a belief in the superiority one's own social or cultural group.

☹ a. Culture shock is the feelings of confusion and anxiety experienced by somebody suddenly encountering an unfamiliar cultural environment.

☹ c. Transnational is not confined to a single nation, but including, extending over, or operating within more than one.

☹ d. Empathy is the ability to identify with and understand somebody else's feelings or difficulties.

17. a.   Ferraro, 1998 *The Cultural Dimension of International Business*, page 152

☺ a. Empathy is the ability to identify and understand someone else's feelings.

☹ b, c and d. Empathy is about understanding, not giving guidance, coaching or teaching.

18. d.   *PMI® Code of Ethics and Professional Conduct*

☺ d. We do not share proprietary information.

☹ a, b, and c. Getting paid for sharing—sharing for free, or sharing just a little bit—is all wrong when it comes to proprietary information.

19. d.   *PMI® Code of Ethics and Professional Conduct*

☺ d. We should not accept gifts.

☹ a. Our management's permission does not make it right to accept gifts.

☹ b. Other suppliers accepting gifts does not make it right.

☹ c. Passing the gift onto your management does not make it right.

20. d.   *PMI® Code of Ethics and Professional Conduct*

☺ d. We have the responsibility to report violations.

☹ a and b. Your colleague is in violation of the policies of PMI and thus the violation needs to be reported to PMI.

☹ c. If we have factual information we need to report the violation.

RERERENCES

Ferraro, Gary P. *The Cultural Dimension of International Business.* 3rd ed. Upper Saddle River, N.J.: Prentice Hall, 1998

Frame, J. Davidson. *Managing Projects in Organizations: How to Make the Best Use of Time, Techniques and People.* Rev. ed. San Francisco: Jossey-Bass, 1995

Maslow, Abraham H. *Motivation and Personality.* New York: Harper and Row, 1954

McGregor, Douglas. *The Human Side of Enterprise.* New York. McGraw-Hill, 1960

Project Management Institute Standards Committee. *A Guide to the Project Management Body of Knowledge, Third Edition (PMBOK® Guide).* Newtown Square Penn.: Project Management Institute. 2004

Project Management Institute. PMI® Code of Ethics and Professional Conduct.

Meredith, Jack R., and Samuel J. Mantel, Jr. *Project Management: A Managerial Approach,* 5th ed. New York: John Wiley and Sons, 2003

Rosen, Robert, Patricia Digh, Marshall Singer and Carl Phillips. *Global Literacies: Lessons on Business Leadership and National Cultures.* New York: Simon& Schuster, 2000

Verma, Vijay K. *Human Resource Skills for the Project Manager.* Volume 2 of T*he Human Aspects of Project Management.* Upper Darby, Penn.: Project Management Institute, 1996

Verma, Vijay K. *Organizing Projects for Success* Volume 1 of T*he Human Aspects of Project Management.* Upper Darby, Penn.: Project Management Institute, 1996

Walker, Danielle Medina and Thomas Walker, Joerg Schmitz, *Doing Business Internationally: The Guide to Cross-Cultural Success.* New York: McGraw-Hill 2003

Final Comments-

Congratulations to you on making the commitment to obtain your PMP® credential. The Project Management Professional (PMP®) credential is designed for project managers who actively lead and direct project tasks. This designation, and the knowledge gained by achieving it, will set you apart from your peers and help you achieve higher levels in the performance of your work. AME Group Inc. hopes this book benefits your greatly on your path to success. Please send any comments or suggestions for improvement directly to the author at **aileen@amegroupinc.com**. Finally, good luck in all future endeavors.